# The Fuzzbox Diaries

# The Fuzzbox Diaries

*the blessings and bruises of a journeyman guitarist*

## Jeffrey Lee Campbell

Deeds Publishing | Athens

Published by Deeds Publishing in Athens, GA
www.deedspublishing.com

Printed in The United States of America

Cover and title page photo by Ned Matura, NYC
Back cover photo by Vincent Fay

Cover design by Mark Babcock

ISBN 978-1-950794-73-7

Books are available in quantity for promotional or premium use. For information, email info@deedspublishing.com.

First Edition, 2022

10 9 8 7 6 5 4 3 2 1

*For my parents, Jim and Nancy*
*You paved the way with unconditional love and support*

# Contents

# Preface

Melvin Ragin, aka "Wah Wah Watson," is one of my all-time favorite guitarists. Ragin's impressive discography includes Michael Jackson, Marvin Gaye, The Supremes, and Herbie Hancock. But if you want to bear witness to Melvin's true genius, check out "Papa Was a Rollin' Stone" by The Temptations. Pure funk magic. *Wah chicka chicka wah.*

During my freshman year at the University of Miami, I received a letter (no emails back then) from my longtime pal, Mark Sloan. As a playful homage to Wah Wah Watson, Mark had addressed the envelope to:

### Jeff "FUZZBOX" Campbell

For the uninitiated, like a wah wah, a fuzzbox is an effects pedal that alters the sound of an electric guitar. My dormmate from across the hall, Ron, strolled into my room and glanced at my stack of mail. He burst out laughing, "Fuzzbox?!?"—and the nickname stuck (at least every time Ron saw me anyway). I always loved the playful alias, so with a tip of the hat to Mark Sloan's wit, I give you: The Fuzzbox Diaries.

# We Interrupt This Program

I was sitting in the orchestra pit of Broadway's newest tenant, *Mrs. Doubtfire*, shooting the breeze with my fellow guitarists, Brian and Cameron. As we awaited the conductor's downbeat, our conversation veered toward the new, mysterious, embryonic villain known as COVID-19. I'd been following news reports closely enough to offer a prediction to my stablemates. "Gentlemen, I have a feeling we're about to get a little vacation." I was half right. Vacation, yes; little, no.

We were only in our third night of previews at the Stephen Sondheim Theatre when Broadway—and New York City for that matter—came to a screeching halt. We didn't know what hit us. A month earlier, *Mrs. Doubtfire* management had hosted a meet-and-greet luncheon at New 42 Studios in Times Square. Before we chowed down on the sumptuous deli platters, producer Kevin McCollum asked the group to form a large circle. One by one, we took turns stating our names and sharing an interesting factoid about ourselves.

*Hi, my name is Jeff. I'm one of the guitarists in the band, and tomorrow is my 33rd anniversary of moving to New York City.*

As the communion unfolded, a playful cast member introduced himself before jokingly adding, "And I just flew in from

Wuhan, China." The entire room laughed. Sigh. The *joke* would quickly be on us.

Whistling past the graveyard, we all naively thought COVID-19 was a faraway, foreign problem. But reality hit home on the afternoon of Thursday, March 12, when my phone lit up with this ominous message:

> *Tonight's show is cancelled.*
> *Do not report to work.*
> *We will update you ASAP.*

By the next day it was official: EVERY Broadway show was closed... "temporarily."

*(New York, NY) March 12, 2020 — Under the direction of Governor Andrew Cuomo, Broadway shows in New York City will suspend all performances immediately in support of the health and well-being of the theater going public, as well as those who work in the theater industry. Performances will commence the week of April 13, 2020.*

April 13? Okay, I guess I could use a month off. God just chuckled. Three weeks later, that timeline grew.

*(New York, NY) April 8, 2020 — In accordance with guidelines from the Centers for Disease Control (CDC) and the continued direction of Governor Andrew Cuomo, Broadway shows in New York City will extend the current suspension of all performances through June 7, 2020.*

Gulp. My one-month break has now grown into a three-month break and I'm at a loss. Musicians are accustomed to dry spells, but this is unprecedented. There is no work—zilch, nada, "*Smoke 'em if you got 'em!*" Typically, in the music biz, when your Plan A isn't available, Plan B (or C) is a viable option. It's usually easy enough to take a step or two backward and keep the work flowing. Paydays and cachet may shrink, but at least there's something. That is not the case now. Thanks to COVID-19, there are NO gigs. No good gigs, no bad gigs. Live entertainment is shuttered.

I guess it's liberating in an odd sort of way. After decades of hustling, I can actually exhale. (I might as well, there's nothing to hustle for.) The playing field has been leveled—or more accurately, decimated. Musicians are no longer categorized into winners and losers, we're all in the same sunken boat. One cynical muso cracked, "We need to get back to work so I'll know who to be jealous of!"

I'm still trying to process the situation. Is this a holiday? An extended vacation? A sabbatical? A dry run at retirement? In golfer speak, I'm definitely on the "back nine" of my career. (In all honesty, I can see the clubhouse.) Could this be my OFFICIAL retirement?

I played my first paying gig at the tender age of 13. And owing to the immutability of math, this means I'm closing in on 50 years in the biz. (50!?! How the hell can that be?) I've had my ups and downs, but I've somehow managed to carve out a life making music. Singer/guitarist Bonnie Raitt once described being a musician as "the ultimate case of arrested development." I agree with Bonnie. My entire life has basically been a variation on a theme. In the broadest of strokes, every Saturday night is still *"Johnny B. Goode!… in A!… 1, 2, 3!"*

A quick glance at my resumé and I feel a nap coming on. It's difficult to wrap my head around such a circuitous and wacky path. Grooving with Sammy Davis Jr? Chicken wings with Aretha Franklin? Placating Andrew Lloyd Webber? Helicoptering with Jon Bon Jovi? And then there's that mind-blowing year I spent circling the globe with a certain *mononymous* rock star. (No, not Björk.)

In my late twenties, I relocated from my home of Carrboro, North Carolina to New York City in search of fame and fortune. A mere eight months into my NYC gambit, Sting plucked me from obscurity and hired me to play guitar on his *Nothing Like the Sun* World Tour. (Talk about starting at the top.) It was the most amazing—and prestigious—year of my life, but it was still only one year. Which begs the question: "What about all the others, Jeff?" Well, there were some tough stretches along the way, but I'm still standing—and still strumming. Considering the abundant challenges and pitfalls in showbiz, that is no small feat.

As a youngster with a head full of rock-n-roll dreams, I would've gladly signed up for a career with a fraction of my accomplishments. I've been incredibly blessed—and as I always say: playing music beats the hell out of working for a living. But my sparkly credits only tell part of the story. Amid the marquee gigs, I've performed at plenty of awkward proms, smoky roadhouses, empty hotel lounges, and downright dangerous venues. Whether I was playing menacing biker bars in the South (with my racially integrated cover band) or mobbed-up catering halls in the Northeast (in my polyester tuxedo), there's been many a night I was just happy to crawl into bed with all my limbs intact.

Of course, I've forgotten more gigs than I remember, but the ones that have survived in my memory bank have survived for a reason (be it good or be it bad). COVID-19 has turned NYC into a ghost town — and I'm left contemplating my navel. With apologies to Talking Head David Byrne, "How did I get here?"

# The Curse

Like most guitarists of my generation, one can place the blame squarely on Mr. Mel Bay. Growing up, I spent a lot of time with my maternal grandmother, who worked part-time as a babysitter. I'd occasionally tag along, and one night *we* were babysitting for a family who happened to have a cheap guitar and a Mel Bay chord book laying around. I was looking for something to distract me for a few hours ... and accidentally stumbled onto a distraction that lasted a lifetime. Translating Mel's chord diagrams from the page to my fingers was instinctive and intoxicating. I was immediately hooked.

Not long after my chance encounter with a random guitar, my older brother, Mike, won a cheap acoustic 6-string in a department store raffle. He took a few lessons, but sparks didn't fly. I seized the opening and appropriated my brother's discarded axe for my own. Finders keepers.

I strummed day and night. As my obsession grew, I pleaded with my parents to buy me an electric guitar. Mom and Dad were open to the idea, but decided if I was truly serious about guitar, I should study *serious* guitar first. Accordingly, my parents rented a classical guitar (with foot stand and metronome) and enrolled me in private guitar lessons. Their intentions were good, but in hindsight, woefully naive. Despite its air of legitimacy, classical music is probably the most difficult place for a musician to actually earn a living. I gave classical guitar a shot for a few months, but I was miserable. I eventually reached the point where tears would well up in my eyes as Mom drove me to my guitar teacher's house across town. My parents strived to instill a solid work ethic in their children, but they always led with compassion. Feeling my pain, Mom and Dad humanely called off the baroque experiment. Goodbye Bach; Hello Jimi!

Freed from my metronome, I flourished. I was much more interested in pursuing the sounds I heard coming from our family's AM radio—or my pal Larry Riggsbee's portable record player. Larry's teenage sister, Jean, had a *girly* carrying case filled with 45 rpms from artists like Sam & Dave, James Brown, Sly and the Family Stone, Aretha Franklin, and lots of funky one-hit wonders. Larry and I spent untold hours sprawled out on the floor spinning Jean's soulful discs. I didn't realize it at the time, but class was in session. I was a sponge. Those magical platters had a huge influence on my musical development.

On occasion, my parents would allow me to raid my piggy bank and purchase a "Today's Top Hits" songbook from the local music store. I'd devour every page, eagerly trying to crack the code of pop music. A song's genre was immaterial, I'd tackle anything. Whether it was "Hey Jude" or "Harper Valley P.T.A.", I was transfixed. Not surprisingly, there were plenty of complex chords I didn't understand, but I was undaunted. When stumped, I'd simply substitute an easier chord—or skip over the tricky part entirely.

My outside interests fell by the wayside as guitar consumed my imagination. I was a member of the Cub Scouts, but my attendance gradually started to suffer. My frustrated troop leader lost patience one day and barked, "Scouts or guitar—choose!" That ultimatum brought an abrupt end to my half-hearted pursuit of a Webelos badge.

As my guitar skills improved, my parents were forced to face the facts: their middle son was a musician. (Or as we musos like to say, I had "the curse.") My perseverance and dedication finally paid off when *Santa Claus* gifted me with a flashy Teisco electric guitar from Sears.

Owing to the massive popularity of The Beatles, practically every kid in the late 60s had an electric guitar (or a bass guitar or a drum set). Consequently, garage bands sprouted up everywhere. Most of my friends on Simpson Street preferred riding bikes or playing football, but carport concerts were my passion. I'm sure neighborhood parents dismissed my exploits as unbridled noise, echoing my Lawrence Welk-loving grandfather's take, "If that's music, the woods *is* full of it." But I was impervious to any doubters. In my adolescent mind, I was a rock star.

By the time I reached middle school, the *noise* from my guitar was beginning to resemble music. Thanks to proceeds from mowing lawns (and the matching funds from my supportive parents), I became the proud owner of a slick Fender Mustang guitar and a booming Fender Twin Reverb amplifier. Now all I needed was an audience.

In 7th grade, I teamed up with some older guys and put together a band for the school's talent show. My classmates cheered wildly as our ragtag outfit took the stage. I remember thinking, "I like this!" We kicked off our two-song showcase with Santana's latest hit, "No One to Depend On." In pursuit of ethnic authenticity, our drummer, Mark Sloan, had gone the extra mile by foraging an old tom-tom from a thrift store some-where and covering it in shiny aluminum foil. Voila: a timbale! (Of course, it didn't sound anything like a timbale, but at least it kind of looked like one.) In addition to our imitation Latin percussion, we also delivered imitation Latin lyrics. We'd tried to decipher Santana's bilingual vocals but had no idea what they were saying. Out of desperation, we resorted to hillbilly phonet-ics. "No tengo a nadie" ("I have nobody") became "NO TANG WAH NODDY." *¡Viva los gringos!*

Transitioning from San Francisco rock to Houston soul, we wrapped our mini set with "Tighten Up" by Archie Bell & The Drells. Friend and mentor Keith Crittenton had shown me the song's boogaloo bass line a few months earlier, and I'd tried to teach the part to our bassist, but it had proven too compli-cated. Our band was determined to "Do the Tighten Up," so I volunteered to play bass on the finale. Larry Riggsbee hap-pily loaned me his four-string and slipped into the wings. I laid down the bubbly low-end while our rhythm guitarist, Greg Darden, strummed the funky (and for us, sophisticated) major 7th chords.

It's worth noting, from my FIRST day in first grade, my public school system was fully integrated. Despite the South's reputation for bigotry, I grew up in a world where black and white kids learned, frolicked, and broke bread together in rela-tive harmony. When I went away to college and started meet-ing people from up North, I was stunned to hear about their es-sentially segregated upbringing. Turns out, us Southerners were more progressive than a lot of my Yankee pals.

Thanks to Grey Culbreth Junior High's blended student body, the crowd went crazy when we broke into Archie Bell's infectious anthem. African American classmate James Cotton jumped on stage and grabbed the microphone to lead our below-average white band to the promised land. (*"Now make it mellow!"*) This was my first taste of rock stardom. I wanted more.

Basking in the afterglow of our triumphant performance, we agreed our group needed a name. After much deliberation, we settled on "Lotus"—and I was in my first serious band. Our bassist Larry decided he wasn't cut out for showbiz and graciously stepped aside. We marched onward, filling Larry's shoes with high-school ringer, Floyd Knight. In addition to Floyd's impressive bass skills, he owned a Jeep AND a trailer—perfect for hauling musical equipment. Things were falling into place.

The band slowly gelled and, thanks to our determination, I earned my first dollar as a musician. An admiring classmate convinced his adult next-door neighbor she needed live entertainment for her upcoming backyard soirée. After the briefest of salary negotiations with the hostess, we settled on the *hefty* sum of forty dollars for our quartet's appearance (ten dollars per man). On a summery Saturday night, Lotus set up on Carol Porter's carport and unleashed a couple of hours of primitive rock on her inebriated guests. I don't know if they actually liked us, or just found our band of youngsters curiously amusing, but we accomplished the most crucial goal of every gig: we got paid. Ka-ching! I was 13 years old and officially a professional musician.

In addition to my first musical payday, I also notched my first *pas de deux* with alcohol. (This was the beginning of a long, and ultimately dysfunctional, love affair.) The party featured a large plastic garbage can filled with a tasty but lethal fruit punch, and I guzzled numerous cups throughout the evening. Being a precocious rocker, I figured getting drunk was the perfect way to fast track my path to adulthood. Meanwhile, I'd had the mischievous foresight to plan a sleepover at our rhythm guitarist's house. Consequently, I was at liberty to get wild and loose. My thrilling evening of firsts culminated with me hugging Greg's toilet while the bathroom spun like a carousel. I philosophically chalked up my liquor-induced nausea to the cost of doing business, and a necessary rite of passage. Over the next twenty years, I rarely played a gig without a buzz (at bare minimum). Alcohol and rock n roll were inseparable in my mind.

Lotus ultimately expanded, adding new-kid-in-town Tony Bowman on keyboards and vocals. Tony's audition was held at our *swanky* rehearsal space...Floyd's father's garage. After we exchanged awkward teen hellos, Tony took a seat behind an old combo organ Floyd had laying around. We couldn't get the dusty instrument to power on, so we cracked open the lid to investigate. Mystery solved. A mummified mouse was curled up in a nest inside the organ. We all fell out laughing as Floyd tossed the furry carcass into his backyard. Regaining our composure, we dove into some of our classic rock n soul numbers. It was magical. Tony's talent burned bright, so we excitedly invited him to join our band.

We took full advantage of our newest member and quickly moved rehearsals to his house. God bless Tony Bowman's parents for welcoming us into their spacious basement. We shook the rafters, but I assume Hague and Avie decided they'd rather put up with our amplified racket than have us out carousing around town in search of teenaged trouble. Their parental wisdom paid off. Our idea of a fun Friday or Saturday night was convening in Tony's basement for an extended jam session. We'd plug in our instruments, lower the lights to set the mood, and attempt to recreate *The Allman Brothers Live at The Fillmore East* note for note. And while we deserved an A for effort, the advanced 11/4 meter of "Whipping Post" confounded our youthful shaggy heads.

Owing to our deep reverence of the Allmans, we took the radical step of adding a second drummer to our ranks. High-schooler David Tyson joined the band to help us achieve our flammy dream. Twice the drummers, twice the cacophony! Unfortunately, not long after the expansion, our lead drummer, Mark Sloan, was shipped off to boarding school. We hated to see Mark go, but Lotus was on a mission. The band absorbed the personnel blow and (wisely) reverted to a single drummer lineup.

Lotus ultimately reached a level of proficiency that warranted legitimate, salaried gigs. Our primary venues were the fraternities at the University of North Carolina in Chapel Hill—real-life versions of *Animal House* that proved to be an excellent training ground. (The pressure of satisfying paying, drunken customers will sharpen your musical instincts in a hurry.) There were lots of keg parties and lots of shenanigans. One crazy night, I wound up on the shoulders of a plastered frat brother *during* a song. (I would call him a frat "boy," but at the time, they all seemed like men to me.) I was wailing away on a guitar solo when my bucking bronco stumbled and lost his balance. We both came crashing to the floor, successfully toppling one of our Shure Vocal Master PA columns in the process. The IZOD-clad mosh pit roared with approval. I'd fulfilled every kid's fantasy: I'd joined the circus.

I craved all things rock n roll. Accordingly, I went to every concert possible during my teens. I attended shows by artists including Alice Cooper, The Hollies, Raspberries, B.B. King, Fleetwood Mac, The Beach Boys, The Doobie Brothers (with jazz-fusion drummer Billy Cobham as the opening act), Santana, Herbie Hancock, Grand Funk, Average White Band, Seals and Crofts, and my prize catch, Led Zeppelin—still the best $7.50 (!!!) I ever spent.

One of the more memorable shows was Gregg Allman's *Laid Back* Tour. A gang of my friends wanted to attend the concert, but none of us were old enough to drive, so my dad took one for the team and offered to chauffeur/chaperone. The minute the lights went down, Duke University's Cameron Indoor Stadium *lit up*, quickly creating the effect of being inside an arena-sized bong. My friends and I played dumb, keeping our eyes straightforward as an unsteady Gregg Allman was escorted to his Hammond B3. After a couple of tunes, some benevolent hippie on our row offered my father a hit off a joint. Time stood still as I awaited Dad's reaction. I feared the stoner's friendly gesture might trigger an abrupt end to our rock-n-roll field trip, but my father just smiled and waved the guy off. I let out a huge sigh of relief and dug back into "Midnight Rider." My dad was the coolest—a driving force (literally and figuratively) in my success.

Our local music store, Burgner Music, became my home away from home. I loved hanging out around guitars, amplifiers, keyboards, drums, and most importantly, like-minded misfits. I took guitar lessons at Burgner Music and ultimately ended up teaching guitar there as well. I made a pest of myself at the store but wearing out my welcome produced two lifelong friendships: guitarist Bill Baucom and drummer Bob Christian. Bill and Bob, both students at UNC, worked at Burgner's and led a popular cover band, Sunny Day.

Lotus continued to burnish its standing around town. Meanwhile, a couple of Sunny Day's members determined it was time to move on, and as a result, Bill and Bob found themselves in need of new blood. Deciding to roll the dice on youth, they approached Lotus with a proposal of band consolidation. Sunny Day had a solid reputation around the area (and a lot of gigs on the books), so the opportunity offered real advancement for us high schoolers. Unfortunately, like most business mergers, there was the thorny issue of redundancy. When the dust finally settled, Sunny Day only needed a keyboardist and guitarist, so Tony and I were the only Lotus alums to make the transition. Egos were bruised and friendships were strained, but that's showbiz. As a musician friend once joked, "There are three certainties in life: you're born, you die, and your band will eventually break up."

Since Tony and I were still in high school, our parents had some reservations about us joining a band of college-aged guys. Our folks were concerned Sunny Day's older members might be a bad influence on their impressionable teens, so a sit-down was arranged to discuss the situation. Bill and Bob were (and are) upstanding citizens, and they easily convinced our dads there was nothing to worry about. Ironically, our parents' qualms were entirely misplaced. Tony and I wound up being the band's resident bad boys, proving to be perfectly capable of juvenile delinquency without any prodding.

One night, our drummer Bob invited a friend to sit in with Sunny Day at a local fraternity party. Mid-set, saxophonist Jim Henderson made a grand entrance, rolling his trunk of horns through the crowded Sigma Phi Epsilon basement. The long-haired Jim broke out both his alto and tenor sax and proceeded to play them … simultaneously. Jim was a one-man horn section, a mind-blowing combination of jazzer Rahsaan Roland Kirk (known for playing multiple horns at once) and the soulful King Curtis. Jaws dropped as Jim showcased his musical dexterity, while our keyboardist Tony playfully urged the partygoers to "throw coins" in Jim's horns. Despite Sunny Day's desire to maintain healthy profit margins, we immediately asked Jim to join the band. 45 years later, Jim Henderson is still a good friend and one of my favorite humans.

On a prescient note, while I was busy honing my cover band skills, I got my first whiff of Broadway. Chapel Hill High School's drama department mounted a production of *Bye Bye Birdie*, and I was asked to play in the orchestra. The musical, inspired by the Elvis Presley phenomenon, included plenty of guitar-centric numbers that allowed me to strut my stuff. One night after a performance, an audience member approached our band director to specifically compliment the guitar work. The fan was convinced our school had hired a ringer to enhance the teenaged ensemble. (Elvis voice: "*Thank yuh vury much!*") My brief foray into musical theater provided a fun and challenging change of pace, but it felt odd to be strumming while sitting down. Little did I know, I'd end up spending a good deal of my life hunched over in a darkened Broadway pit.

Sunny Day continued gigging throughout my high school years, but college eventually beckoned. I was dead set on studying music and had heard nothing but praise for the University of Miami's jazz program. (*Jaco! Metheny! The beach!*) I eagerly applied to the faraway school and was thrilled when I received an official letter of acceptance. With my bandmates facing looming conflicts as well, we pulled the plug on Sunny Day.

Before heading off to college, I treated myself to a high-school graduation gift: a trip to New York City. One of Sunny Day's original members, Vic Lipscomb, had relocated to NYC, and he'd invited a few of us up for a visit. Bill Baucom, drummer Larry Duckworth, and I piled into Bill's Datsun pickup and tackled the 10-hour journey to Manhattan. Bill handled the driving duties while Larry and I took turns riding *al fresco* in the back of the truck. Human cargo traveling in the uncovered bed of a pickup? With no seat belt? On the Interstate? No way that was legal.

My grasp of northeastern geography was rudimentary at best, so I had no idea Manhattan was located just across the river from New Jersey. Consequently, I was confused when I spotted two tall towers on the horizon as we made our way up the Jersey turnpike.

"Wow! Does New Jersey have Twin Towers too?" I naively asked Bill.

Bill passed on a perfect opportunity to mock me and politely replied the clump of skyscrapers in the distance was in fact New York City. (Duh!) But I figure I've redeemed myself. Forty-some years later, I know Manhattan like the back of my hand.

NYC blew my small-town mind. We embraced our role as yokels and hit all the touristy spots we could afford. We went to the top of the World Trade Center, took in a Broadway show (the original production of *Chicago* at the 46th Street Theatre with Chita Rivera and Jerry Orbach), and strolled around the sleazy, porn-filled Times Square—while desperately trying to keep our provincial eyes from popping out of our heads.

But the highlight of our trip was a visit to a small, unassuming jazz club on Manhattan's Upper West Side called Strykers. The joint was located in the bottom of a brownstone and featured live music nightly. With great anticipation, we hit Strykers on a Monday evening to catch The David Matthews Big Band (not to be confused with Virginia's noodly jam-rocker, Dave Matthews).

At the time, the legal drinking age in New York was 18, but I was still a few weeks shy of that arbitrary threshold of adulthood. Due to my small physical stature and youthful appearance, I'd never had much success sneaking into bars back home—but NYC felt like the Wild West compared to North Carolina. I had a hunch my underage status wouldn't be an issue in the Naked City, so when the waiter asked for our drink orders, I lowered my voice an octave and mumbled, "Budweiser." The server didn't bat an eye. Woo hoo, it's party time!

The David Matthews Big Band was filled with NYC hotshots, and they sounded incredible (especially to my young ears). But the most memorable point of the evening occurred while the band was on break. I'd gone into to the men's room to relieve myself, and I couldn't help but eavesdrop as two of the musicians chatted over the stalls.

"Hey man, are you on that Art Farmer date [recording session] next Tuesday?" asked one of the guys.

"Yeah man, I'll see you there," his bandmate replied.

This was the most exciting conversation I'd ever heard. Art Farmer? I owned a couple of the jazz trumpeter's albums — and now I was standing in a poorly ventilated room with two of his colleagues. I thought to myself, "Damn, these dudes are the coolest!" From that moment on, my fantasy was to become one of the *cats* on the New York music scene. It took me ten years to get back to NYC, but I ultimately achieved my goal in spades. Whenever I'm feeling a bit low, I think of that night at Strykers and remind myself, "Chin up, Jeff. You did it!"

It was mid-July, and the city was sweaty and steamy. Vic was a gracious host, but three extra bodies crashing in his one-bedroom apartment quickly reached a tipping point. After a few days of urban stimulation, we climbed back into Bill's pickup truck in the late afternoon and headed home. A couple hours into our trip, we turned on the radio to hear frantic news reports of a massive blackout in New York City. Looting and vandalism was widespread, and thousands of people had been arrested. Yikes! Talk about dodging a bullet. We missed the infamous NYC blackout of 1977 by a matter of hours.

## GPA & SPF

August rolled around and punched my ticket to Miami. At the time, my father owned a small, independent TV store in Carrboro named Tar Heel TV, so he commandeered the store's delivery van to transport me (and my college freshman junk) to the southern tip of Florida. Road-trip ready, my dad, mom, younger brother, Will, and I piled into the van — which sported a large

Tar Heel logo (blue foot with black heel) on its side—and set out on our 800-mile adventure. I'm not saying we were as countrified as The Beverly Hillbillies, but I have been called "Jethro" at times.

With no interest in tackling the entire 15-hour drive, we planned a stopover in Orlando to visit Walt Disney World. The theme park was relatively new (Epcot was still just a twinkle in Mickey's eye) but compared to the Midway at our annual State Fair, The Magic Kingdom delivered plenty of wow. We gorged ourselves on rides and attractions, covering as much ground as possible in a single day. However, the most memorable part of our Orlando experience occurred post-Disney.

After an exhausting day of wonderment (and excruciatingly long lines), we returned to the motel to recharge our batteries. Dad snored peacefully as the rest of us lounged in our pajamas, reliving the day's highlights. The TV was playing quietly in the background when I noticed a "Breaking News" banner flash across the screen. I turned up the volume to hear: "The King is dead!" 42-year-old Elvis Presley had died from a heart attack earlier that afternoon. People always compare tales of "where were you?" when a historic piece of news broke. Disney World offered a bounty of memories, but when I think of Orlando, I think of Elvis's untimely demise.

We set out for Miami the following morning and four hours later we were gawking at palm trees and a steady parade of bronzed bodies. We checked into a cheap motel across from campus and spent the next couple of days buying college kid necessities and moving me into my dorm room. Once I was settled, it was time for the emotional farewell. I'm sure it was difficult for my parents to surrender their middle child to unsupervised adulthood, but I have to wonder if a few of my dad's tears weren't triggered by the thought of retracing his marathon drive in the opposite direction.

\* \* \*

I felt incredibly lucky to be enrolled at the University of Miami. UM is a private school—"private" of course being code speak for "expensive"—and while our family wasn't poor, we weren't rolling in the dough either. My parents did a wonderful job of providing for us kids, but extravagance was not in our playbook. Nevertheless, I boldly/foolishly applied to only ONE school: the pricey University of Miami. My mom had suggested I also apply to my hometown University of North Carolina (which would've offered a solid—and much less expensive— education), but I was hellbent on chasing my musical dreams. My mother justifiably saw UNC as a good fallback plan, but I didn't want a fallback plan. I feared if I was presented with an exit ramp, I just might take it. My mantra was "Miami or bust." Fortunately, I was accepted to UM, and my unconditionally supportive parents vowed to make it happen (somehow).

I'd submitted an audition tape to Miami in hopes of receiving a music scholarship, but in retrospect, I was delusional. Music scholarships are reserved for the heavy hitters, not bush leaguers like me. Luckily, my high school grades were strong enough to snag a small academic scholarship, and combined with a low-interest student loan, a work-study job, and my parents' loving—but overburdened—wallet, The University of Miami became financially doable (barely).

Miami was an eye-opening experience for this small-town kid. Being on my own for the first time in my life was equal parts exciting and daunting. I met people from all over the world and quickly learned about true diversity. Growing up in North Carolina, my ethnic interactions had essentially been limited to two flavors: black and white. But in Miami, I was exposed to a global community pulsing with Italian, Irish, Jewish, Arab, Asian, and Cuban heritage.

On the other hand, the lack of diversity in Miami's weather ultimately proved unsettling. People love to romanticize sultry climes, but after growing up with four distinct seasons, I eventually tired of Miami's redundant "hot and sunny" forecast. I missed the anticipation of an autumn sweatshirt, a wintry blanket of snow, and the blossoms in springtime. Life can be enough of a rut without having the thermometer stuck on 85° most of the year. I discovered I much prefer seasonal change. For me, it serves as a perfect palate cleanser for the soul.

As a student in the Studio Music and Jazz program, I found myself surrounded by real jazz musicians. I'd naively considered myself a jazzer because I knew a 13th chord and a few Wes Montgomery licks, but UM tossed me into the deep end of the pool with highly skilled players from around the country. Hearing my classmates navigate sophisticated compositions from unfamiliar artists like Charles Mingus or The Mahavishnu Orchestra was sobering. I struggled to keep up, but I was handicapped by my pop music upbringing. Or was I?

I was laboring through a private lesson one afternoon, when my guitar teacher, Steve Watson, cut me off and scratched his head.

"It's weird, Jeff, you don't know nearly as much as most of my students — but somehow you sound better than a lot of 'em."

I smiled and embraced the backhanded compliment. After being subjected to a fair share of overly technical players at Miami, I realized my formative years of gigging at frats and proms had been a blessing. I might not have spent enough time in the woodshed playing complicated bebop transcriptions with a metronome, but learning how to keep paying customers on the dance floor had clearly strengthened my musicality. Bottom line: metronomes don't boo.

At the end of my freshman year, my guitar teacher graciously shared his summer contact info with me. Steve said he was heading to Williamsburg, Virginia to spend a couple of months playing in a rock band led by his pal, and former UM classmate, Bruce Hornsby. I fancied myself a bit of a jazz snob—and of course had no idea who Bruce Hornsby was (or would become)—so I questioned Steve's voluntary *downgrade* to pop guitarist. Steve scoffed at my blinkered attitude and assured me Hornsby was something special. Steve obviously knew what he was talking about. Less than ten years later, Bruce Hornsby won the Grammy for Best New Artist—and he's gone on to release 14 albums (two of which went platinum).

I returned for my sophomore year at Miami armed with hometown reinforcements. After a year of study at East Carolina University, my longtime friend and musical partner-in-crime, Tony Bowman decided to transfer to UM. I'd bragged about the school's hip jazz program and had successfully persuaded Tony to join me down *south*. (Miami is at the southern end of Florida; but culturally speaking, it's the most *northern* city in the state.)

I'd spent my freshman year living on campus in a high-rise

dorm—and one year of dorm life had been more than enough. I hated being warehoused with rowdy, debauched knuckleheads wielding weapons-grade stereo systems. Although Miami's music program was competitive and demanding, the university at large was known as a notorious party school. The student body was full of rich-kid snowbirds with minimal academic interest, hence the derogatory nickname, "Suntan U." (It could have just as easily been called "Quaalude U.")

Tony and I decided to look for off-campus housing and found a small house that fit our (or more accurately, our parents') limited budget. Our new living arrangements were nothing fancy, but college kids ain't exactly picky. We had a two-bedroom bachelor pad with a large refrigerator to chill our beer and a spacious back yard for grilling out—everything else was gravy.

Our humble neighborhood featured a blue-collar mix of American and Cuban American families living in small squat houses with chain link fences and snarling guard dogs. Tony and I didn't possess the bandwidth to care for a pet, but our yard occasionally played host to the stray iguana or two. It was wild to wake up in the morning and stumble out the back door barefooted to pull my breakfast from our towering grapefruit tree—while a jumbo, neon-green lizard eyeballed me from a nearby branch. Tropical Miami proved to be an exotic adventure for us Tar Heels.

Being in the big city meant I was much closer to the big time. Miami was a hotbed of music in the late 70s and The Bee Gees ruled the roost. Guitar slinger Eric Clapton had recorded his iconic *Derek and the Dominos* album at Miami's Criteria Studios, and he'd recommended the facility to his Bee Gee pals. The Brothers Gibb heeded Clapton's suggestion and chose

Criteria to forge their smash disco soundtrack, *Saturday Night Fever*. Putting the finishing touches on their masterpiece, The Bee Gees enlisted Miami's Boneroo Horns. The in-demand horn section, led by trombonist (and top local contractor) Peter Graves, featured a couple of UM alums, as well as our Director of Jazz Studies, saxophonist Whit Sidener.

I loved being under the tutelage of a guy who moonlighted as a pop musician. Whit played sax on numerous hit records by artists including The Bee Gees, KC and the Sunshine Band, Bobby Caldwell, Dr. John, etc.—and his real-world experience bestowed instant credibility in my book. From time to time, Whit would pull back the showbiz curtain and entertain us students with behind-the-scenes tales. One afternoon, as we pumped Whit for *Saturday Night Fever* gossip, he quietly confided he'd been paid triple scale for the Bee Gees recording sessions. Whit went out of his way to praise the Gibb's generosity but confessed (tongue firmly in cheek) the substantial payday eventually started to feel meager after hearing "Stayin 'Alive" or "Night Fever" on the radio for the *millionth* time. Whit's open-mindedness toward commercial music helped broaden the attitudes of Miami's jazz department and made this budding popster feel right at home. I took advantage of UM's pliable boundaries and spent more time transcribing guitar solos from rockers like Steely Dan, Tower of Power, and Gino Vannelli, than jazz artists like Jim Hall or Pat Metheny.

I was a diligent college student—maybe to a fault. (In my defense, my scholarship money was contingent on maintaining solid grades.) For better or worse, attention to detail is in my DNA. I never grasped the concept of average. I knew how to make an A; I knew how to make an F; but understanding how to finesse a C always escaped me. In retrospect, I wish I'd skated through some of my elective courses and worked a bit harder in the practice rooms. I'm convinced my peers were wisely focused on becoming better guitarists while I was hunkered down in the campus library, cramming for yet another meaningless history exam.

Wrestling with my priorities, I sought guidance from my guitar teacher (and department chair), Randall Dollahon.

Randall replied thoughtfully, "Well Jeff, moderation can be elusive. But if I was forced to choose between being overly conscientious versus being slack, I know which lane I'd pick."

Randall's wisdom hit home and has served me well throughout my life. Based on my experience, it's better to care too much than too little. In the big leagues, "good enough" never is.

On the upside, my type A personality helped me land work in Miami. Despite having to play catch-up early on, I eventually rose to the status of assistant teacher. Randall's schedule was jam-packed, so he recruited me to instruct some of his fringe students. Expectations were lower for guitarists pursuing non-performance degrees (music therapy, music business, etc.), so I was charged with tutoring a handful of the department's not-ready-for-prime-time players. (I'll refrain from calling them "dregs" because the fusion/twang cult band, Dixie Dregs, were proud sons of the UM School of Music.)

### Sunrise Services

Before its hipster renaissance in the late 1980s (and the resulting influx of beautiful people), Miami Beach was essentially viewed as a vacation/retirement spot for old folks. The area featured numerous luxury hotels that showcased well-known entertainers—which consequently provided a ton of work for local musicians. The touring acts were usually geared toward the retiree demographic…but not always. I saw James Brown perform at an intimate nightclub in a Miami Beach hotel, and despite the occasional bursts of loungey jive, the evening was nothing short of a pilgrimage. During his final number, Brown invited audience members to join him on stage. I sprang from my seat and ended up grooving right alongside The Godfather of Soul, busting my baddest moves in my 3-piece pinstripe suit and platform shoes. (Damn I wish I had a photo.)

In addition to the Miami Beach hotels, the Sunrise Musical Theater was a major source of work for sidemen. (The city of Sunrise, located 35 miles north of Miami, boasted a brand new 3700-seat performing arts center.) The joint was basically *Vegas South*, playing host to a variety of Sin City stalwarts from Sinatra to Rickles. Trombonist Peter Graves (leader of the Boneroo Horns) was the contractor at the Sunrise Theater, and often used members of Miami's faculty—and, at times, the student body—to flesh out his orchestra. Most of the acts traveled with a rhythm section, so local horn and string players were the biggest winners. But there were occasions when a guitarist was needed.

I was hired to play numerous shows at the Sunrise and was lucky enough to work with venerable artists including Mitzi Gaynor, Jerry Vale, Billy Eckstine, Henny Youngman, Don Rickles, and Sammy Davis Jr. Being an unwashed teenager, I didn't begin to grasp the depth of showbiz wisdom I was absorbing from the Sunrise bandstand. Sure, most of the performers were past their prime (and borderline cheesy), but it was a highly educational experience — musically and socially.

Actor/singer/dancer Mitzi Gaynor is probably best known for her role in the film version of Rodgers and Hammerstein's *South Pacific*, and although my week with Ms. Gaynor wasn't exactly high art, it did open my eyes a little wider.

One night during Mitzi's run, I was wandering around backstage before the show when one of her dancers struck up a conversation with me. The hoofer was primping in a stray dressing mirror and offered a friendly hello as I passed. After a bit of banter, he inquired about my heritage.

"Are you Greek? You look Greek."

I told him my last name was "Campbell," so I assumed my lineage was Scottish. He paused for a moment, and then batted his eyelashes.

"Maybe you're Scottish ... *and* Greek."

"Hmmm, not sure," I shrugged innocently, before wishing the dancer a "good show" and moving on.

During the performance, my new pal kept looking over at me as he twirled across the stage. Our eyes awkwardly met at one point — and he smiled and winked. Then it hit me: "Greek" was his euphemism for homosexual. Duh. Being a painfully naive (and straight) teen, I was oblivious to the dancer's veiled flirting. I guess I was flattered, but I took the easy way out and steered clear of the amorous chorus boy for the rest of the week.

I was super excited when I got the call to play Don Rickles's week-long stint at the Sunrise (with Italian crooner Jerry Vale serving as Don's opening act). I couldn't wait to see the comedy legend *lovingly* denigrate his fans as they hooted and hollered and begged for more.

Typically, the guitar chair at the Sunrise was buried amidst the orchestra, often on the back row near the drums. But as we settled in for the Rickles rehearsal, I discovered my seat was located downstage, just behind the piano—and right in Don's crosshairs. The older band members howled, labeling me "a sitting duck." Based on my boyish appearance, the Sunrise veterans assured me I'd be the target of nonstop abuse. I steeled myself for a barrage of wisecracks, but my bandmates' predictions were ultimately unfounded. To my chagrin, Rickles didn't lay a glove on me. I sat fifteen feet away from "Mr. Warmth" for an entire week and never once basked in the glory of a personalized zinger.

During our afternoon rehearsal, Don's musical director walked the band through a general roadmap of the show. Rickles, an equal opportunity offender, took aim at all ethnicities, and one of the show's dependable highlights was his impersonation of Marlon Brando's Mafia boss from *The Godfather*. Rickles would stuff tissues in his jowls and proceed to mumble insults at the considerable number of Italians in his audience.

The conductor looked over at me at rehearsal and said, "When Mr. Rickles goes into his mobster bit, I'll cue you to play a few bars of the *Godfather* theme. Be ready!"

I nodded while the harried conductor moved on to the next order of business. As he doled out further instructions to the band, I frantically scanned the previous chart in search of any notation for the classic "Speak Softly Love" melody. It was nowhere to be found. Against my better judgement, I timidly raised my hand and interrupted the conductor to point out my music did not contain the requested motif. He stared at me blankly and—without saying a word—tugged on his ear lobe.

Translation: *You're a professional musician, you should be able to HEAR that line.*

I got the message and quickly hunched over my guitar, hunting and pecking until I could fake my way through the passage. The teachable moment left a bruise, but I can still play "Love Theme from *The Godfather*" on command.

Don Rickles's set was fueled by rapid-fire trash talk, but he'd eventually run out of snark and wish his audience "good night." On cue, the band would play Mr. Rickles off the stage as the crowd cheered wildly. But like every show since the beginning of time, the goal was an encore. The house lights would stay "at half" as the masochistic fans chanted for more. Despite the ovation, there was always a group of early birds who'd jump from their seats and start rushing toward the exits. After milking the applause within an inch of its life, Rickles would answer his curtain call—and hit the roof when he discovered a traffic jam of backsides in the aisles.

"Jeez, I don't get you people," Rickles would steam. "You wait all week long for a night out, you spend your hard-earned money, and then, for some crazy reason, you can't wait to get home. In an hour, you'll be sitting on your couches staring at the clock on the wall saying, 'Well, Marge, at least we didn't get stuck in traffic.' Come on folks! Sit your butts back down and enjoy the rest of the show." A few people might sheepishly return to their seats, but most of the exodus had their minds made up.

Rickles may have not convinced his defectors, but his rant

made a lasting impression on me. What's the hurry? Enjoy yourself! Decades later, a friend and I spent some of our "hard-earned money" on a pair of New York Knicks tickets. The ballgame became a lopsided blowout in the 4th quarter and my pal kept nudging me, asking if I was ready to leave. The distant voice of Don Rickles echoed in my head. Nope, I was staying put until the final buzzer.


The highlight of my tenure at the Sunrise Musical Theater was a week spent in the presence of showbiz royalty: Mr. Sammy Davis Jr. I'd shrugged when I got the call, ignorantly lumping Sammy into the category of yet another schmaltzy Vegas act. I could not have been more wrong. (As Sammy famously sang, "What Kind of Fool Am I?") Looking back, Sammy is one of the most talented guys I ever worked with.

As always, school was in session at the Sunrise, and I learned a lot from Sammy. But despite his best efforts, one specific lesson never completely landed.

"Mr. Bojangles" was one of Sammy's biggest numbers of the evening. Between his evocative vocals and "the old soft shoe," the song was a reliable showstopper. Unfortunately for me (or maybe Sammy), the arrangement began with a brutally exposed guitar part. The "Bojangles" chart eventually surfaced at our afternoon rehearsal, and Sammy's musical director, George Rhodes, counted off the folksy waltz. We'd only made it through a few bars when Sammy turned and stopped the band. He wandered over to huddle with his conductor and, after a brief exchange, the pair started making their way in my direction. (Uh oh, nobody ever wants to be the reason a rehearsal grinds to a halt, especially not the youngest guy on the bandstand.) All eyes of our 28-piece orchestra shifted toward me as the intimidating tag team leaned over my music stand. The imposing George Rhodes, who towered over the diminutive Sammy, spoke first.

"We need to take a look at the top of this song. It feels a little stiff. Let's hear you play it."

I was on the hot seat as my fellow musicians sat staring at me with their arms crossed. I strummed for a bit until Sammy waved me off.

"Relax Baby!" Sammy urged. "Pretend like you're an old man sitting on the front porch of his shack on the Louisiana Bayou."

I took the note (to the best of my ability) and gave "Bojangles" another shot before asking, "Is that better?"

George and Sammy looked at each other—then Sammy broke the awkward silence and humanely let me off the hook. "Yeah, that'll do."

Sammy's hollow endorsement stung, but my teenaged musical well was only so deep at that point. In my defense, by the end of the week, there was some loose talk about me possibly joining Sammy's road band. (Apparently, they'd just fired their regular guitarist—which was why I was on the bandstand in the first place.) Despite the rumor, I was never offered the gig. Fast forwarding to today, I'd give anything for a chance to redeem myself with "Mr. Bojangles." Having a few more decades of strumming (and life) under my belt, I'm confident I could satisfy Sammy's discriminating ear. Maybe in the next world?

During our breaks, the band would retreat to a spacious greenroom backstage. Sammy employed a full orchestra representing a wide range of ages, so cliques were only natural. Most of the horn players were hipster college teachers or grad students, while the string section was largely made up of older players. It was funny to watch the musicians split off into their respective tribes to partake in age-appropriate vices. Greying violinists sipped coffee and smoked cigarettes at one end of the room, while a couple of shaggy sax players snorted bumps of cocaine in the other corner. What can I say? It was the 1970s and coke still had a somewhat decent reputation. *It gives you energy! It helps you focus! It's a wonder drug!* Sound too good to be true? It was. As a wise friend once observed, "With cocaine, the first hit is too much...and the last hit is never enough."

Sammy Davis Jr. was a force of nature. The dude could sing, dance, tell a joke, and play numerous musical instruments. During one rave-up number in the show, Sammy would make his way around the bandstand, stopping off to play trumpet, vibraphone, and drums, before returning to center stage. My chair was located right beside the drum kit, so I had a ringside seat to Sammy's nightly razzle-dazzle solo. Sammy would look over at me as he pounded the skins and flash an ear-to-ear grin. The image of Sammy's sweaty, smiling face, with his roving glass eye, is forever etched in my mind. (Sammy lost his left eye in a car accident decades earlier.)

Performing with Sammy Davis Jr. is one my most treasured memories. I started off the week as a clueless skeptic but walked away a true believer. Like a typical know-it-all teenager, I'd impulsively prejudged Sammy without stopping to consider his body of work. *Come on Jeff, connect the damn dots!* Sammy was a core member of Sinatra's Rat Pack—which alone should've removed any doubt about the man's *bona fides*. (Although I was probably guilty of dismissing Sinatra back then too.) For years, I downplayed my Sammy Davis Jr. credit, fearing it made me look like an old-timer. But I made peace with that silly notion long ago. Today, I'm incredibly proud to say I worked with THE man. And on top of being an amazing talent, Sammy was a class act. On closing night, he gifted each orchestra member with an expensive bottle of Scotch. I held onto that keepsake for years before finally cracking the seal and raising a toast to "Mr. Show Business."

The Sunrise Theater also hosted Broadway touring productions on occasion. During my junior year, the well-trodden *Man of La Mancha* hit town for a month-long run. The show had a nylon-string guitarist traveling with the company, but they hired an extra picker at every stop to add heft and volume. My guitar teacher, Randall, got called for the gig, but he needed a dependable understudy as *La Mancha's* Wednesday matinees clashed with his academic schedule. I was excited (and flattered) when Randall asked if I'd be interested in covering his conflicts. I loved any opportunity to play with the big boys, and the extra money came in handy for this financially strapped college kid.

The *Man of La Mancha* guitar book contained many challenging flamenco-esque strumming patterns and odd-metered charts, but luckily my job description was to simply mirror Guitar 1. This scenario lessened the pressure, but it also lulled me into a false sense of security. I thought I was playing the *ink*—until fate intervened and revealed just how much I'd been unwittingly cheating off my 6-string neighbor.

My ineptitude was exposed one afternoon when the regular guitarist, Bob, arrived at the theater and realized he'd left his axe back at his hotel. There wasn't enough time for Bob to retrieve his guitar, so we went with the only option available: Bob would use my instrument, and I would twiddle my thumbs for the next three hours. We decided against mentioning our single-guitar scheme to the conductor (for obvious reasons), and fortunately, the ruse had a chance of going undetected. Due to space limitations in the pit, the conductor had been exiled to the theater's mezzanine—with the orchestra following the maestro via a video feed. In short, we could see him, but he couldn't see us.

We (figuratively speaking) played the first act, and then held our breath at intermission. Amazingly, our subterfuge seemed to be working as the conductor was all smiles. Convinced we were in the clear, we (figuratively speaking still) dug into the second act on cruise control. Everything was going along swimmingly—until we got cocky and spiked the ball prematurely. At the end of the show, Bob asked if I wanted to play the bows. I said sure and grabbed my guitar for the push across the finish line. *This* is when I realized I didn't know how to play *Man of La Mancha*. Without Bob as my sonic crutch, I stumbled through the final number. I was completely embarrassed and apologized profusely to my fellow guitarist. Bob just grinned and shrugged it off...but then the conductor appeared.

"What the hell was going on at the end?" the conductor groused.

An honest explanation would've landed both of us in hot water, so we chose to play dumb. Fortunately, the storm passed. I bet Bob never forgot his guitar again.

*Man of La Mancha* was originally scheduled for a four-week run, but brisk ticket sales resulted in a two-week extension. A month of Don Quixote's "Impossible Dream" had driven my guitar teacher Randall to distraction, so he offered me ALL the remaining shows. Normally, I would've jumped at the windfall, but the extra bloc of work included Thanksgiving—and I'd made plans to fly home for the holidays. Consequently, I hesitated when Randall asked if I was available. (Full disclosure: I suffered from chronic homesickness throughout my years in Miami. I missed my family, my friends, and the seasonally appropriate temperatures. Worst of all, I'd made the painful mistake of falling head-over-heels in love with a Carolina girl just before I left for college. Colossally bad idea.) I confessed to Randall I'd already made arrangements to be in North Carolina for Thanksgiving, and I was really looking forward to my trip. Randall stared at me stone-faced. He wasn't the least bit sympathetic to my plight and, in so many words, delivered a heavy-handed ultimatum of "take the gig ... *or else.*" I may have been young, but I was no dummy. Keeping my overlord happy was a top priority, so I cancelled my travel plans.

Instead of sitting around my parent's kitchen table snuggling with my girlfriend Betsy, I consumed my turkey and pumpkin pie at a hotel buffet on Miami Beach with bassist (and fellow Tar Heel) Tim Smith. After our bluesy bachelor lunch, I made my way to the Sunrise for an evening performance of *Man of La Mancha.* I felt sorry for myself at the time, but in hindsight, that day represented a significant rite of passage for me. Punching the clock while most Americans were relaxing helped set the tone for the rest of my life. Today, when someone asks what I'm doing on any given holiday, I proudly and humbly reply, "Entertaining people who are lucky enough to have the day off." It's a badge of honor.

Things started getting pretty loose as *La Mancha* dragged on. I began to see flasks and spliffs making discreet appearances

IN the pit. Accentuating the slack atmosphere, a football fan in the orchestra brought a portable black-and-white television to the theater so we could watch NFL games—*during* the show. Accordingly, my duties expanded to include dimming the TV screen whenever leading man Richard Kiley made his way to the edge of the stage.

Despite the shenanigans, I was surrounded by some incredibly talented musicians. Early in our run, I watched in awe as trumpeter Bill Purse memorized his part after only a few repetitions and never bothered to open his music again. But that was just a peek at Bill's virtuosity. One afternoon, our oboist failed to materialize, and the conductor fretted over certain exposed passages in the show. Bill calmly offered to save the day. "No problem, Maestro, I'll play the [oboe] cues on trumpet."

I was astonished. Not only had Bill memorized his book, he'd also memorized some of the other players' parts as well. (Actually, "memorize" is the wrong term. Bill could just "hear" it.) It was damn impressive. But this wasn't the first time I'd borne witness to Bill's prodigious talent. During my stint with Don Rickles and Jerry Vale, Bill had flexed his versatility by playing trumpet for Jerry's portion of the show before relocating downstage to serve as Don's pianist. It's easy to stay humble when you've laced 'em up with players of this caliber.

Friends often accuse me of being overly self-deprecating about my musical abilities, but I assure you I'm just calling balls and strikes. Yes, I'm tall enough to ride the ride, but there are some insanely talented people out there who run circles around me. I've been in the presence of enough *Mozarts* to know where I stand in the grand scheme of things. Even on my best day, I feel like a serviceable *Salieri*.

But we play the hand we're dealt, and I've come to see my limitations as a blessing. I used to envy artistic genius, but after watching so many of my heroes struggle and ultimately flame out, my envy has morphed into sympathy, if not pity. Being saddled with mid-pack skills has kept me honest, grounded, and to be blunt, vertical. (Living on the edge can be exciting—but also hazardous to your health. Meanwhile, it's hard to fall off the middle.) My mere-mortal status has forced me to stay focused and apply myself. Lucky for me, a strong work ethic can carry you a long way. Calvin Coolidge, 30th president of the United States, agrees:

*"Nothing in the world can take the place of persistence. Talent will not; nothing is more common than unsuccessful men with talent."*

## Heading Back North (to the South)

By the end of my third year at UM, my love affair with jazz was on the rocks. My *ears* were definitely wandering. College offers a path of self-discovery—and I'd discovered I was a pop/rock/soul guy at heart. Meanwhile, my roommate, Tony, had reached the same emotional impasse. He'd landed a steady gig at a nightclub in Miami's Coconut Grove and had decided to quit school to become a full-time musician. I was happy for Tony but feared this situation could potentially create conflict around the homestead. It was easy to envision a *Felix and Oscar* scenario where I'd be gearing up for morning classes while Tony was gearing down from a late-night of funk n roll. Then fate took the wheel.

Whenever Tony and I headed home for Christmas or summer break, we'd throw together some incarnation of our old band, Sunny Day, and book a few gigs for fun and profit. Summer was upon us, so we'd started discussing possible band personnel. Deciding to aim high, we set our sights on one of Chapel Hill's most coveted singers, Carter Minor. Carter was a good-looking, soulful singer (and a few years older than us), so I felt pangs of nervousness as I dialed his number. My fears were unfounded, Carter couldn't have been friendlier. Carter said he was between bands and would love to work with us—before adding he had a PA system and a van. We'd hit the trifecta.

Returning to North Carolina, Tony and I assembled the latest edition of Sunny Day—with Carter Minor on vocals//harmonica, Greg Darden on bass, and Morgan Davis on drums. The band had never sounded better, and it was clear something special was brewing.

In addition to Sunny Day's repertoire of pop/soul covers, we dabbled in original music. With the band clicking on all cylinders, we decided to book some time at TGS studios to record a few of our songs. Local bandleader Bill Bolen was impressed when he heard our demo and passed it on to a childhood friend with international connections. Somehow our tape wound up on the desk of German impresario Bernd Palmein—and he was blown away. *Herr* Palmein excitedly made plans to visit North Carolina to record more music with us. Staring at a rosy future that included talk of a possible European record deal, the University of Miami lost what little luster it had left. The intoxicating combination of having my musical dreams *and* my girlfriend within reach proved irresistible, so I worked up my nerve and approached my parents about quitting school. I expected pushback, but my folks were surprisingly onboard. (I think they missed me as much as I missed them.)

With nothing but blue skies ahead, Sunny Day flourished. Our steady stream of gigs helped tighten our sound and vision. Meanwhile, the smitten German producer eventually came to town, and we returned to the recording studio. As the sessions played out, our European mentor urged us to consider a name change. We were eager to please and had no objections to a fresh start. (The name "Sunny Day" was essentially a path-of-least-resistance holdover from years gone by.) We kicked around a few ideas and somebody proffered "Steps." That name did nothing for me, but our ESL producer liked the *sound* of it, and since he held the keys to the kingdom, we deferred and agreed to re-brand the group.

*Will you welcome—from Chapel Hill, North Carolina—ladies and gentlemen: STEPS!* (Trigger warning for cynics: nothing ever came from our German suitor.)

### Can You Surry?

Shortly after re-establishing my Carolina residency, I received a cryptic phone call. The voice on the other end of the line told me he was passing through town and wanted to hear some live music. The mystery man said a mutual friend, Michael Sachs, had suggested he give me a call. Michael, a drummer from NYC, had relocated to Chapel Hill years earlier, and we'd played in a local jazz group when I was still in high school. (Yet again, I was surrounded by musical elders. I was lucky that way.) I did my best to give the caller the polite brush-off, passively recommending a few places where he might be able to catch some music. He tipped his hand (a bit) and confessed he specifically wanted to hear ME play.

"Sorry, but I'm not working anywhere tonight," I replied. "Maybe next time?"

He finally came clean and identified himself as the tour manager for singer/songwriter Laura Nyro. Now he had my attention. I was a fan of Nyro's work thanks to her chart-topping compositions for The 5th Dimension ("Stone Soul Picnic" and "Wedding Bell Blues"), Three Dog Night ("Eli's Comin'"), and Barbra Streisand ("Stoney End"). The road manager said Laura had just finished playing some shows in Florida and they were on their way back to New York. He expressed disappointment over my empty performance calendar and asked if I'd be willing to meet with Laura.

I answered, "Sure!"

The next afternoon, I swung by the Holiday Inn on the edge of town for a friendly rendezvous with Ms. Nyro. The tour manager greeted me in the lobby and escorted me to Laura's room. After handling the introductions, he excused himself and retreated to the band bus parked outside Laura's door.

Laura asked if I wanted anything to drink. "Coffee, tea…beer?" I'd *never* said no to a beer, so my host dialed room service and ordered a couple of Heinekens. Laura and I sat and sipped, talking about life and music as her toddler lay sleeping in a nearby crib. There was an electric piano set up in the room—and an acoustic guitar *just happened* to be leaning in the corner. After chatting for a bit, Laura asked if I'd like to play a little music. I said yes and grabbed the guitar as she took a seat behind her keyboard. My memory of our impromptu jam session is blurry, but I do remember segueing into Curtis Mayfield's "People Get Ready" at one point. As we talked between tunes, I gushed about how happy I was to be out of Miami and back in North Carolina with my girlfriend and a killer band. I was so infatuated with my new lease on life I didn't grasp I was in the middle of an audition with an established recording artist. Based on my home-sweet-home testimonial, I can't blame Laura for concluding I had no interest in joining her band and moving to New York City. Accordingly, she kept her cards close and never dropped any hints about a potential job offer. After an hour or so, I thanked Laura for the hang (and the beer) and wished her well.

It took a few days, but I finally realized the error of my ways: I'd foolishly ignored the sound of opportunity knocking. My regret intensified after friend and fellow guitarist Scott Sawyer pointed out the obvious: *Dude! Laura Nyro! NYC! WTF?* I scrambled to make a few corrective phone calls, but the window had closed. Laura was back in New York looking at other players after I'd unwittingly convinced her I wasn't the man for the job. The experience taught me an important (and possibly expensive) lesson: keep an open mind and listen to the universe. Don't dismiss things right off the bat. Leave yourself some wiggle room in case your gut instinct betrays you.

Who knows what would've happened if I'd signed on with Laura Nyro and moved to New York in 1980? It still feels like a missed opportunity, but I was young and blinded by love: love for home, love for my new band, and love for my girlfriend—who, by the way, broke up with me only a few months later. (I clearly did not see that coming.)

Seven years after blowing my chance with Laura Nyro, I made the move to NYC—and things ended up working out pretty well. I'm philosophical about it. I've learned to approach life with the attitude of "you're always exactly where you're supposed to be." Sadly, I never crossed paths with Laura again and she died of ovarian cancer in 1997.

## Dues: The Right Thing

Steps continued to grow, and as our popularity increased, so did our payload. We went from being able to haul our equipment in Carter's humble van, to needing to rent a tandem U-Haul trailer, to ultimately buying a cargo truck. In hindsight, our Gear Acquisition Syndrome (G.A.S.) seems completely overblown, but we were desperate to stay competitive with the other bands on the circuit. Regrettably, we got caught up in a ridiculous—but arguably necessary—arms race.

We bought more and more equipment (power amps, speaker cabinets, lighting), but still didn't hold a candle to the big boys. Some of our peers actually had tractor-trailer trucks and crews of roadies. These *posers* were determined to act like rock stars—despite the fact they were playing cover tunes in regional dives. Certain club owners openly griped about our relatively modest PA system, but I maintain we had plenty of gear—and my cranky back would agree. I once asked my NYC chiropractor about my chronic issues, and he responded with a string of Latin words.

"What the hell does that mean?" I asked.

He smirked, "Old bones."

Although Steps employed a soundman (Tim Hildebrandt) and a light man/driver (Tom Merkel), we never achieved a level of financial success that justified hiring a road crew. Consequently, EVERYBODY was required to pitch in on the dirty work. We eventually reached the bloated point where it took us two hours to unload and set up our gear, and an hour to tear it down and put it back in the truck afterward—with a sweaty four-hour gig sandwiched in between. Adding to the glamour of it all, our budget only allowed for two motel rooms on the road. Do the math: seven guys divided by four beds. Yep, six grown men (note I didn't use the term "adult") were forced to double up, while one lucky guy took his turn in the rotation with a private bed.

We played gigs all over the Southeast, burning up the blacktop between Washington, DC and Atlanta, while consuming massive quantities of beer (and other mind-altering substances). We were popular with college crowds, so we hit a lot of campuses. But nightclubs and roadhouses also accounted for a sizable part of our portfolio—and that's where things could sometimes get sketchy.

One of our more memorable gigs was at a sleazy nightclub in an old, renovated movie theater in West Virginia. We'd pulled into the sleepy town midday and were unloading our equipment in front of the venue when a father and his young son walked by.

The inquisitive kid pointed toward the building's entrance and asked, "Daddy, what's in there?"

The disgusted dad shook his head, "A hellhole, son…it's a hellhole."

The band laughed—but *Daddy* was right.

We rolled our gear through the darkened club, trying not to disrupt the owner's afternoon poker game. Cigarette smoke rose from the beer-strewn table, while a snarling German Shepard stood guard. Topping off the depravity, an eager-to-please dwarf was running back and forth to the bar, cheerfully fetching drinks for the shady group of gamblers. (I swear I'm not making this up.) The joint was high-octane nightmare fuel, a depressing and scary cross between *Deliverance* and *The Sopranos*.

Our weekend residency at *Bada Bing South* was a complete bust. We played set after set to an empty dance floor as the surly patrons ignored us with a passion. Adding insult to injury, the moment the DJ took over during our breaks, the dance floor was immediately packed.

Depending on our destination, we had to contend with covert and *overt* racism on occasion. Our lead singer, Carter, was African American, so he bore the brunt of our dubious environs. Even though we're talking the 1980s, it sometimes felt like the 1950s. And it didn't take a sociologist to figure out when we were in for a long night (or two).

One weekend, we held our collective breath as we set up shop in a dicey lounge at a motor lodge in western South Carolina. Steps was dedicated to spreading the *groove*, so our repertoire leaned heavily on music from funky artists like Prince, Earth, Wind & Fire, and blue-eyed soulsters Hall & Oates. This could sometimes be a problem. Every band has been there at one time or another; you're not the right fit, but the show must go on.

After our first set, a skanky waitress delivered a note from two bearded motorcycle gang members sitting in the back of the club. The missive, scrawled on a cocktail napkin, cut to the chase:

*Stop playing the n\*gger music*

Uh oh, now what? It wasn't like we could turn into a Lynyrd Skynyrd tribute band on the spot. We kept our heads down and finished out the evening, before scurrying to our inclusive one-star accommodations and bolting the door. Unfortunately, we still had to honor our contract and endure a second night at *Club KKK*. The next afternoon, we returned to the scene of the crime for a quick soundcheck—and discovered Carter's microphone was missing. We looked around for the mic, but it was nowhere to be found. I guess somebody had decided to send another *message*. We reported the theft to the club owner, but he just shrugged. Hell, he was probably in on it. We survived the weekend and made a note to never accept another gig at that venue. I doubt they would've wanted us back anyway.

Although Steps paid its bills by playing cover tunes, we continued to pursue our original music. Like most bands, our goal was fame, fortune, and MTV. We eventually signed a record deal with a regional indie label, Dolphin Records, and released a four-song EP. Our local record store hosted a release party, and our hometown radio station gave us a little love, but lightning refused to strike. We sold a few copies of our album along the way, but we were never able to break through. Meanwhile, tastes were shifting, and our soulful, hook-oriented pop was falling out of fashion. Our smooth musical stylings began to feel relatively tame compared to the edgier sounds (and haircuts) of New Wave and College Radio. Bands like U2, R.E.M., and A Flock of Seagulls hijacked the conversation and put us out to pasture. After five years of faithfully paying our dues, Steps made the painful decision to call it quits.

Steps was a great learning experience, both musically and personally. I became a better player during those years and cemented lifelong friendships. Nevertheless, I sometimes wonder if we may have set the bar too low—or in the wrong place altogether. In retrospect, focusing our energies and resources on having a truck full of gear and "the best Sly and the Family Stone medley in the Southeast" seems shortsighted. But we'd all been raised playing in Top 40 bands, so we did what we knew. Maybe we should have steered clear of the cover-band wars and concentrated exclusively on our original music. Who knows? Success is a fickle beast. It's easy to second guess oneself, but it's hard to *zig* when *zag* is putting money in your pocket. At least we took a shot.

# Start Spreading The News

I was 25 years old, a college dropout, and unsure of my next move. One thing was certain: I needed to find a source of income to maintain my starving artist lifestyle. My only appreciable skill was strumming a guitar, so, for better or worse, my job search was narrow. Society band leader Bill Bolen offered me a spot in his "orchestra" (which was usually just a quartet), and I readily accepted. I bought a tuxedo (and a flask), learned a bunch of oldies, and hit the country club circuit. The gigs were much more laid back than what I was accustomed to, but I welcomed the change of pace. There's something to be said for playing Cole Porter tunes at a low volume from a seated position (with a vodka on the rocks by your feet). I was happy to be out of the music-industry rat race, no longer chasing long-shot dreams of stardom and ruining my back in the process.

With things on autopilot, I decided to take a mini vacation. One of my college pals, Doug Travis, had moved to New York after graduating from Miami and he'd been urging me to pay a visit. I finally took Doug up on his offer and unwittingly changed my life. I came, I saw, and—like Sinatra—my little town blues melted away. New York City was exciting and alluring and I wanted in on the action. The scales fell from my eyes, and I vowed to return to "the center of the universe" on a full-time basis.

I spent a couple more years in North Carolina, honing my wedding band chops with The Bill Bolen Orchestra, while squirreling away enough money to relocate to the big city. Bill's tutelage was invaluable; learning the ins and outs of the country club scene served me well. Entry-level music jobs in NYC almost always involve a bow tie and a functional repertoire of crowd-pleasing hits from across the musical spectrum. These society gigs — known as "clubdates" in New York, "casuals" in LA, and "GB (general business)" in Boston — are the bread and butter for many a musician, sometimes for their entire careers.

Ironically, although clubdates are often ghettoized by musicians, the job is incredibly demanding. The band basically functions as a human jukebox, so players are required to know a *million* tunes from multiple decades. Band members need to be well-versed with material from George Gershwin to The Rolling Stones to the latest pop hits — and practically everything in between. I've performed on some of the biggest stages in the world, and I still contend playing in a wedding band is one of the most challenging ways for a musician to earn a dollar.

I scrimped and saved and finally reached the point where I felt I was ready to make my move. After staking a claim on a fold-out sofa in a one-bedroom *share* in midtown Manhattan, I set out to slay the dragon. I had $3,500 in my pocket and plenty of fire in my belly. I may have been naive, but I was also fearless.

In search of work, I opened the Yellow Pages and started cold-calling clubdate offices. Friends had given me the names of some of the bigger/busier bands, so I figured, "Why not start at the top?" *Fortune favors the bold.* New York's premier society orchestras were led (ostensibly) by Lester Lanin and Peter Duchin—although I assume both Les and Pete had hung up their batons by the time I made the scene. Nevertheless, these venerable bands—cultivated in the ballrooms of The Waldorf Astoria and The St. Regis Hotel—marched onward, and I was determined to join their ranks. Maybe the contractors were amused by my audacity (and/or my Southern accent), but both offices surprisingly agreed to give the bumpkin a shot. However, to be clear, these designer-label orchestras had multiple bands performing under their corporate umbrella, so I'm sure the new kid was dispatched to one of the lesser outfits. I didn't care, I was officially a working musician in New York City.

My debut to NYC society came courtesy of The Lester Lanin Orchestra at The Plaza Hotel. I showed up at the designated time in the designated ballroom and introduced myself to the bandleader. He welcomed me (in his dismissive New York way) and proceeded to lay down the law. First and foremost, I was told to turn my guitar volume OFF during "the American music," I was only permitted to play on "the rock n roll." *Um, okay?* As the other players filtered in, it was clear I was going to be the youngest guy on the bandstand; I was definitely the only guy with a full head of hair. The band leader begrudgingly introduced me to the pianist, who turned out to be jazzer Steve Kuhn. I knew the name well. I'd played compositions by Kuhn in college and was aware of his extensive resumé. *Welcome to NYC, Jeff! Tonight you'll be hacking your way through a clubdate with a pianist who's worked with saxophone genius John Coltrane.* Gulp.

The gig started and, as instructed, I kept my volume off as I faked along with the band. The vibe was formal and stiff, with the musicians sitting in chairs lined across the back of the stage. I felt like I was at a spelling bee. After the band reeled off a few tunes (tunes I absolutely knew how to play), I got tired of being window dressing. I steeled my courage and turned up my guitar, slowly creeping into the mix on "The Girl from Ipanema" while discreetly glancing around the stage. Surprisingly, my bandmates were smiling. In fact, when the clarinet solo was over, the leader nodded for me to take an improvised chorus. The elders seemed impressed that some kid with a red Stratocaster could navigate one of their sacrosanct "American" songs.

Halfway through our second set, a drunken woman approached the band and begged us to play some contemporary music. She slurred, with a hint of booze-fueled anger, "We want to PARTY!" Like synchronized swimmers, every head on the bandstand turned toward me. Aha! Now I get it—I was the designated rocker. Once the crowd grew bored with the jazzy standards, it was my responsibility to lead the band to the promised land. I'm not much of a singer, but I knew clubdate guitarists were expected to be able to bark out a few classic pop/rock numbers, so I answered the bell. I turned to the band as I stepped up to my mic and shouted, "Signed, Sealed, Delivered." The balding bassist just looked at me and shrugged. *You've got to be kidding. This guy doesn't know Stevie Wonder's Motown smash?* I punted. "Okay, 'Twist and Shout' in C ... 1, 2, 3!" I knew I was in for a long night.

We stumbled through a couple more upbeat tunes as the dance floor filled. The band leader smiled at me and motioned for me to keep it going. Next, I called John Cougar Mellencamp's relatively current hit, "R.O.C.K in the U.S.A." As I was working my way through the rave-up, I noticed pianist Steve Kuhn leaning in, signaling for help. I obliged, yelling out the chords in between my warbling, while desperately trying to land the plane. Despite the fog of war, I was acutely aware I was shouting at a guy who once played with *Trane*. I was intimidated, but also thrilled. THIS is why I moved to NYC.

On the other hand, New York didn't always live up to its hype. I was excited to book a gig with the prestigious Peter Duchin Orchestra, but the experience was deflating. I showed up for an afternoon wedding reception at a tiny, second-floor restaurant in Greenwich Village. (This was clearly not Duchin's top unit.) I dragged my gear up the flight of stairs and introduced myself to the band leader. To call the guy unfriendly would be charitable. I disregarded the chilly vibe and started setting up. After getting my guitar rig in working order, I connected my vocal mic and turned to the leader.

"Here's my microphone cable. Where's the PA mixer?"

He rolled his eyes. "There is no PA. Plug your mic into your amp."

My amp? I was incredulous. I don't care how small a room is, singing through your guitar amp is an unacceptable low-fi solution. Complete amateur hour.

The band was as thrown together as any I've seen. These dubious types of gigs are affectionately known as "screamers." Translation: the band leader *screams* out the title of the next song as his ragtag lineup clumsily segues from one worn-out tune to the next. I also learned a hard and fast clubdate rule in those early days: NO shaking hands on the bandstand. God forbid the client gets the impression the band doesn't know each other. (We usually didn't.) Meanwhile, no telling how much the bride and groom paid to have THE Peter Duchin Orchestra play their wedding. *Caveat emptor!*

Continuing to make my way down the list of area clubdate offices, I reached out to Steven Scott Entertainment. Their contractor expressed interest and asked me to come to his office for an interview/audition. Unfortunately, Steven Scott's office wasn't located in Manhattan, but rather on Long Island. I didn't care, I was on a mission. I went to Penn Station, bought a ticket on the Long Island Rail Road and set out for the village of Great Neck. Arriving at my stop, I exited the train and started following my hand-written directions. I'd been told I didn't need to bring a guitar; I could use the one at the office. This turned out to be a blessing as I had to climb through a hilly, overgrown field to reach my destination. (Cue "Ain't No Mountain High Enough.")

I identified myself to the receptionist and was directed to a small office. I knocked on the door and introduced myself to the contractor. We chatted for a few minutes, then he asked me to grab the acoustic guitar in the corner.

"Play something for me," he grunted.

I took a deep breath and dug into a sophisticated arrangement of the jazz standard, "All the Things You Are." The cigar chomper nodded when I finished.

"Nice job kid, but I want to hear you play a tune from *this* decade. We're looking for pop players."

I changed gears as requested and unleashed Huey Lewis's "The Heart of Rock & Roll."

The guy beamed, "Beautiful! We'll call you if we need you." They never called.

Despite the dead end, I learned a huge lesson that day. Jazz (or classical) skills are impressive but, more often than not, pop music is what puts food on the table. Whenever guitarists reach out to me in search of work, I'm much more interested in their practical experience than their academic achievements. A salty Broadway colleague puts a finer point on it. "I don't give a shit if a guy has a master's degree from Juilliard, I want to know if he's ever been yelled at by an old bluesman on a late-night bar gig." I concur with this take. And so would my younger brother, Will.

I'm very proud of my *baby* brother. A highly skilled saxophone player, Will is the Director of Jazz Studies at The University of North Carolina at Charlotte, and has scaled the heights of academia, earning a Doctor of Musical Arts degree from the University of Illinois Urbana-Champaign. Will has also paid his real-world dues, touring the globe with Harry Connick Jr.'s big band in the early 1990s. Nevertheless, a gig at a Fort Worth nightclub remains one of Will's richest educational experiences.

While still in college at University of North Texas, Will was booked to play a couple of shows with legendary session cats, guitarist Cornell Dupree (Aretha Franklin, Bill Withers, Donny Hathaway) and bassist Chuck Rainey (Aretha Franklin, Steely Dan, Quincy Jones). The band was hanging out backstage before the gig when Cornell offered my brother a sip from his flask.

"I should probably pass," Will replied prudently. "If I start drinking, you might not like my playing."

Cornell sniffed, "I might like it better."

Spoken like a true journeyman. Don't make your life about music; make your music about life.

\* \* \*

Although I'd managed to start at the top of the wedding band heap, water seeks its own level. Thanks to a referral from fellow University of Miami guitarist John Hart, I was able to land some semi-steady employment with The Frank Terris Orchestras in Yonkers. (John Hart is a world-class player, and now heads our alma mater's guitar department.) Frank Terris wasn't on par with the big boy offices in Manhattan, but I wasn't in a position to be picky. Hell, I was just happy to be earning the occasional buck as a NYC musician. Most of Frank Terris's work was in the outer boroughs (Queens, Brooklyn, The Bronx, Staten Island)—or New Jersey or Long Island, but I'd come *physically* prepared for this scenario: I owned a car. Being emotionally prepared was another story. Driving around NYC was an intense, sometimes frightening experience compared to laidback North Carolina, but I eventually adapted to the traffic insanity.

I didn't know my way around the tri-state area, so I felt like Magellan every time I set out for a gig. Whenever I was lucky enough to have a booking, I'd call Frank Terris's secretary, Kathy, for directions to the venue *du jour*. (God bless the ever-patient Kathy.) I'd scribble down the info and say a prayer before hitting the road. This was long before the advent of GPS, so handwritten instructions were your only method of navigation. It was tricky enough finding your way to the gig, but the real *fun* started afterward. Your daunting task was to decipher the crumpled directions backwards—usually in the dark, and usually with angry drivers flipping you the bird as they whizzed by.

But even after successfully making my way back to the city, I wasn't home free. I still had to survive the harrowing hike from my parking lot to my apartment. After moving to New York, one of my first orders of business had been finding nearby, *affordable*, 24-hour parking. (There was no on-street parking in my midtown neighborhood, and many of the garages closed by midnight—an unfriendly hour for working musicians.) I ultimately signed a monthly lease at a giant outdoor lot located underneath an elevated section of the West Side Highway down by the Hudson River. The graveled plot of no-man's-land was surrounded by a 10-foot chain link fence topped with razor wire, making the facility look more like a car prison than a car park. The desolate area, lined with industrial warehouses, was sketchy during daylight hours, so you can imagine what it was like in the middle of the night. Remember, we're talking the late 1980s, a few years before NYC's touristy renaissance. Manhattan was still a dangerous place—especially after dark.

After parking my car, I'd literally make a run for it (often in my tuxedo and dress shoes). The CBS Broadcast Center was only a couple of blocks away, so I always felt a little safer once I made it to the well-lit complex. (I could slow from a sprint to a jog.) Meanwhile, if things ever got really dicey, the fallback plan was to walk in the MIDDLE of the street while loudly talking to yourself. The goal was to make the night creatures afraid of YOU.

Fast forwarding to today, I'm amazed when I stroll by the former location of my parking lot. The once-forsaken stretch now features luxury high-rise buildings with 24-hour doormen. I could've used their watchful eyes back in those scary days and nights of 1987.

Despite the occasional gigs, I was still having trouble making ends meet. I finally conceded I'd have to look for an additional source of income, and this inconvenient truth landed me behind the concession stands of Broadway. Fortunately, since I was still new to town, everything—including hawking candy and cocktails in theaters on The Great White Way—felt glamorous. I was a concessionaire during the week (working alongside a fledgling playwright named Aaron Sorkin), and, when lucky, a wedding band guitarist on the weekend. I had no complaints; I was doing it in New York City.

### *Not Even in my Wildest Dreams*

Four months into my new life, things got crazy...FAST. I met a keyboardist named Delmar Brown, and he hired me to play in his fusion band, Bushrock. We embarked on a low-budget summer tour of Europe, playing a month of gigs around France and Italy. A couple of weeks into the campaign, Bushrock crashed Perugia's Umbria Jazz Festival for a nondescript gig at a local club. But, as fate would have it, rock god Sting was also in town, and he wandered in off the street to check out Delmar's band of unknowns. The rest, as they say, is history. My life exploded a couple of months later when Sting recruited me to play guitar on his *Nothing Like the Sun* World Tour. In the span of two whirlwind weeks, I went from selling candy in Broadway theaters to playing on *Saturday Night Live* with Sting. A month after that, I was in Rio de Janeiro performing in front of 250,000 people. I didn't know what hit me. I'm not going to re-plow those *Fields of Gold* here, but the year-long, mind-blowing experience—and its humbling aftermath—is chronicled in my book, *Do Stand So Close: my improbable adventure as Sting's guitarist.*

## *On the Road Again*

After a year of orbiting the earth with Sting, I burned on re-entry and splashed down in NYC. I welcomed the break at first but started getting antsy when my phone refused to ring. Then, after four months of radio silence, I finally got a nibble. Sting's management company fielded a call inquiring about my availability for a tour with Virgin Records artist Sam Phillips. I didn't know anything about the *female* Sam Phillips (not to be confused with the legendary *male* Sam Phillips, who founded Sun Records back in the 1950s), but I was the definition of available. I contacted Sam's management and we scheduled an audition. After a long, quiet winter, I felt reborn.

I was instructed to learn two songs from Sam's new album, *The Indescribable Wow*, before meeting with her and producer, T Bone Burnett. Although I didn't know Sam, I was aware of T Bone's heavy-hitter status. T Bone had started as a sideman, touring with Bob Dylan's Rolling Thunder Revue, before branching out as a critically acclaimed solo artist and an up-and-coming producer with acts like Los Lobos and Elvis Costello. T Bone had produced Sam's latest album and was helping her assemble a band for her upcoming tour. (I later learned, in addition to being business partners, Sam and T Bone were married to one another.)

My audition took place at the venerable (now demolished) Mayflower Hotel on Central Park West. On the appointed afternoon, I strutted into the elegant lobby and approached the front desk.

"I'm here for a meeting with T Bone Burnett."

The receptionist stared at me blankly. "Is Mr. Burnett a guest?"

"Yes."

I waited as the clerk typed away on her computer.

"I'm sorry sir, but we don't have anybody registered under that name."

Huh? Was my coveted job offer already in jeopardy? I asked again and waited nervously as the clerk conferred with other hotel employees. Thankfully, the mystery was eventually solved, and I was directed upstairs.

I exited the elevator and wandered down a long hallway in search of the slippery room number. I knocked on the door and was met by a tall, clean-cut, red-headed dude with nerdy Malcolm X browline glasses. He smiled and extended his hand, "Hi, I'm T Bone." I was caught completely off guard. I'd never seen any photos of T Bone, so I was expecting an archetypal rocker—clothed exclusively in black and covered in tattoos. T Bone was the exact opposite. He was a towering, soft-spoken Texas gentleman dressed in conservative attire. (Defying all stereotypes, I later learned T Bone was also a "scratch" golfer—in other words, very good at the game.) T Bone has since gone on to become one of the industry's top record producers with credits including Robert Plant and Alison Krauss, John Mellencamp, and Brandi Carlile, as well as the soundtracks from *The Big Lebowski, O Brother, Where Art Thou?* and *Crazy Heart.*

T Bone invited me inside, offering a beverage and a seat. I was getting settled when Sam appeared from another room in the suite. T Bone handled the introductions. Sam's hip chanteuse persona perfectly matched her fresh alt-rock sound. She was slinky, charming, and understated—just like her music.

The three of us chatted for a few minutes, then T Bone handed me the acoustic guitar leaning on the couch. Sam and

T Bone listened intently as I played the requested tunes. After I finished, the duo complimented my skills and thanked me for my time. I thought I acquitted myself nicely, but, like most auditions, I was clueless as to how my jury felt. Plus, I had no idea how many other guitarists were on their list. Now the waiting.

I got a call a couple of days later saying I'd passed muster and the gig was mine if I wanted it. Woo hoo! Back in the game.

T Bone subsequently told me he knew I was "the guy" the moment I started playing, saying my "touch" had sealed the deal. I was flattered. Like T Bone, I've come to realize music is primarily in the hands—and, of course, the heart. I've worked in numerous Broadway pits over the years and seen multitudes of players pass through as subs. (Chair holders maintain a stable of substitutes.) It's wild to hear various people play the *exact* same notes on the *exact* same instrument—yet sound completely different. Each player's touch is as individual as their fingerprints. It ain't the arrow, it's the archer.

I definitely wanted the Sam Phillips gig, but details needed to be ironed out. Not surprisingly, I was offered a substantially lower salary than my Sting paycheck, but the amount was acceptable for the condensed six-week commitment. On the other hand, the proposed lodging arrangements created a sticking point. Although we'd be spending most of our time on a tricked-out tour bus, there would be hotel accommodations at certain stops. Sam was hiring three musicians for the tour, but management only wanted to provide TWO hotel rooms for the boys in the band. As a result, the sidemen would be expected to share a room on a rotating basis. This was a deal breaker for me. I was much too old to be cohabitating with a strange adult. (And trust me, most musicians are *strange*.) I was resolute and prepared to make a counteroffer: a pay cut in exchange for a private hotel room. Fortunately, before I could broach the subject, management reversed course and declared each band member would get their own room. Sold! Let's do this.

Tour rehearsals were set to begin the following month in Los Angeles. I was excited to be back in the saddle, jetting off to the West Coast to make music with a major-label artist. Since we were only a trio (plus Sam on vocals), T Bone decided to conduct rehearsals at his beachfront apartment in Santa Monica. Lucky us! Instead of being locked in a windowless, soundproof bunker for days on end, we sprawled out across T Bone's living room and watched the waves roll in as we assembled our lean, mean, power trio. The band also included David Miner on keyboards/bass, and Michito Sanchez on percussion.

After a week in sunny California, the band (and our three-man crew) boarded a cross-country flight to chilly, gray Canada. We survived open night jitters at Toronto's Diamond Club, and then played Ottawa and Montreal (opening for The Cowboy Junkies) before making our way back to the US. We wound our way down through the Northeast, but like all tours, our itinerary involved some circuitous routing. We played shows in Boston and Providence, and then, despite having a New York gig on the books, headed south to Philadelphia first. I'd only been on the road for three weeks, but I felt pangs of homesickness as I watched Manhattan's skyline whizz by on our way to Philly.

After Philadelphia, we performed at DC's famed 9:30 Club before backtracking north to New York. I was ecstatic our tour included a stop in NYC, and I was doubly pumped because we were playing CBGB (the legendary rock venue known for launching artists like Talking Heads, Debbie Harry, and The

Ramones). Unfortunately, my first visit to the hallowed halls of CBGB was underwhelming, if not traumatic. I walked in and thought, "*This* is CBGB? What a dump!"

CBGB was dark, dingy, and reeked of stale beer. In addition to a nicotine-colored veil, the club's walls were covered with years of tattered band flyers and stickers, creating the effect of the world's largest (and messiest) bulletin board. Meanwhile, the CBGB bathroom made your average gas station toilet seem downright luxurious. CBGB's men's room was located at the bottom of a poorly lit, narrow staircase in the back of the club—and it may be the nastiest place I've ever unzipped my pants. (Please keep all jokes to yourself.) The door-less latrine featured a rusty sink, a pair of urinals, and a single commode perched atop a pedestal—with NO stall. (The euphemism "throne" has never been more accurate.) My sympathies go out to anybody who's ever had to conduct any *personal business* in that graffiti-covered hellscape.

Despite my initial impressions, I ultimately came to appreciate the downtown magic of CBGB. The sound system kicked ass, and the stage was filled with some of punk rock's coolest ghosts. I wound up playing the venue numerous times over the years and grew to love the place—until their doors closed in 2006. RIP CBGB. The space now houses a John Varvatos clothing store, but at least the boutique retained some of the club's punk decor and character. Could be worse; could be a bank (like The Fillmore East).

Sam's band was gelling nicely, which meant we were overdue for an off night. *Hello CBGB!* Unfortunately, high-stakes NYC isn't the best place to uncork a shaky show. I experienced technical problems throughout the evening (including breaking a couple of strings), and when things started unraveling, I think Sam let it get to her. We soldiered through our set, but the bad juju continued to snowball. The result was passable, but we didn't exactly blow the roof off the joint. Oh well, I'd been around long enough to be philosophical about it. *We'll get 'em tomorrow!*

Over my decades of gigging, I've learned there's a simple litmus test to measure professionalism: How good is your bad? Executing is easy when you're in the zone, but what happens when the fairy dust is nowhere to be found? Can you still deliver when anxiety kicks in and things start spinning out of control? Pros can.

Sam's band was composed of seasoned vets, so our *bad* was good enough—but Sam seemed shaken by the crowd's lackluster response. Adding to the snakebit evening, our tour bus wouldn't start after the gig. We were supposed to drive to Chicago overnight, but that plan had to be scrapped until a mechanic could be found. Sam's tour manager, Dan, told me to go home and get some rest. He'd give me a call when it was time to hit the road.

I was thrilled by the thought of sleeping in my own bed (if only temporarily), so, after a few post-gig cocktails, I hailed a cab to my Upper West Side apartment. Welcoming myself home, I flopped onto my futon without grasping the fatal flaw in my plan: the telephone/answering machine was in my roommate Doug's bedroom...and out of my earshot. (No cellphones back in 1989.) When I awoke the next morning and realized I was still in NYC, I wandered out of my bedroom in search of coffee. Doug was standing in the kitchen.

"Hey Jeff, the phone rang a few times during the night.

Some guy named Dan was looking for you. You might want to check the machine."

I rushed to Doug's bedside table and nervously pressed play on the blinking box. Dan had left numerous messages, starting with "Jeff, the bus is fixed. We're ready to leave for Chicago. Meet us at CBGB," and eventually ending with an exasperated, "OK dude, we're heading out. Getting to Chicago is now your problem." Oops.

I called Sam's management and explained my predicament. They shrugged; nothing surprises managers, they've seen it all…twice. Sam's office handled my travel arrangements while I got my ass to the airport. Touching down in The Windy City, I made my way to the hotel and called Dan to let him know I was back in the fold. Not surprisingly, Dan was less than happy with me—but dealing with knuckleheads is a big part of a tour manager's job. Dan bluntly informed me, due to the fact I'd gone AWOL, I was responsible for the cost of the airline ticket. I balked, and we haggled back and forth until finally agreeing to split the expense. Considering the screwup was entirely my fault, I gladly accepted the compromise.

I was surprised to see T Bone Burnett materialize in Chicago. Despite being our de facto musical leader, T Bone wasn't an actual band member, so he'd stayed behind in LA as Team Sam racked up the miles. I can't speak for T Bone, but touring loses its appeal rather quickly for a lot of musicians. The glamour fades and the road becomes a necessary evil to spread the gospel and keep the cash flowing. T Bone had been around the block a time or two, so he certainly didn't need to be advancing his odometer on our account. That said, Sam had apparently sent up the bat signal after our bumpy CBGB gig, and her loving husband had jetted to her side. I don't blame Sam one bit. Performing is incredibly stressful and living out of a suitcase is lonely as hell.

As we chilled in the Park West green room before the show, Sam asked T Bone if he'd be willing to join her onstage for a song. His reaction was ambivalent at best. T Bone was a friendly yet retiring type of guy (he kind of reminded me of me), but I was still young enough to assume everybody craved the limelight. After initially resisting Sam's overture, T Bone acquiesced and agreed to play a number. I was puzzled by T Bone's reticence and, lacking much of a filter, nosily asked him about it. T Bone laid some deep truth on me.

"The way I see it, you don't need an audience to be an artist. Picasso didn't paint in front of a crowd."

T Bone's words struck a chord with me. As I've grown older (and similarly lukewarm about performing), I've found refuge in T Bone's wisdom. Being an artist *and* an entertainer frequently overlap…but they don't have to. I've discovered I don't need the roar of the crowd to feel fulfilled. I'm perfectly happy scratching my artistic itch in the relative seclusion of an orchestra pit or a recording studio—or in total seclusion with my computer, tinkering in ProTools or Microsoft Word.

Playing in Chicago gave me a chance to catch up with my pal—and one of the city's hippest citizens—bassist Darryl Jones. I'd been a Darryl fan for years, captivated by his work with Miles Davis, jazz guitarist John Scofield, and, of course, Sting's *Dream of the Blue Turtles* band. Darryl wasn't a member of Sting's group during my tenure, but we'd met and bonded on Amnesty International's *Human Rights Now!* World Tour (which featured Sting, Bruce Springsteen, and Darryl's boss at the time, Peter Gabriel).

I called Darryl, told him I was in town, and invited him out to Sam's gig. He said he'd be there. I felt like such a big shot as I added Darryl's gold-plated name to our guest list and was thrilled when he poked his head backstage before the show. Doing my best impersonation of a power broker, I puffed out my chest and introduced heavyweight producer T Bone Burnett to heavyweight bassist Darryl Jones. T Bone was familiar with Darryl's work and seemed psyched to meet him. Not that T Bone didn't already respect me but being friends with Darryl might have banked a few extra brownie points.

After the show (that indeed featured a cameo by Mr. T Bone Burnett), we had a couple of hours to kill before tackling our overnight drive to Minneapolis. The tour manager told everybody to be back at the hotel by 1am for "wheels up," so Darryl suggested he and I grab a bite to eat. A one-on-one hang with my bass idol? That's an easy sell. We jumped into Darryl's car and hit the streets of Chicago in search of midnight grub. We eventually found a suitable joint and settled in for a quick nosh. As we caught up on current events, I shared a juicy (and potentially lucrative) piece of gossip with Darryl.

While in LA for Sam's rehearsals, I'd spent some time with my old Carolina/Miami partner-in-crime, Tony Bowman. (When I'd headed north to NYC, Tony had chased his musical dreams west to Los Angeles.) Tony and I were out carousing around town one night when we bumped into his friend and colleague, Niki Haris. (At the time, Niki was working as one of Madonna's primary backup singers and dancers.) Niki and I were shooting the breeze when Darryl's name came up.

"Jeff, you played with Sting, do you know how to get in touch with Darryl Jones?"

"Sure, why?"

"Madonna wants Darryl to play bass on her next tour."

I assumed Niki was just making small talk, and I was confident Madonna's management could track down Darryl in a heartbeat, but I made a mental note.

Over our fashionably late supper in Chicago, I told Darryl about my conversation with Niki.

"Madonna huh?" Darryl said, eyebrow raised. "Hmmm, I've got some work on the books with Herbie Hancock, but I might have to look into that." Almost as an afterthought, Darryl smiled and added, "I definitely dig her new tune, 'Like a Prayer.'"

Sure enough, a year later, Darryl wound up playing bass on Madonna's *Blonde Ambition* World Tour. (I'm still waiting for my commission…I'm kidding!) Darryl's career has been nothing short of astounding. After stints with Miles Davis, Sting, Peter Gabriel, Herbie Hancock, and Madonna, he somehow managed to top himself by joining The Rolling Stones. Darryl deserves every bit of his success. The dude is a monster.

Glancing at my watch, I told Darryl we should probably grab the check and head back to the hotel. I was already in the doghouse for missing the bus to Chicago, so I didn't want to notch any more demerits. We paid our tab and jumped into Darryl's car, driving for several blocks until Darryl made a startling confession.

"Uh Jeff, I don't remember where your hotel is."

Say what?!? I felt a surge of panic but forced myself to stay cool. (Being in Darryl's presence requires permanent cool.) Darryl and I zigzagged through downtown Chicago in search of my mislaid hotel as the departure clock ticked down. I felt like a rock-n-roll Cinderella and feared Darryl's car would become my pumpkin of doom. Luckily, my prayers were answered when we rounded a corner and saw Sam's idling tour bus. Praise the Lord! I thanked Darryl for his hospitality, gave him a hug, and urged him to reach out to Madonna. Wiping the sweat from my brow, I climbed aboard our Minneapolis-bound bus.

I loved our tour bus. It may seem counterintuitive but traveling by bus—as opposed to a plane—has its advantages. My year with Sting was spent exclusively in the air, and although we enjoyed the luxury of a private plane on the domestic legs of our tour, everything outside of North America entailed commercial airlines. And who the hell likes airports? Plus, I'm no fan of flying in general, so I find the *terra firma* aspect of a tour bus extremely appealing.

But more to the point, unlike airplanes, band buses have sleepers. This is a HUGE perk. Touring often requires early morning starts, and when air travel is involved, you are doomed to social interaction. Between the van ride to the airport and waiting to board the plane, your day has begun, ready or not. Last, and definitely least, you're herded onto a flight filled with self-centered strangers, all bumping and shoving as they attempt to wrestle their swollen bags into the overhead bins. It is dependably brutal—especially with a sleep-deprived hangover.

But with a tour bus, those inevitable crack-of-dawn lobby calls require the bare minimum of consciousness (and clothing). Throw on some gym shorts, a hoodie, flip flops, stumble downstairs, grunt at your bandmates, crawl into your bunk and go back to sleep. It's a softer, gentler way to temporarily greet the day after a late night of debauchery.

Unlike a commercial airliner, a tour bus is more of a rolling home. Whenever you finally decide to spill out of your curtained cubbyhole, you have access to a small kitchen stocked with your handpicked goodies, a comfy couch, and a TV—usually playing *This is Spinal Tap* on a loop. But, in the spirit of full disclosure, the bathroom situation on a tour bus is suboptimal. Unless it's an emergency, certain bodily functions are reserved for Truck Stops along the Interstate.

On long haul days, I'd stay in my sweatpants and stocking feet for the duration. I'd pour myself a tumbler of grapefruit juice (spiked with plenty of vodka) and slide into the shotgun seat for hours of windshield time. Our driver, Bob, was an easygoing, good ol' boy from Tennessee, so we bonded over our shared Southern heritage. Bob was straightforward and plainspoken but, after years of transporting musicians, also a man of the world. Much to my delight, Bob had just finished a tour with one of my favorite groups, Public Enemy. And thanks to his prolonged exposure to the political rappers, Bob was sporting a fresh coat of *woke*. I'd sit back and watch America whir by, as Bob expounded on the progressive social theories of Chuck D, interspersed with colorful anecdotes from Flavor Flav. Bob was pretty fly for a (fellow) white guy.

Sam's tour was hit and miss when it came to our venues. Some stops found us performing in front of huge crowds at large halls, other nights I felt like I was in a bar band. *Hello Wisconsin!* Despite our quartet's modest footprint, the tiny stage at Madison's Club de Wash didn't come close to accommodating our cubic needs, and, as a result, I was forced to spend the evening straddling the bandstand. I played our entire set with my left foot on the stage and my right foot precariously perched on a stack of milk crates, as we rocked *tens* of people.

Piling up the mileage, we made our way to the Pacific North-west, playing shows in Canada's Vancouver and Victoria, as well as Seattle and San Francisco (performing at Boz Scaggs's club, Slim's). Five weeks and 17 cities later, Sam's tour came full circle, closing things out in Los Angeles. Fittingly, the band was ensconced at the notorious rocker hangout, The Hyatt on Sunset. Affectionately known as the "Riot Hyatt," I was honored to be staggering in the historical footsteps of bands including Led Zeppelin, The Who, and The Rolling Stones. We played our final show at the Hollywood hotspot, Club Lingerie, before retreating to the hotel for the requisite end-of-tour blowout. As usual, I overdid it (by a long shot) and paid dearly the following day.

Although the tour was finished, Sam and I were scheduled to do a live radio interview in the late afternoon. I consumed a couple of medicinal margaritas at my farewell lunch with pal Tony Bowman, but still felt like shit when I arrived at the radio station. The receptionist asked if she could get me anything to drink, so I eagerly requested a beer. The young woman disappeared for a few minutes before returning with tragic news. "I'm sorry, but alcohol isn't allowed in the studio." Damn, there would be no (additional) "hair of the dog" for me. I played it off, but I was hurting. Luckily, I was able to power through my fogginess and bang out a couple of Sam's tunes on command. After we wrapped the wobbly interview, Sam thanked me for being a part of her tour and gave me a goodbye squeeze. I told her I really appreciated the gig and then slumped into the car of an A&R guy from Virgin Records. I was LAX-bound to catch the redeye back to NYC—and the unemployment line.

## Because I'm Thirsty

I returned to New York and a completely empty calendar. I picked right back up where I'd left off: sitting around waiting for my phone to ring—and drinking heavily. I still had some money left over from the Sting tour, but thanks to my incessant partying, my resources were dwindling fast. I'd always had a taste for alcohol—and my Sting success had poured gasoline on that fire. New York City has a bar on practically every corner, with some of the hardcore establishments opening as early as 8am. When you factor 4am closing times into the equation, you end up with a city that never sleeps...or sobers up.

My Hell's Kitchen neighborhood featured numerous dive bars and I clocked many an hour on their tattered stools. Sometimes I drank alone, sometimes I had help. (Yeah, I'm looking at you Mike Olsen.) Rudy's Bar & Grill, located just around the corner from my apartment, was one of my favorite watering holes—and apparently Donald Fagen's as well. The first verse of Steely Dan's "Black Cow" famously name-checks the joint. "I saw you in Rudy's, you were very high." I don't remember ever seeing Fagen at Rudy's, but then again, I was usually "very high."

My other home away from home was the Dwyer Brothers Pub on West 42nd Street. Hoo boy, if those walls could talk. I spent many a late night boozing it up with local lushes, pimps, prostitutes, and wayward NYPD detectives. It was wild to see real-life versions of Superfly, Coffy, and Kojak all hanging out together, bending elbows (and powdering their noses) in harmony. And even though closing time was technically 4am, that just meant the omnipotent bartenders, Chris and "Tommy Towel," were required to lock the doors. The neon beer signs in the window would flicker off, but our private bacchanal plowed forward unabated. The night wasn't over until Chris and Tom proclaimed it was over—and usually by that point, Shorty was opening the door at Rudy's. *Free hotdogs!*

### In a Fixx

Digging into another lost evening at the Dwyer Brothers, I struck up a conversation with a fellow barfly. We did the usual dance of strangers, cautiously revealing bits and pieces about ourselves as we sized each other up. (You could never be too careful around Times Square.) After determining I wasn't conversing with a psycho killer, I introduced myself and mentioned I was a musician. My bar-mate, Adam, confessed he was also in the biz—before casually adding he was the drummer for the British New Wave band, The Fixx. (I was a fan of the group thanks to their catchy hits like "One Thing Leads to Another" and "Saved by Zero.") Following Adam's lead, I told him I'd recently toured with Sting. Adam broke into a smile. Turns out, The Fixx had served as one of the opening acts for The Police on their farewell *Synchronicity* tour. This cemented our cosmic connection.

Adam said he was in town working on The Fixx's latest album and invited me to swing by the studio sometime. When I asked where they were recording, Adam replied, "Electric Lady." I suppressed a grin and eagerly accepted Adam's offer. I was psyched. I'd finally get a chance to visit "The House that Jimi built."

A few nights later, I made my way down to Greenwich Village, giddy over the thought of hanging with The Fixx...at Electric Lady Studios! (I relished *any* whiffs of my former life as a contender.) I pressed the intercom and stated my business. The sacred portal buzzed open, and I floated downstairs to the subterranean temple responsible for some of my favorite records from Jimi Hendrix, Stevie Wonder, David Bowie, Chic, and Led Zeppelin.

Adam waved me into the lounge area and introduced me to a few of his bandmates. We chatted a bit before Adam ushered me into the control room where Fixx leader, Cy Curnin, and the engineer were hunched over the console. The duo looked up and mumbled a quick hello before burying their heads back into their work. I plopped down on the leather couch in the control room and listened as the mix took shape. One section of the tune seemed to be giving the pair a problem. They kept hitting rewind over and over, attempting to identify the issue. After a few stops and starts, I decided to add my two cents. (What the hell was I thinking?) I offered my unsolicited input, and the room went dead quiet. Cy and his co-pilot slowly turned and looked at me with dead eyes. After a very pregnant pause, I broke the awkward silence.

"But that's just my opinion, maybe I should shut up."

Cy and the engineer chimed in unison, "YES...you should."

I was thoroughly humiliated but attempted to mask my shame with a stiff upper lip. I remained in the control room for a face-saving amount of time before quietly slipping back out into the lounge. I made myself a cup of tea and nervously hung around for a bit, but the minute I deemed it acceptable, I said my goodnights and tucked tail back uptown. Moral of the story: studio guests are like children—they should be seen, and not heard.

Ironically, years later, I wound up doing some guitar work on one of Cy Curnin's solo projects. A mutual friend had recommended me to Cy, and thanks to my trusty Sting credit, we hit it off. (Fortunately, Cy didn't remember me from the Electric Lady incident, and I wasn't about to remind him.)

I spent a week in the studio with Cy—and learned a highly valuable lesson in the process. I was a couple of years removed from my Sting glory, so my swagger had all but deserted me. Compounding the problem, I found myself somewhat starstruck by Cy's chart-topping success and heavy rotation on MTV. My combination of timidity and deference created a clumsy energy in the studio and, as a result, my contributions lacked conviction. I saw Cy as the musical guru in the room, and repeatedly looked to him for guidance. Cy eventually became exasperated with my passivity and fumed, "Come on, Jeff—sell me some goddam snake oil!"

The moment was a revelation. People hire professionals for a reason; they *want* us to bring our expertise and self-assured opinions to the table. When it comes to rock n roll, the meek shall inherit jack shit. No one has ever tiptoed their way to the top. From that day forward, I never let doubt cloud my musical choices. Even if I was unsure (or intimidated), I forged ahead with feigned confidence. Thanks for the tip, Cy. *Snake oil! Don't leave home without it.*

\* \* \*

One slow season bled into another. I picked up a few gigs here and there, but I was still struggling with the harsh reality I was no longer a rock star (or at least playing guitar with one). I had some near misses along the way with loose talk of maybe hitting the road with Hall & Oates, or a possible stint with NYC cult rocker Garland Jeffreys. There was also some chatter about another tour with Sam Phillips (opening for Elvis Costello), but none of these leads panned out. I began to wonder if I'd used up every last drop of my luck landing the Sting gig.

I was 30 years old, and afraid I'd peaked professionally. (In a narrow sense, I had.) But what was I supposed to do? Retire? That option seemed a *bit* premature—and, more importantly, financially untenable. At a crossroad, I was faced with the emotional, psychological, and economic challenge of working my way *down* the ladder of success. But thanks to perspective, I've come to realize life isn't a ladder; it's really more of a jungle gym. Careers involve a host of moves: up, down, sideways, stationary…all while trying not to fall and bust your ass.

### Catskills/Dogskills

Among my varied projects, I did a handful of shows and recording sessions with singer/songwriter/social justice activist Billy Sparks. One of our more memorable gigs was performing at Woodstock's 20th anniversary concert. I'd never visited the hallowed site, so I was psyched. We were booked in an early evening slot, but like most multi-artist affairs, the concert fell way behind schedule. Our gang sat backstage, twiddling our thumbs and drinking much too much tequila as we waited our turn.

We finally took the stage around 2am. I was frustrated (and exhausted) from the interminable wait, but I got a much-needed burst of adrenaline when the soundman started blasting Jimi

Hendrix's fuzzed-out "Star-Spangled Banner" through the PA system. Standing on the same plot of land where Jimi had unleashed his "bombs bursting in air" was powerful.

During our final tune of the night (ahem, *morning*), I walked to the edge of the stage for my guitar solo. (I still had my wireless transmitter from the Sting tour, so I was able to wander about freely.) As I leaned into my dramatic feature, my guitar tone started randomly changing from one sound to another. I was confused until I glanced over at my rig. Mystery solved. A stray dog had made his way up onto the bandstand, and he was pawing at my pedalboard—engaging and disengaging stomp boxes while cheerfully wagging his tail. *Is that you, Jimi?* I burst out laughing and scurried over to shoo the mischievous canine back into the wings. The free-spirited moment felt quintessentially Woodstock. Fido let his freak flag fly!

It was too late to drive back to NYC after our set, so we started looking for lodging. Unfortunately, concertgoers had snapped up all the local hotel rooms, so we were forced to search for quite a while before finding shelter.

We finally scored rooms at the Concord Hotel, the legendary Catskills resort that primarily catered to Jewish vacationers from the NYC area. (Think "Dirty Dancing.") A poster on an easel in the lobby told me everything I needed to know. *Comedian Buddy Hackett appearing this week in the Imperial Room!* The desk clerk gave our motley crew a sideways look as we checked in for the night. Who could blame him? We didn't exactly fit the profile of the resort's typical clientele.

I awoke the next morning with a howling tequila hangover. Self-diagnosing my condition, I prescribed a pre-breakfast cocktail. I made my way downstairs to the lobby bar, grabbed a stool, and ordered my old reliable: vodka and grapefruit juice. Gaining my bearings, I suddenly felt like an extra in a Woody Allen nostalgia film. The Concord was offering free cha-cha lessons, and the lobby was brimming with blue-haired ladies honing their skills. (I guess their husbands were on the golf course.) The scene was borderline surreal — and quite entertaining. An hour or so later, I joined my bandmates for breakfast in the Concord's restaurant and cemented my full-fledged *goy* status by asking the waiter for a side of bacon — in a strictly kosher establishment. Duh. I was definitely a work in progress. Guess I still am.

## Soul Caged

Gigs remained sporadic and uneventful, certainly nothing to write home about. Meanwhile, my mother was set to undergo surgery, and I was overdue for a visit, so instead of writing home, I went home. My cobwebbed schedule presented no obstacles, so I decided to take a breather from NYC and help Mom get back on her feet.

During my North Carolina hiatus, Sting came through town on his *Soul Cages* World Tour. I was excited about the co-incidence and couldn't wait to reconnect with Sting and catch up with some of my old pals on the crew. Although I'd been replaced with guitarist Dominic Miller, there weren't any hard feelings on my part. (If you can't handle rejection, do NOT go into showbiz.)

I called Sting's management office a few days before the concert and asked for a handful of complimentary tickets. The junior staffer on the other end of the phone had no idea who

I was and seemed indignant over my request. This was ridiculous; I knew how things worked. When I toured with Sting (in a nine-piece band), each musician was allowed four comps per show—at least. (I'd been granted TWENTY tickets when we played my hometown on the *Nothing Like the Sun* tour.) Despite the standing perk, band members often don't need the freebies, so the tickets are simply kicked back to the box office.

Fast forwarding to *The Soul Cages* concert, Sting had downsized to a quartet—and two of the guys were British—so I knew there'd be plenty of spare comps at the North Carolina stop. Accordingly, I didn't think twice about asking for the professional courtesy. Sting's minion hemmed and hawed, sighing "I'll see what I can do." I held firm. "Please just tell Billy that Jeff Campbell would like eight tickets." (Billy Francis, Sting's tour manger, was a good friend and I was certain he'd take care of me.) After keeping me hanging for a couple of days, the assistant finally called to say he'd spoken with Billy. Verdict: eight comps were no problem; they'd be under my name at the will-call window. I felt vindicated.

The night of the show, I picked up the tickets, got my entourage seated, and made my way backstage to say hello. The crew welcomed me with smiles and hearty back slaps before escorting me to Sting's inner sanctum. My former boss lit up and gave me a big hug when I entered his dressing room. I told Sting I was in town visiting my parents and couldn't wait to hear his new band. We spent a few minutes talking about life, and then Sting casually asked if I wanted to sit in on a song. No arm twisting required. We kicked around some ideas and agreed upon "Set Them Free."

In addition to guitarist Dominic Miller and drummer Vinnie Colaiuta, Sting's new group included keyboardist David Sancious. David is an incredibly talented multi-instrumentalist with credits including Bruce Springsteen, Eric Clapton, Santana, and Peter Gabriel. (David and I knew each other from our time together on Amnesty International's *Human Rights Now!* World Tour, when he was a member of Peter Gabriel's band.) Although David's primary responsibility with Sting was keyboards, he also played a bit of guitar during the show, so Sting suggested I might use David's rig for my cameo. Sting summoned a roadie to lead me to the band's dressing room to hammer out logistics. David Sancious greeted me warmly and said he'd be happy to loan me his Stratocaster—with requisite rockstar wireless transmitter of course. I thanked David, wished the guys a good show, and headed back out to my seat.

The lights went down, and Sting's new streamlined quartet proceeded to kick ass. The band had been over twice that size when I was in the fold, and while it had been an honor to work with Sting's jazzy all-star lineup (including Branford Marsalis, Kenny Kirkland, and Mino Cinélu), there was a part of me that had longed for some lean, straight-up rock n roll à la The Police. I guess there was a part of Sting that felt the same. He'd returned to stripped-down basics with his *Soul Cages* band, and I loved it.

Sting had instructed me to make my way to the stage during "King of Pain," so I slipped out of my seat when I heard the percussive plinks of the anthem's minimalist intro. A roadie waved me through the security barricade and guided me to the side of the stage with his trusty flashlight. I climbed the steps to find David Sancious's personal tech sheepishly holding a cheap off-brand guitar...and a brutally short cable. David's wireless Strat was nowhere in sight. The roadie shrugged, "Sorry man, I have NO idea where this piece of shit came from."

I guess David had rethought his offer—and decided to stick me with a stray mutt instead. I'm not picky so I wasn't fazed by the pawn shop special, but the lack of a wireless transmitter was a blow. Rather than roaming the stage freely and mixing it up with the boys, I'd be tethered to David's guitar amp with a 10-foot cable. (Trust me, ten feet is very short for a concert stage.) I don't know if I was the victim of a little good-natured hazing—or straight-up sabotage, but I took the passive aggressive dis in stride. I had no choice. After three *long* years out of the limelight, I sure as hell wasn't going to miss an opportunity to step back on the big stage with my rock-star pal.

## *Tux for the Memories*

My Carolina sabbatical was restorative, but I eventually had to return to New York and face the music (or the lack thereof). After treating Chemical Bank's ATM as my primary source of income for a couple of years, the jig was up: I needed a job. I'd exhausted my short list of long shots, so I had no choice but to return to the wedding band racket. I contacted my previous employer, The Frank Terris Orchestras, and threw myself at their mercy. After the proper amount of groveling (and a humbling re-audition), I was brought back into the *family*. But since the bulk of Frank Terris's work took place outside of Manhattan, I was once again in need of wheels. I'd sold my first "city car" after landing the Sting gig, but I'd sadly come full circle. It was time to revisit the joys of urban automobile ownership. I bought a beat-up Honda Civic for $600 and rented a monthly parking space at a nearby outdoor lot. Look out world! (again)

Each weekend, I'd don my emotional suit of armor and navigate the expressways of Greater New York in my rusted-out rattletrap. My car had no air conditioning or radio, so I'd cruise (or creep) down the highway with my head sticking out the window, ear glued to my transistor radio as I tried to decipher the traffic reports on 1010 WINS.

My car was such a piece of junk, it was debatable if the vehicle could even pass New York State inspection. But luckily, I had connections. My bandleader, saxophonist Tommy G (who reminded me of Wolfman Jack) told me not to worry—he knew "a guy." I gave Tommy fifty bucks at a gig one night and, a week later, he slipped me an automobile inspection sticker on the sly. In his thick Brooklyn accent, Tommy whispered out of the side of his mouth, "Put this thing on in the dark. Do not let ANYBODY see you do it."

I loved Tommy G. He was a gruff sweetheart who took great pleasure in cracking corny jokes and busting chops. (Whenever a band member noodled on stage before a gig, Tommy would bark, "Practice at home!") Most important of all, Tommy wound up playing a pivotal role in my sobriety. But that day of reckoning was still a ways off. I needed to do a little more *research* first.


Every clubdate musician has a bottomless supply of commuter horror stories. I've broken down in tunnels, sat in 3am traffic jams, ridden black-tie in a tow truck operated by two guys just sprung from prison (they stopped to buy a six-pack of beer along the way), and willfully euthanized my terminally ill Honda by ignoring the pinned temperature gauge as I cursed the Cross Bronx Expressway. But one particular experience deserves its due.

After a late-night wedding gig, I was heading home on the six-lane racetrack known as the Long Island Expressway (aka the L.I.E.). I'd upgraded to a marginally less clunky VW Jetta, but I was having problems with the car bucking and knocking off at random. Unfortunately, the issue was just intermittent enough to go unsolved. (My mechanic *eventually* determined the culprit was a faulty fuel pump.)

I was cruising along, grooving to my radio when the display went dark, and the music stopped. *Hmmm. What's that about?* As I looked at my dashboard for clues, the high-beam indicator light above my speedometer mysteriously started glowing blue. This curious combination of circumstances got my attention, so I slowed my roll and merged right. Just after I made my move to the granny lane, my car started jerking violently and lost power. By chance, I was near an exit ramp, so I put on my emergency flashers and coasted up the hill to a stop. Whew, that was close! A breakdown in the middle lane of the L.I.E. could have been catastrophic—or even deadly.

I was able to restart my car and I made it home safely. But as I replayed the events in my head, I struggled to connect cause and effect. (Abrupt silence? An inexplicable warning light?...then loss of power?) I've been known to casually thank my "angels" from time to time, but I'm typically skeptical of the supernatural. Coincidences are usually just coincidences. But in this case, I was stumped—and humbled. I truly believe I was the beneficiary of divine intervention that fateful evening; nobody will ever convince me otherwise. Thank you, whoever and wherever you are.

\* \* \*

On the domestic front, after years of going through the motions in an undefined relationship long past its expiration date, I found myself a bachelor. The breakup was in the best interests of both parties, but since I was the *dumpee*, the rejection still hurt. I was slogging along aimlessly, in desperate need of a wake-up call, when Cupid charitably intervened.

I bumped into a female acquaintance from the neighborhood one afternoon, and the chemistry was undeniable. Kentucky native Patty Murray was friendly, attractive, and exactly what this lonely boy needed. Patty, an actor and a singer, knew I was a guitarist, and mentioned she was teaching herself the instrument. I applauded her initiative and said I'd be happy to give her some tips. She accepted my offer; on the condition she could buy me dinner afterward. We had an enjoyable evening…and we've now been married 28 years.

Patty and I somehow navigated the early years of our relationship despite my heavy drinking and battered self-esteem. After experiencing the big time with Sting, my return to the wedding band trenches seemed like cruel and unusual punishment. Shitty gigs (and prodigious amounts of vodka) had broken my spirit and made me extremely self-conscious about my fall from grace. Accurate or not, I felt like people were whispering behind my back, "What the hell happened?" I wondered the same thing.

## *Loathe Boat*

The lowest point of my once-thriving career was a recurring gig on a Long Island *booze cruise*. The ignominious party boat sailed from Port Washington to the Statue of Liberty (and back) and left me scarred for life. The captain set sail at 6pm, which meant my commute from the westside of Manhattan to Exit 36 on the Long Island Expressway inevitably coincided with the heart of rush-hour. Attempting to calculate my departure time, I was always faced with arriving much too early, or a tiny bit late — and late was not an option. The phrase "missed the boat" took on a literal meaning with this gig. Legend has it, a tardy musician once had to hire a dinghy to catch up to the cruise already in progress. My ostensibly manageable 25-mile trip usually ended up taking approximately two hours. (Cue Hendrix's "Crosstown Traffic.")

The four-hour gig was, in a word, brutal. The typical evening featured a drunken array of suburban knuckleheads, often sprinkled with obnoxious bridesmaids and rowdy off-duty firemen. (I'd spend half the night wresting my microphone away from liquored-up, wannabe vocalists.) The band played on the open-air, upper deck of the boat, which resulted in an ongoing battle with sea sickness. You haven't lived until you've strummed your way across a choppy Long Island Sound in a sweaty tuxedo. I should've sought an endorsement deal with Dramamine.

The *Voyage of the Damned* involved a specific, structured repertoire. We always kicked things off with Christopher Cross's "Sailing" as we pulled away from the city dock; we'd play Elvis's "Jailhouse Rock" when we passed Rikers Island jail in the East River; and the evening's *coup de grâce* was a cheesy medley of Lee

Greenwood's "God Bless the U.S.A." and Billy Joel's "New York State of Mind" when we reached the Statue of Liberty. Pure, un-adulterated schmaltz.

Like many gigs, there was a constant back-and-forth between management and musicians over volume. After repeated run-ins, the boat's crew eventually moved the PA mixer to a locked cabinet. The band had no control over the knobs and had to request permission (and a key) to make any adjustments. Each night when I got home, Patty would lovingly ask, "How was the gig?" She already knew the answer, but she'd listen sympathetically as I grumbled about "goddam sailors doing sound."

Adding final insult to injury, I was paid the paltry sum of $100 for my Herculean effort. Yep, I made a lousy hundred bucks for those four hours of floating torture (and the dependable snail-like commute). I should've contacted Amnesty International about the ongoing abuse.

Today, with over twenty years between me and my nautical nightmare, it's sometimes easy to lose sight of those bad old days. But whenever I catch myself whining about some trifling luxury problem (or hear the opening arpeggio of "Sailing"), I pause and picture "the boat"—and a wave of gratitude washes over me. When I landed my first full-time Broadway show, Patty gave a me a simple but powerful good luck charm: a small photo of a party boat circling the Statue of Liberty. Two decades later, that treasured memento is still working its magic. Each time I start a new show, my first order of business is taping that tattered picture inside the back of my locker. I want to keep that memory fresh—forever.

\* \* \*

Augmenting my tent pole job as a wedding band (and boat) guitarist, I performed with singer/songwriters in downtown clubs, played on low-budget indie recordings, and occasionally landed the rare jingle session—whenever the first *twelve* go-to guys weren't available. Jingles are highly coveted because, in addition to the session fee, musicians receive residual payments if the ad continues to run after its initial 13-week cycle. The reuse amount per spot is nominal, but it can add up for the busier players. Truth is, it's virtually impossible to gig your way to financial security—there are only so many hours in a day. But if you can get on the royalty train, you have a shot at earning a respectable income. I made years of "mailbox money" for a simple two-chord tag I played on an ad for the children's toy, Magna Doodle. The goal is to get paid while you're sleeping.

Unfortunately, due to advances in technology and tastes, the jingle business has all but evaporated for sidemen. Today, staff composers can often create the entire music bed on their laptop computer—no pesky, expensive musicians required. Exacerbating the situation, jingle houses now face the stiffest competition of all: rock stars. No longer afraid of being labeled a "sell out," successful artists are willing to license their catalogs for commercial use. The next time you hear The Beatles on a Nike ad or Led Zeppelin hawking Cadillacs, light a candle for NYC's starving session musicians.

## *See Me, Fire Me*

As I nickeled and dimed my way to keeping the lights on, a new resource appeared on the horizon: Broadway. *The Who's Tommy* was heading for The Great White Way, and in need of guitarists with authentic rock and roll sensibilities. I got a call from John Miller—an accomplished bassist and one of Broadway's top musical contractors—to gauge my interest. My answer was a resounding "Hell yes!" Unfortunately, my first foray into musical theater was humbling.

I was asked to audition for the Guitar 2 chair in the *Tommy* orchestra. (Guitarist Kevin Kuhn had played *Tommy's* pre-Broadway run at the La Jolla Playhouse in California, so he already had the Guitar 1 slot sewn up.) I had no idea what the numerical designation meant, but I didn't care; I was simply happy to be in the mix. I was told to learn "Pinball Wizard" for my audition, so I swung by Tower Records to pick up a copy of the *Tommy* CD. I thought, "Hey, it's just Pete Townshend. How hard can it be?" This blend of arrogance and naïveté would ultimately blow up in my face.

As instructed, I showed up at the producer's midtown apartment for my audition. Contractor John Miller greeted me at the door and invited me in. As I entered, I saw my pal and ace guitarist Jon Herington packing up his instrument. (Jon is currently the guitarist for Steely Dan—a position he's held for the last 20 years.) I said hi to Jon in passing, and then turned to meet musical director Joe Church. I took a seat on the couch and pulled my acoustic guitar out of my gig bag.

"Where's your electric guitar?" Miller asked.

This is where my tale starts to unravel.

When I dissected "Pinball Wizard" to prepare for my audition, I heard two guitars: electric and acoustic. I assumed the electric guitar would be considered Guitar 1, so, by the process of elimination, I figured the acoustic guitar *had* to be Guitar 2. Right? Accordingly, I only learned the acoustic part—and only brought an acoustic guitar to my audition. Wrong! The "powers that be" had expected me to prepare ALL the guitar parts to showcase my skills. I tried to play off my rookie mistake by shifting the blame to a straw man. *Nobody told me to bring an electric guitar.* Tsk tsk. I doubt my bullshit attempt at deflection scored any points with the brass, but fortunately my relatively fresh Sting credit provided sufficient cover for my blunder. I played the *acoustic* part to "Pinball Wizard" as the listening heads nodded approvingly. The jury thanked me for coming and said they'd be in touch. I exited the apartment and rang for the elevator, while resisting the urge to punch myself in the face.

John Miller called a few days later with the verdict: NYC stalwart John Putnam had been hired to play Guitar 2. I thanked Miller for the opportunity, and was in the middle of apologizing AGAIN for my audition faux pas when he interrupted, "However…"

I was all ears.

At the time, Broadway orchestras still employed "walkers"—a somewhat questionable practice stemming from a clause in the musician's union contract that requires shows to hire a minimum number of players. (Orchestra minimums are based on the size of the theater.) In this specific instance, *Tommy* was booked at the St. James Theatre, and the collective bargaining agreement between The Broadway League (producers) and Local 802 (musicians) stipulated productions at the St. James

HAD to employ a minimum of 25 musicians. But here's the rub: *Tommy* only needed 17 players to perform its score. This discrepancy meant the show's producers were obligated to add eight *non-playing* musicians to the payroll. These extra bodies were known as "walkers." The name referred to the cushy job description: go to the theater, sign in, and *walk* away. But by this point, the situation was even cushier. Walkers were no longer required to show up at all. (In our union's defense, the well-intentioned rule was implemented to prevent unscrupulous producers from using skeletal bands or even worse, prerecorded music. Broadway patrons pay good money for their tickets; they deserve a professional product.)

Long story short, although I hadn't been hired to play *Tommy*, I'd been designated as one of the show's walkers. This setup sounded too good to be true. Patty (still only my girlfriend at the time) had a neighbor who played trombone on Broadway, so she asked him for the inside scoop on walkers. He replied sarcastically, "Well, there is one catch…you have to swing by the theater once a week to pick up your check." Wow, I'd hit the jackpot: a no-show job. (Cue *The Sopranos* opening theme.)

Patty and I drove down to North Carolina for Christmas, and I spent the holiday break raising glass after celebratory glass to good ol' 802. But duty eventually called. I had a New Year's Eve commitment with The Frank Terris Orchestras so, after a week of extreme overindulgence, Patty and I headed back to NYC. The year-end gig was your typical *Auld Lang slog*—and my post-holiday hangover (emotional and physical) weighed a ton. But the real gut punch was lurking just around the corner.

My phone rang on New Year's Day. I picked up to hear *Tommy* contractor John Miller on the other end.

"Hey buddy, I've got a bit of bad news."

I braced for impact.

John continued, "The producers have decided to make some changes...and your walker position has been rescinded. Sorry man."

I hung up and let out a long sigh. *Easy come, easy go?* I didn't (nor couldn't) fully process the financial blow at the time—but *Tommy* wound up running over two years. Crunching the numbers, I lost out on more than $100,000 of *no-strings* income. Ouch seems inadequate. But being brutally honest, losing the phantom job was probably for the best. My drinking was out of control by that point. I'm not sure giving free money to a drunk was such a good idea.

I accepted my fate but attempted to salvage the situation by signing on as a substitute guitarist. Kevin Kuhn had asked if I'd be interested in subbing his Guitar 1 chair, and I'd readily said yes. (I had no idea what I was in for.) Following sub protocol, I sat in the pit with Kevin for a couple of shows, made a cassette recording of the performance, and xeroxed the book. Then it was homework time. My *it's just Pete Townshend* assumptions were quickly dismantled.

*Tommy* was quite challenging—and being a Broadway newbie, I made all the classic mistakes. My biggest blunder was faithfully memorizing my pit recording without factoring in the nightly variances of a *live* musical production. I failed to grasp things change (big and small) at each performance.

When my first shot came, I buried my head in my music stand and played the version of the show I'd learned from my cassette tape—giving little regard to the conductor. This is NOT how it's done. I survived...barely. I was told I'd played well enough to earn another crack, but I needed to pay better attention to the podium.

I absorbed the notes and took a second pass at the show. Unfortunately, my sophomore effort was equally shaky. I'd grown up playing in garage bands, so I didn't understand what all that arm waving was about. Being a dumb guitarist, I'd never played in the wind ensemble or marching band, and, as a result, had no idea how to follow a baton. I was given a third try, still made too many mistakes, and was asked not to return. Feeling utterly defeated (and embarrassed), I waved the white flag and declared Broadway was not for me. This *hot take* would ultimately prove to be way off-base.

# Last Call

After living in sin for two years, Patty and I were married at the United Nations Chapel in NYC. My life had been rudderless, if not sinking, so settling down was just what I needed. A couple of weeks before the wedding, I was barhopping with a few pals when somebody asked if I was having a bachelor party. My dear friend (and pickled partner-in-crime) Richie Douglas interjected, "Why bother? Jeff's whole life has been a bachelor party!"

That pretty much summed it up. Although I'd never been much of a Casanova, I was a BIG drinker. But that clock was ticking.

Less than one year into our marriage, the bill for my heavy drinking came due. After a long weekend of multiple club-dates—and obviously not enough alcohol—I suffered a withdrawal seizure at the Greentree Country Club in New Rochelle. (For what it's worth, I tried to drink responsibly whenever I had to drive. But I'd overindulged the night before at a local Manhattan event, and the thirsty gorilla on my back needed his fix. Situational temperance was my undoing.) The gig had just ended, and I'd gone to the men's room before tackling my commute home. Next thing I knew, I was waking up in our lead singer's arms. (Our vocalist, Paul Rich, found me flopping about on the tiled floor and held me until the convulsions ended. Paul later told me when I fell limp, he feared I was dead. I still feel guilty about putting my friend through this ordeal.) Thank God the seizure occurred before I climbed behind the wheel of my car; I'm literally lucky to be alive. I spent a couple of days in the New Rochelle Hospital undergoing a battery of tests, with my supportive—but clear-eyed—wife by my side. Patty had recognized my drinking problem early on, but fortunately saw a light inside of me and patiently helped me find my way. The doctors sent me home with an unambiguous diagnosis: stop drinking.

I didn't touch a drop of alcohol for months and I felt like a million bucks. Convinced I had a handle on things, I determined it was safe to resume drinking. I'd seen the error of my ways and vowed to embrace moderation. (Vodka laughed.) Despite my best intentions, I quickly spiraled back into excess. After falling off the wagon with a resounding thud, I showed up at a wedding band gig completely sloshed. My bandleader, the lovable but straight-shooting Tommy G, assessed my condition as soon as I walked through the door. He should've pulled me aside and read me the riot act, but his disappointment apparently eclipsed his anger. Tommy confronted me, eyes filled with pity, and gently whispered, "Jeff, go wash your face."

Boom!

You'd think your moment of truth would be more dramatic, but Tommy's hangdog expression triggered my rock bottom. Thoroughly disgusted with myself and tired of disappointing loved ones, I quit drinking.

Unfortunately, my previous brush with death notwithstanding, I'd somehow missed the memo: alcohol withdrawal can be life-threatening. I stupidly went cold turkey and, right on cue, suffered another seizure…on stage…during a set at a midtown rock club. (The crowd got their money's worth that night.) My commitment to immediate sobriety was admirable, but ill-advised. Moral of the story: Do NOT try this at home; seek medical attention. After 20 years of hard drinking, booze had knocked me on my ass. I was down for the count, but as the saying goes, "The view from the canvas can be quite instructional."

Getting sober absolutely saved my life—and, for better or worse, altered the trajectory of my career. Without alcohol, I suddenly found the extroverted nature of my job less enjoyable. I'm reminded of the old Grateful Dead gag:

Q: What did the Deadhead say when he ran out of drugs?
A: This band sucks!
(Calm down Dead fans, it's just a joke.)

Much like the dry Deadhead, once I "ran out" of drink, gigs weren't nearly as much fun. Believe me, I envy the *cowboys* who can't wait to jump on stage, rev up the crowd, kick out the jams, and maybe even consume a couple of drinks. But I'm not a cowboy (at least not anymore). I've realized I'm more of a *sheriff*, a law-and-order type who flourishes in the controlled setting of a recording studio and/or a Broadway pit. This may sound boring or unglamorous (or just plain sad) to some, but we play the hand we're dealt. And I've found contentment—and creativity—in my solitude.

\* \* \*

*(New York, NY) May 12, 2020 — With the ongoing suspension of Broadway performances due to COVID-19 continuing until further notice, the Broadway League is updating information regarding performance cancellations and ticketing protocol. While a date to resume performances is yet to be determined, Broadway theaters are now offering refunds and exchanges for tickets purchased for performances through September 6, 2020.*

Yikes. My *vacation* has now stretched to six months. This is going in the wrong direction. Help!

## Indie Hunt

In the early years of my sobriety, I tackled as many projects as possible. I was determined to throw myself back into my work and rebuild my reputation. Clubdates provided the bulk of my income, but I also played in several original bands to keep the creative fires burning. NYC is full of gifted, ambitious artists in need of sidemen, and while these gigs are typically low-paying, they do offer musicians a shot — albeit a long one — at fame and fortune. (Like the Lotto pitch says, "You can't win if you don't enter.") In addition to my hired-gun endeavors, I formed a "garage soul" band with my wife, Patty. It was nice to be in at least one group that performed songs I'd had a hand in writing.

These original bands played the usual downtown circuit of clubs (CBGB, The Bottom Line, The Bitter End, Tramps, etc.)

with the same goal in mind: lure an A&R guy to the gig, land a major label deal, strike it rich, and build a guitar-shaped swimming pool behind your mansion (or at least a guitar *amp*-shaped swimming pool). We all had occasional whiffs of interest from the dream makers, but none of us ever hit the jackpot.

Experience has taught me success is unpredictable, elusive, and sometimes downright random. I've met and worked with a ton of talented people over the years—and only a select few of them have hit it BIG. (In fairness, I'm talking "cover of the *Rolling Stone*" big, but I can literally count these conquering heroes on one hand.) Right place/right time is often more important than talent—and getting the cosmos to align is beyond our mortal reach. The only thing we really control is our effort, so that's where I place my focus. Forget about wins and losses, I'm most proud of my perseverance. I want my tombstone to read: "I tried."

### Taxi!

I kept tilling the soil and, in addition to my blue-collar/black-tie workload, I was able to occasionally land gigs with more established artists; you know, people you've actually heard on the radio. One of my first prestige gigs (in sobriety) was with renowned pianist, and forefather of smooth jazz, Bob James. Bob has had a stellar career as a performer, arranger, and producer, but he's probably best known for his song "Angela"—aka the theme from the 1970s TV hit, *Taxi*. Bob had recently collaborated with vocalist—and daughter—Hilary James on a new album, *Storm Warning*, and the duo needed a backing band to play some promotional dates.

My connection for the gig came from bassist Stu Woods (whose impressive discography includes Jim Croce, Bette Midler, Barry Manilow, and Todd Rundgren). Remember those first three *exposed* bass notes on the intro of Todd Rundgren's, "Hello It's Me"? ...that's my buddy Stu. When I asked how he managed to swing that memorable bass *solo*, Stu responded sarcastically, "They didn't know any better." Stu and I worked for the same clubdate office, playing a slew of gigs together over the years. One evening, the bandleader called the disco chestnut, "Turn the Beat Around," but told Stu to lay out because the bass part was already programmed into the keyboardist's synthesized sequence. Stu shrugged, "Okay ...but you do know I played bass on the original recording, right?" (Move over Rodney Dangerfield.) Stu also played bass on Tony Orlando's chart-topping "Tie a Yellow Ribbon Round the Ole Oak Tree" and has the distinction of appearing on the very first episode of *Saturday Night Live* (née *NBC's Saturday Night*) with singer Janis Ian. Stu is the real deal, an authentic NYC *cat*.

Stu got the call for the Bob/Hilary gig, and generously recommended me for the guitar slot. As my close pal (and successful keyboardist) Jeff Kazee says, "The good gigs come from knucklehead gigs." Kazee is right, every cool job I ever landed sprouted from some unglamorous seed I'd planted along the way. My humdrum clubdate alliance with Stu Woods had yielded a sweet dividend.

Over the next year or so, I played a handful of shows with Bob and Hilary James, as well as doing multiple recording sessions with the pair. I was thrilled to be in the presence of a man of Bob's talent and stature. From Quincy Jones to Sarah Vaughan to Roberta Flack, Bob James reeked of musical gravitas.

Our first gig was in Detroit, so we flew to the Motor City a couple of days ahead of time to assemble the band. We set up shop in a vacant downtown theater and spent the afternoon/evening honing a song list culled from Bob and Hilary's new album — plus some of Bob's tasty classics. During one of our breaks, I decided to wander outside for a breath of fresh air and a reprieve from the arctic air conditioning. I fancied myself a tough New Yorker, so I didn't think twice about taking a little stroll around Detroit. This was a miscalculation on my part; my spidey senses started tingling after only a couple of blocks. Despite being the middle of the day, the streets were eerily quiet. I'd been an urbanite long enough to know empty streets breed trouble — muggers prefer working without an audience. I kept noticing shady characters loitering in doorways, so I quickly corrected course back to the comfy (secure) theater.

We were scheduled to perform the following night at the Chene Park Amphitheatre on the northern bank of the Detroit River. (I was surprised to learn Windsor, Ontario was on the southern bank. Yep, Canada is south of Detroit. A map will bear me out.) It was the dog days of July, and the Midwest was in the throes of a brutal, record-breaking heatwave. Awaiting our lobby call, I stared out of my hotel window in awe as the blackened sky dumped golf-ball sized hail on the lawn. The storm let up before we made our way to the venue but reared its head anew during soundcheck. Flash-flood waterfalls rushed down the amphitheater stairs, while giant barges on the Detroit River disappeared into angry squalls. The downpour transformed the summer afternoon into something akin to a scene from *Apocalypse Now*. There was even talk of cancellation, but the weather calmed enough for the concert to proceed.

At one point in our show, a gust of wind barreled across the stage, scattering sheets of Stu's music though the air. Despite the liberal number of clothespins ringing his music stand, our bassist's efforts proved no match for Mother Nature's temper tantrum. I internalized a sigh of relief; glad I'd gone to the trouble of memorizing the music. Once again, my pride (or OCD) had saved my ass.

My next gig with Bob and Hilary took me to the lush Caribbean nation of the Dominican Republic. Much like my time with Sting, traveling with Bob James meant I enjoyed first-class accommodations. We stayed at the exclusive Casa de Campo Resort, a sun-kissed playground for the rich and famous that featured three private beaches, seven restaurants, and three award-winning golf courses. I was in the lap of luxury. (The snorkeling was amazing!) Bob was an avid golfer and mentioned over dinner he couldn't wait to hit the links. Fishing for an invite, I dropped numerous hints of my love for the game, but confessed my skills were (ahem) "limited." Bob wisely didn't take the bait. The last thing a serious golfer wants is a duffer like me spoiling his mojo. Bad golf is highly contagious.

We were performing at the Heineken Jazz Festival in Altos de Chavón, a replica 16th century Mediterranean village nestled in the heart of the Dominican countryside. I was doubly excited because the artist lineup included "El Rey de los Timbales," Tito Puente. I was a big fan of Puente's Latin jazz stylings—and the teenaged rocker in me was thrilled to be sharing a bill with the man who composed Santana's crossover hit, "Oye Como Va."

Killing time before our set, I wandered backstage in search of a beverage. I stepped into the bustling kitchen area and came face-to-face with *El Rey* himself—but the scene was far from majestic. The solitary Puente sat slumped in a metal folding chair, looking like a man in desperate need of a vacation (or possibly retirement). Tito's posture and weary expression seemed to reflect every hard mile of his 50-year career. I smiled and nodded but resisted the urge to say hello. I respectfully let the Latin legend be, and quietly made my way to the soda fountain.

The concert was held at a picturesque stone amphitheater, transporting me back to fond memories of my Italian travels with Sting. The Dominican crowd loved our set, but despite playing at a *legit* jazz festival, the biggest cheer of the night came when we broke into Bob's "Theme from *Taxi*." Even with an arguably discriminating audience, the pop hit won the day.

Post show, Bob treated the band to a celebratory late-night dinner. Camaraderie counts, so I played along with the festivities—cheering on my rowdy bandmates as they consumed shot after shot of tequila while I sipped my virginal ginger ale. I know feelings ain't facts, but nursing a *Shirley Temple* made me feel like a total outcast. (Boozing is a dependable and popular form of bonding—maybe nowhere more so than the music biz.) As the bash gained steam, I kept sneaking glances at my watch, painfully aware of our pre-dawn lobby call for the airport. I didn't want to be labeled a party pooper, so I hung until the bitter end. As a result, my head didn't hit the pillow until almost 3am. I knew my efforts were futile, but I was desperate to at least grab a ceremonial catnap before my 4:30am wake-up call. I'm no fan of flying, and lack of sleep only exacerbates my anxieties.

I rose before the Dominican roosters, packed my bag, and dragged myself to the hotel lobby. Our tour manager pointed me toward an idling minibus parked out front. I climbed aboard the vehicle and searched in vain for a secluded seat. (Turns out, we were sharing a ride to the airport with Tito Puente's band. Those poor guys were flying north to New York before immediately jumping on another plane and reversing course for South America.) I sat in the back of the darkened bus—exhausted yet anxious, surrounded by hungover (or still drunk) musicians giggling, farting, and snoring. And people wonder why I don't like "the road."

I exhaled as our plane took off from Santo Domingo, happy to be homeward bound. Then, only a few minutes after the flight had leveled off, our pilot came on the intercom and started speaking—in Spanish. *¿Qué pasa?* I had no idea what our captain was saying but my seatmate obviously did. He began squirming and tugging at his necktie while frantically peering out the window. (It did seem like we were losing altitude.) I wanted to tell the guy to calm his ass down; "nervous flyer" was *my* job. A flight attendant eventually explained (in English) a warning light was flashing in the cockpit, so we were returning to the airport to investigate the issue. We landed safely and a maintenance crew boarded the plane to nose around. After a half hour or so, we were cleared to resume our flight. Take two! And people wonder why I don't like "the road." (Is there an echo in here?)

A couple of weeks later, The Bob and Hilary show hit the skies again, destination Los Angeles, to perform at a multi-artist benefit for the Boys and Girls Club of Pasadena. Saxophonist Kirk Whalum was hosting the event and he'd invited us, keyboardist George Duke, and vocalist James Ingram to join the party. I was always psyched to head for the Left Coast, but the trip provided an eye-opening geography lesson: Pasadena ain't Hollywood. The City of Roses was beautiful, but they rolled up the sidewalks a lot earlier than the LA I was accustomed to. Finding late night food or drink was the equivalent of a scavenger hunt.

I was a big fan of George Duke, so I couldn't wait to see his set. Unfortunately, I was underwhelmed by Duke's offering. Instead of stretching out into hip, jazz-fusion territory, George played it safe, primarily leaning on pop tunes from his sideman/producer discography. All due respect, but I don't consider Deniece Williams's "Let's Hear It for the Boy" to be the ideal vehicle for showcasing George's virtuosity.

On the other hand, crooner James Ingram blew me away. I knew Ingram from his hits, "Just Once," "One Hundred Ways," and one of my all-time faves, "Yah Mo B There" with Michael McDonald, but I wasn't prepared for his high level of intensity. (Is *smooth intensity* a thing?) Despite staying in mellow mid-tempo for the entire evening, Ingram killed it. His evangelical delivery converted me into a true believer.

The crowd loved the Bob James portion of the show, but I had a rough night. To simplify logistics, every band had agreed to use the same "backline" (rental amplifiers), and the same stage configuration. This strategy was efficient and pragmatic, but regrettably placed me only a few feet from Bob's piano—and WAY too close to his sensitive eardrums. I fiddled with the unfamiliar amplifier throughout our set, struggling to get my desired sound and tone. Compounding my anxieties, Bob kept shooting subtle but dirty *you're too loud* glances in my direction. My angst came to a humiliating head when I lost my fretboard bearings during a guitar solo and ended up on an objectively wrong note. Disgusted with my amateurish choke, I flashed back to an NYC singer/songwriter gig earlier in the week, where I'd *marveled* at how good I sounded.

But that was then, this was now. Performing with Bob James at a packed theater in LA had upped the ante, and I'd buckled under the stress. It was a humbling reminder of how pressure can mess with your head. My *bad* wasn't very good that night.


### Gangsta Lean

Back in New York, I was invited up to Bob James's house in Westchester County to add some guitar parts to Hilary's latest tracks. Living out every musician's fantasy, Bob had a fully appointed, state-of-the-art recording studio—in his basement. I was supremely jealous; commuting to work in your bedroom slippers seemed like heaven.

In addition to Bob's extensive career as an artist and producer, he'd stumbled into a lucrative *third act* as one of hip-hop's most sampled artists. Turns out rappers (including Run-DMC, Eric B. and Rakim, and N.W.A.) loved spitting rhymes over Bob's smooth grooves. Hilary told me Bob would spend hours in his studio, listening to demos from rappers seeking permission to use his music. She chuckled, "You wouldn't believe some of the explicit lyrics I hear drifting through Dad's door."

Ironically, I wound up in the middle of one of Bob's hip-hop negotiations. Brooklyn rapper Buddha Monk had constructed a track around a 2-bar section of Bob's "Winding River," and he'd sought Bob's blessing to use the mellow snippet. I don't know if Bob refused, or Buddha balked at the price, but the two were unable to reach an agreement.

When an impasse like this occurs, rappers typically choose Plan B and create a "replay" (a note-for-note replica of the desired track). Going the replay route circumvents the need to license the master recording—an expensive proposition that requires every musician on the *original* session to be paid (again). Long story short, Buddha Monk opted to record a sound-alike of the Bob James sample (which featured guitarist Earl Klugh), and I got the call. I was a longtime fan of Klugh's nylon-string stylings, so I was happy to oblige.

I was hired for the Buddha Monk date by an old pal from the Bronx, drummer/A&R man John McNally. John emailed me an mp3 of the Buddha demo for reference and asked me to bring a classical guitar and an electric bass. When I pointed out the original Bob James track used upright bass, John shrugged, "Bring your P bass anyway."

The recording session took place at Giant Sound Studios, located at 1776 Broadway. (The same *historic* building where I first met with Sting's manager Kim Turner to schedule my audition with destiny, but I digress...) Walking into the studio lounge, I encountered a boisterous three-ring circus shrouded in marijuana smoke. John waved hello and introduced me to the man of the hour, Buddha Monk. Buddha, a larger-than-life character with a jovial attitude, welcomed me to the festivities before introducing me to his female manager (who was clearly immune to all the off-color language flying around the room) and his large posse of hangers-on. After a bit of banter, I made my way out to the studio and started setting up my guitars.

One of Buddha's fresh-faced cohorts trailed me into the isolation booth and started asking questions about my instruments. The bubbly teen said he was an aspiring bassist and asked if I had any tips. I gave him the same advice I give all fledgling musicians: try to imitate your favorite players. He nodded.

I dug deeper. "What bands do you like?"

He paused and gazed upward...before answering with a huge, enthusiastic grin, "Blood, Sweat & Tears!"

Huh? You could have knocked me over with a feather. The FIRST album I ever purchased as a kid was the self-titled, *Blood, Sweat & Tears*, so I was literally a lifelong fan. I never expected to hear an adolescent hip-hopper name-check the venerable jazz/rock ensemble. I smiled and urged the young man to follow his bliss.

The engineer finished tweaking sound levels and pressed the record button. Copping the Earl Klugh line was easy and straightforward. Again, it was only a 2-bar section of music, and I was simpatico with Klugh's chill vibe. Next, I laid down the bass line—which was ultimately dumped for upright bass. (I tried to tell 'em.) Buddha Monk liked my work, but felt the track still need something extra, something "gangsta." At the risk of being politically incorrect, when Buddha mentioned gangsters, my mind went directly to the catering halls of Brooklyn. I reflexively channeled my wedding band experience and started playing single note fills that simulated a *Godfather*-esque mandolin. Buddha exploded, "Yeah *boyee*, that is THE shit!"

The primary goal for any session player is to make the artist happy, so I gave Buddha Monk what he wanted—and then some. Since the recording was still a work in progress, I purposely overplayed throughout the five-minute opus. I filled every hole in the song, leaving Buddha tons of options to choose from, before imploring him and the engineer to please use the mute button liberally. After I'd finished adding WAY too much Neapolitan noodling, Buddha slapped me on the back and sent me packing.

The next morning, after a couple of cups of coffee, I called my friend John to make sure his client was satisfied. I dialed John's cell phone around noon. He answered right away.

"How did things end up last night? Everything cool?" I asked.

"End up?" John groaned. "We're still here!"

Yikes! 12 hours later and the session/party was still going strong.

The following week, I got a call from John asking if I wanted to drop by the studio to hear the final mix. I lived in the neighborhood, so I said sure and made my way back over to Giant Sound.

I walked into the control room and was greeted by the same throbbing entourage. Buddha Monk leaned back and signaled for the engineer to press play. I was unprepared for what came next. I was standing in front of one of the wall-mounted speakers when the downbeat exploded. The concussive blast scared the ever-loving shit out of me; I bet I jumped a foot in the air. It was the loudest music I'd ever been exposed to. It almost stopped my heart.

After playback, Buddha asked if I liked the track. I diplomatically said yes — electing not to mention the completed version contained every single note I'd *overplayed* on the session. They hadn't cut a thing. Forget "less is more," when it came to my gangsta guitar fills, more was more.

A few weeks later, I received an unexpected call from one of Bob James's producers, Michael Colina — who somehow knew I'd played on the Buddha Monk recording. Apparently, Bob had heard Buddha's finished product, and wasn't convinced it was a "replay." To Bob's ear, the music bed sounded a whole lot like his original track. I assured Michael I'd recut the Earl Klugh part but covered my ass by pointing out I wasn't around for the mix session, so I couldn't definitively vouch for what Bob was hearing. That said, I had no reason to believe Buddha didn't use my Earl Klugh imitation, he sure as hell used ALL of my *guido* lead fills. In the end, I was flattered I'd been able to trick Bob's ears. If Bob James thought I sounded like Earl Klugh, who was I to argue?

To my knowledge, Buddha Monk's "Got's Like Come on Thru" represents my only appearance on the Billboard charts. The song reached #81 on the Hot R&B/Hip-Hop chart and was featured on the soundtrack for *The Big Hit*, an action/comedy mobster film with Mark Wahlberg and Lou Diamond Phillips. The final version of the tune also included a cameo rap by Wu-Tang Clan member Ol' Dirty Bastard. Imagine that, ODB and JLC on the charts together. Life is indeed strange.

## Jughead

Working with Bob and Hilary James gave me an opportunity to meet and play with some of NYC's top musicians. Like most ongoing projects, the lineup of sidemen was a bit of a revolving door, but thanks to the city's endless stream of talent, the quality never waned. After Hilary's concert dates were behind us, we started concentrating on new songs for her next album. By that point, Hilary's rhythm section featured drummer Clint de Ganon and bassist Wayne Pedzwater—both heavyweight cats with major credits.

As the three of us gelled into a cohesive unit, a call came through for a wacky side gig: The Archies. For the uninitiated, "Archie" was the titular character in a comic book series set at fictional Riverdale High School. Created in the 1940s, the popular brand went on to become a syndicated daily comic strip and a Saturday morning cartoon show in the late 1960s. (Apparently there's also an Archie-based teen drama, *Riverdale* on The CW Network. That's news to me, I guess I'm not the target demographic.) The animated cartoon version found the perennially teenaged Archie leading a band, *cleverly* named The Archies. And the man behind The Archies' catchy sound was singer/songwriter/producer Ron Dante. (But Ron was more than just a cartoon character, he also co-produced Barry Manilow's first nine albums.)

In an example of bizarre corporate synergy, Ore-Ida Tater Tots had teamed with Archie Comics to raise money for the fight against cerebral palsy. Parent company Kraft Heinz organized a press event at the Hard Rock Cafe to announce the alliance — and they wanted to mark the occasion with a special (human) appearance by The Archies. Ron Dante accepted the challenge and tapped Clint, Wayne, and me to be his honorary "Archies."

Haters can roll their eyes all they want, but "Sugar, Sugar" was an indisputable smash. (Wilson Pickett even covered the damn thing. If it's good enough for Wilson...) During our rehearsal, Ron filled me in on the bubblegum anthem's impressive success. I knew the tune had been popular, but I was stunned to learn "Sugar, Sugar" spent four consecutive weeks at number one on the Billboard chart — after knocking The Rolling Stones' "Honky Tonk Woman" from the top slot. Cementing its place in musical history, "Sugar, Sugar" was named the top single of 1969 (besting songs by artists including Elvis, The Beatles, and Marvin Gaye).

Adding to the unique nature of the gig, our downbeat was scheduled for a chirpy 9am. With our set consisting of only two numbers: "Everything's Archie" (the cartoon's theme song) and "Sugar, Sugar," I was done—and paid handsomely for my services—by 10am. What a blast! The fun and goofy morning transported me back to the carefree days of my childhood. I've long contended music is the closest thing we have to a time machine.

* * *

Hilary James continued to record new material for her upcoming album on the GRP label. Calling in the heavy artillery, famed producer Phil Ramone was brought onboard. Ramone's spectacular body of work includes Billy Joel's *52nd Street*, Paul Simon's *Still Crazy After All These Years*, and Frank Sinatra's *Duets*. I loved being in the studio with a living legend—and a perfectionist who knew exactly what he wanted. One day, Ramone stopped a session for a full two hours while he awaited delivery of the *right* microphone for the kick drum. That's what I call clout!

I showed up at a downtown studio one afternoon to track yet more guitars for Hilary. I was lounging on the control room couch, awaiting my turn under the microscope, when I saw a notepad lying next to the telephone. I took a closer look and saw the name "John Leventhal" with a phone number scrawled beside it. Leventhal is one of the finest guitarists/producers in NYC, with credits including Shawn Colvin, Marc Cohn, and

Roseanne Cash. I should've been honored to be in such esteemed company, but instead I foolishly felt betrayed. In my mind, I'd been a steadfast and loyal employee, and I resented Hilary *cheating* on me with another player. Of course, this was a ridiculous reaction on my part, but my insecurities got the better of me. I recorded my tracks that day with a pouty chip on my shoulder.

The following morning, after some introspection, I realized my reaction had been childish and amateurish. Luckily, God must have been watching—and decided to grant me a mulligan. A few days later, I got a call from the session producer, Michael Colina.

"Jeff, I have some bad news and some good news."

"Okay."

"The bad news is we accidentally erased all of your guitar tracks and we're going to need you to re-record the parts. The good news is you will be paid again."

I resisted the urge to ask how something like that could happen; I'm sure the engineer felt bad enough. Meanwhile, I jumped at the chance to redeem myself—and double my payday in the process. I returned to the studio and recut my tracks, *this* time with a professional attitude. Being mentioned in the same breath as John Leventhal wasn't an affront, it was an accomplishment.

I really enjoyed my tour of duty with Hilary James. I dug her as a singer and a friend, and she introduced me to a slew of great players (including her father). Maybe most importantly, Hilary provided me with a reputable gig to hang my newly sober hat on. This was a crucial first step toward my career redemption. Unfortunately, Hilary's record deal ended up hitting a snag and none of our hard work ever saw the light of day. Ah, show-biz—one disappointment after another.

## Loeb Rollercoaster

I was excited to hear singer/songwriter Lisa Loeb was auditioning guitarists for her band. I was also frustrated. Why was I learning this information second hand? Why wasn't I on Lisa's short list? I thought I was doing my due diligence as a freelance musician, but this newsflash made me feel invisible. I clearly needed to step up my game.

Miffed over not being on Loeb's radar, I took action and cold-called her management company. Lisa's rep was distant and guarded until I dropped the five-letter word: S-T-I-N-G. Our conversation turned on a dime. (I'm beyond grateful for my industrial-strength Sting credit, I'm certain it—or a mangled facsimile—will follow me around for the rest of my life. One evening, I was standing at a nightclub urinal between sets when a drunken patron slurred, "Hey dude, I heard you used to play with...*Styx*." Yeah, no.) Speaking with Loeb's manager, I expressed interest in auditioning for the gig and immediately received a slot. *He shoots, he scores!* I was told to swing by the office to grab a copy of Lisa's upcoming CD for study purposes.

Lisa Loeb was already a huge pop star, but her new album, *Tails*, was her first major label release. Incredibly, Loeb's "Stay (I Missed You)" climbed all the way to No. 1 on the Billboard chart WITHOUT the benefit of a record deal. (She was the first artist to ever accomplish this feat.) Loeb's improbable ascent came courtesy of her movie-star neighbor, Ethan Hawke. A fan of

Loeb's music, Hawke slipped a recording of "Stay" to his pal Ben Stiller, who was directing the film *Reality Bites*. Stiller added Lisa's tune to his soundtrack and solid-gold lightning struck. After reaching the top of the charts under her own steam, a bidding war ensued for the red-hot free agent, and Geffen Records prevailed. I've always heard, "It's not what you know, it's who you know." That's often true — and New York City is filled with powerful *whos*. Sometimes they live next door.

I was impressed with Loeb's new album. I thought the tunes were great and the musicianship was top-notch. Management instructed me to familiarize myself with three songs for the audition, so I rolled up my sleeves and dug in. After ingesting the material, I called Lisa's office to clarify my mission.

"Should I learn both the electric and the acoustic guitar parts?" (I wasn't about to make the same boneheaded mistake I made with *The Who's Tommy*.)

Management replied, "Only the electric stuff, Lisa will cover the acoustic parts."

I must confess I was skeptical. The album's acoustic guitar work was impressive, so I just assumed a studio ringer had played on the recording. Unfairly jumping to conclusions, I'd lumped Lisa in with the plethora of pop stars — male and female — who essentially *wear* their guitars, treating the instrument more like a fashion accessory than the mystical tool it is. (Folk legend Woody Guthrie claimed his "machine" could kill fascists. Your mileage may vary.) Guitar impostors are easy to spot. They look like they're holding a poisonous snake — and stare at their fingers non-stop. Conversely, real guitarists make the instrument look like an organic appendage. But Lisa Loeb dispelled all doubts at my audition as she navigated her way around the fretboard with the greatest of ease. The woman can play!

My audition took place at Big Mike's/CMS studios in Manhattan's Chelsea district. I was sitting in the lounge area, waiting my turn, when Lisa's assistant poked her head out of the studio and invited me in. The revolving-door aspect of auditioning was in full swing as I passed another guitarist exiting the room. I didn't know the guy, and had no idea how his audition had gone, but the dazed look on his face definitely caught my attention.

I said hello to Lisa and her rhythm section, plugged in my pedalboard, and slung my guitar around my neck. The vibe was friendly, but businesslike. Lisa called a tune and counted it off. When we finished the number, Lisa was complimentary but asked if I could turn down my delay/echo pedal. Ego sufficiently bruised, I complied. I felt chastened, but simultaneously impressed with Lisa's sharp ear and clear musical vision. Lisa Loeb was no empty-headed pop star surrounded by handlers. She was in charge and knew exactly what she wanted.

We played a couple more tunes, then Lisa thanked me for coming down. I packed up my gear, told Lisa I appreciated the opportunity, and made way for the next victim. I felt good about my audition, but you're never sure if the artist shares your view.

I got a call from Loeb's management the following day asking if I could come back for another look-see. Woot! I was still in the mix. I also received a cordial phone call from Lisa's bassist, Joe Quigley, who confided, "In my opinion, you should get this gig." I could feel the specter of Sting working its magic. Little did I realize, that specter was wielding a double-edge sword.

Unlike my first go-round, the second audition was not a cattle call; the CMS lobby was no longer overrun with hungry *gun-slingers*. I played a few tunes with Lisa and the band, then we took a break to hang and chat. I tried to play it cool as Lisa and I sat on the couch making small talk, but, internally, I was anxious. I really wanted the gig—plus I found Lisa's "sexy nerd" persona disarming. Her warm smile and cat-eye glasses brought out the nervous teenager in me.

As we shot the breeze, Lisa told me she was leaving the next day for a promotional trip to Australia. I nodded and asked if she'd ever been to the faraway country. She answered no before returning the question. I replied yes, humblebragging I'd only been once—when I was on tour with Sting. Lisa mustered a smile as an awkward silence ensued. Being in full schmooze mode, I was just trying to bank a few cheap points—but instantly feared I'd inadvertently one-upped my potential employer. Lisa was no doubt aware of my Sting credit, but maybe I should've been a little more measured with my response, instead of flaunting my worldly travels with one of the planet's biggest rock stars. (Muddling the balance of power further, Lisa was an avowed Sting fan.)

Lisa decamped to Australia as I awaited news of my fate. Time passed and my phone stayed quiet. Growing impatient, I worked up my courage and called Lisa's management for an update. They responded with a vague, "She hasn't made up her mind."

I was incredulous. Loeb was scheduled to appear on *Saturday Night Live* in just a couple of weeks, and she still hadn't settled on a guitarist. Complicating matters, I had a clubdate scheduled for that same night. I had to chuckle at my predicament: uncertain if I'd be performing "Live from New York!" on

NBC—or sporting a monkey suit at a Bronx catering hall. Unfortunately, the monkey suit won out. Lisa wound up using guitarist/producer Danny Blume for her *SNL* appearance, and my consolation prize was playing "The Electric Slide" at Marina del Rey. (Lisa ultimately hired guitarist Mark Spencer for the tour.)

I'll always wonder if my throwaway remark about Australia hurt my chances with Lisa. Self-promotion is tricky. Finding the happy medium between humility and tooting your own horn is elusive. You feel like a PR version of Goldilocks; not too hard, not too soft. Objectively speaking, I understood Lisa's dilemma. I can see how an artist might have reservations about hiring sidemen with overly shiny resumés. Leaders want seasoned players—but they don't want to risk hiring someone who might end up looking down on the gig. (Sting's ticklish experience with his all-star *Blue Turtles* band comes to mind.) In my case, nothing could've been further from the truth. I would've loved to have been a member of Lisa Loeb's band. I'm a fan.

### Swede Thing

Indie folk rock singer Ruth Gerson was one my main side projects. Ruth had built a solid following around the NYC area, and, with her visibility on the rise, she'd been asked to appear at a music festival in Sweden. Ruth excitedly called to inform me of our international invitation, but unfortunately, I didn't share her enthusiasm. I'd already experienced Sweden (courtesy of Sting), and I knew the payday would be light, so I apologetically begged off. Thanks to my year of non-stop barnstorming with Sting (181 concerts in 25 countries on six continents), my wanderlust was all but depleted—plus sobriety had drastically changed my attitude toward touring. I never liked flying in the first place, but international air travel without *self-medication* seemed tantamount to torture. By that point in my career, I was only interested in hitting the road if there was a chance of reaping real dividends (professional or financial).

Ruth was disappointed but accepted my decision and agreed to find a replacement guitarist for the gig. Problem solved (or so I thought). Ruth enlisted the services of a fresh-out-of-Berklee youngster, and quickly realized something was missing: experience. Frustrated with her greenhorn substitute, Ruth begged me to reconsider. I'm a compassionate guy and I sympathized with Ruth's plight, so I took a deep breath and acquiesced. *Oh boy! I get to fly over the Atlantic Ocean, in coach class...sober.* Adding to my airborne *pleasure*, the festival was in northern Sweden, which meant our itinerary included two flights: NYC to Stockholm; Stockholm to Luleå (final destination: Piteå).

Groggy and disoriented from jet lag, I awoke in my Swedish hotel room to the news of TWA Flight 800 exploding after takeoff from JFK airport, killing all 230 people on board. Damn, I was just there! I spend a good deal of energy trying to convince myself my fears and phobias are irrational—then reality ups and smacks me in the face. God bless the victims of Flight 800.

Although I'd been to Sweden with Sting, we'd only played Stockholm, which is in the southern part of the country. This time, I was in northern Sweden...in July. This meant it NEVER got dark. I'd heard tales of "the midnight sun," but it was amazing to experience perpetual daylight. An approximation of dusk occurred around 2am, but I never saw true darkness during our stay.

Despite my initial apathy, I embraced our Swedish adventure. I have a steadfast rule: if I accept a job, it's my responsibility to deliver a good attitude (or at least fake one). It's called "being a pro." There is nothing worse than ending up on a gig with someone who doesn't want to be there. If your heart is not in the gig, please spare your bandmates and just say NO.

The highlight of my trip was making the acquaintance of musician/songwriter Eric Bazilian. A founding member of The Hooters, Eric was riding high on his recent success as the composer of Joan Osborne's breakout hit, "One of Us." *Did he just call God a slob?* Eric was staying at our hotel, so we all became buddies. (The loneliness of the road exposes our humanity. Compatriots who blithely ignore one another at home magically bond when meeting abroad.) Taking full advantage of the American camaraderie, Eric asked to borrow Ruth's musicians for his festival appearance.

After years of playing in cover bands, I'm always excited to perform a hit song with the actual composer. I bow before anyone who can crack the code of radio airplay. (I still can't believe I got to play "Every Breath You Take" with Sting...and for an entire year!) To that end, performing "One of Us" with Eric Bazilian was memorable, and not only because he'd written the smash hit, but also because we played it in front of thousands of screaming fans at 1:00am — and I was wearing my Ray-Bans to shield the sun's glare.

I made it back across the Atlantic safely with a few extra bucks in my pocket and only a little worse for the wear. I shrugged off the excursion as a long, exhausting weekend and returned to the grind. A week or so later, I bumped into a fellow muso on the street. When he asked what I'd been up to, I offhandedly mentioned my recent trip to Sweden. He replied excitedly, "Sweden? Wow, cool!"

This exchange taught me a valuable lesson: perception is half the battle. My gig in Sweden wasn't nearly as prestigious as it sounded, but it scored points with my peer nonetheless. From that day forward, "Sweden" became a shorthand descriptor in our household. If a gig comes along that generates more respect than it probably deserves, Patty and I shrug, "It's a *Sweden*."

## Our Lips are Synched

I got an out-of-the-blue phone call from drummer Mark Papazian. Mark and I usually crossed paths on the wedding band circuit, but he'd stumbled onto a situation that offered us a chance to play some music sans bow ties — on TV! I'd answered yes before Mark could finish his pitch. Mark said he'd been charged with assembling a backing band for Belinda Carlisle's upcoming appearance on VH-1's *The RuPaul Show*. Double yes! I'd been a fan of The Go-Go's during their heyday and, like most guys of a certain age, I'd had a sizable crush on their gorgeous lead singer. (Killer bassist and ultra-hipster Brad Albetta rounded out our ensemble.)

*The RuPaul Show* was taped at a TV studio on Eleventh Avenue, only a couple of blocks from our apartment. (The space is now home to Comedy Central's *The Daily Show*.) On the afternoon of the gig, I grabbed the coolest-looking guitar in my arsenal and wandered over to the bland stretch of industrial buildings near the Lincoln Tunnel. Glamorous huh?

I checked in with security and was directed to our "dressing room"—a Winnebago RV parked beside the studio. The Go-Go's had served as an opening act for The Police on their *Ghost in the Machine* World Tour, so I figured my Sting connection would provide a perfect ice breaker with the New Wave diva. (It sounded good on paper.) I climbed aboard our mobile green-room and found myself face-to-face with Ms. Carlisle. She was lounging in the front passenger seat of the motorhome with her nose buried in a book. She looked up from the page long enough to offer a chilly hello before plunging right back into her novel. The "Do Not Disturb" vibe was unmistakable, so I made a beeline for the back of the vehicle. I sat quietly on the rear bench seat, as socially distanced as possible, while Belinda ignored me completely. There we were—alone together. *Where the hell are my bandmates?* For the record, I never got a chance to drop Sting's name.

Our trio's four-minute mission was to sway in the shadows as we faked along to a track from Belinda's new album. I hate lip-synching in principle, but, on the bright side, it eliminates rehearsal time. That said, the selected tune, "In Too Deep" included a short guitar solo, which required a little extra home-work on my part. And I wish I'd done a little more. Unfortunately for me, RuPaul's director was on top of his game, and cut to a close-up of the guitar neck during my six-bar show-case. Upon viewing playback of our pantomime, I'd give myself a squishy B minus. (My hands almost matched the track.) But nobody gave a damn, the gig was the epitome of "phoning it in."

As RuPaul's end credits rolled, our makeshift power trio stood idly onstage, exchanging knowing glances and grins until the broadcast faded to black. Belinda waved to the band as she vanished into the wings, mouthing a blanket "thank you" that rivaled the indifference of her hello. *Wham, bam — your money's on the dresser.* I said goodbye to my cohorts and set out in search of an exit. Wandering down a hallway, I turned a corner and spied Bangles singer/guitarist Susanna Hoffs sitting in a makeup chair. (*The RuPaul Show* taped two episodes a day, and Hoffs was on deck.) Damn, I'd hit the MTV male-fantasy daily double. Susanna's dark smoky beauty rivaled Belinda's Waspy sex appeal. Carlisle and Hoffs under the same roof? Be still my beating heart.

### Sub-servient

We all experience moments that, at the time, seem insignificant, but ultimately turn out to be transformational. Call it luck, call it fate — but I can point to a handful of innocuous encounters that resulted in tectonic shifts in my life. One such moment was a brief exchange with drummer Clint de Ganon. (We'd worked together with Hilary James — and The Archies.) Clint's passing suggestion altered my life forever.

I bumped into Clint on the streets of midtown one day. After exchanging pleasantries, Clint mentioned his pal David Spinozza was playing guitar for the Broadway musical *The Life*, and in need of subs. Clint said he'd taken the liberty of recommending me to Spinozza.

Hold the phone…THE David Spinozza? I didn't know David personally, but I certainly knew of his reputation. David was one of NYC's top-call guitarists, with a resumé that boasted some of the biggest names in the music industry. Spinozza's impressive legacy includes Paul McCartney, John Lennon, James

Taylor, Billy Joel, Paul Simon, musical director for the *Saturday Night Live* band...and on and on.

Clint gave me Spinozza's phone number and urged me to follow up. Not needing any prodding, I called David and eagerly offered my services. It'd been four years since my Broadway crash-and-burn with *The Who's Tommy*, but my life had changed dramatically in the interim. In short: I'd gotten sober. Plus, I'd come to the realization I needed to pursue every income stream available just to keep my head above water. Although I was managing to stay relatively busy with the usual hodgepodge of gigs, I was still barely making ends meet. The life of a freelance musician can be brutal. *"You eat what you shoot."*

Spinozza was game, so we picked a date for me to audit his chair at *The Life*. On the appointed night, I tackled the two-block walk to the Barrymore Theatre, feeling both nervous and excited. The doorman buzzed me in, and I navigated my way downstairs to the band locker room. My friend Warren Odze was playing drums on the show, so I was happy to have an ally on the inside. Warren greeted me and introduced me to the easy-going Spinozza. David shook my hand and cracked a few off-color jokes, before leading me into the cramped orchestra pit. (I felt like I was boarding a submarine.)

The show had an R&B vibe—at least by Broadway standards—so I knew I'd be a good fit musically. I recorded David's performance on my Walkman, borrowed a spare copy of the guitar book, and thanked him for his consideration. Study time!

My mission was to dissect David's work and learn to mimic him as much as possible. When subbing, simply playing the *ink* is not sufficient; the printed page is just a starting point. Chair holders infuse their own personality into the music and subs are expected to dig between the cracks and duplicate that flavor. David's soulful guitar style was in my wheelhouse — but, once again, following a conductor was not. My previous failure on Broadway was based largely on my inability to decipher the *semaphore* coming from the podium. But this time, I had a secret weapon. Technology was slowly creeping into the world of Broadway, and the show's percussionist, David Yee, had made a VIDEO recording of the conductor's performance. This study tool made all the difference.

I spent two months going through my copy of Yee's VHS cassette with a fine-tooth comb, poring over each frame like it was the Zapruder film. I learned to speak fluent *baton* — familiarizing myself with all the moves: pickups, cutoffs, accelerandos, rallentandos, etc. Equally important, I became adept at differentiating between a musical cue and when the conductor just had an itchy nose.

After months of diligent preparation, the big night finally arrived. And I'm happy to report my return to Broadway was a triumph. I received accolades from the band and, more crucially, the conductor. I heaved a huge sigh of relief.

I spoke with Spinozza the following day. He told me his boss was pleased with my work and I'd been greenlit to return. In view of my earlier fiasco at *Tommy*, I felt vindicated — unfortunately to a fault. Flush with confidence, I dropped my guard and, as a result, struggled mightily at my next performance. Chalk up another victim of the dreaded "sophomore slump," a well-known pitfall in subbing circles.

Like many a sucker before me, my initial success lulled me into a false sense of security. Consequently, my second performance was shaky (at best). Post show, the conductor typically gives "notes" to a sub, pointing out specific spots that need to be cleaned up. I waited around after the curtain for my job evaluation. It was concise and lethal.

"Ummm...*guitar*," (the conductor didn't know my name, which is VERY common in sub world) "I started making notes [about your mistakes] during the show, but there were so many, I finally stopped writing. Please go home and learn the music."

I deserved every bit of the conductor's disdain and swore I'd never fall into that trap again. Staying focused for your *first* performance as a sub is easy. You are single-minded as your life is consumed by the task at hand. You study a ton — and then you study some more; fear is a great motivator. One Broadway veteran told me, "When you *think* you're ready, practice two MORE weeks." This is sound advice. Here's another piece of sound advice: IF you survive your first attempt, don't get cocky! Stumbling through round two at *The Life* taught me an invaluable lesson. Moving forward as a sub, I vowed to treat my first FIVE performances of any new show with equal weight and respect. Play it right five times — then exhale.

Working at *The Life* opened other doors. Among the boatload of new faces, I struck up a friendship with guitarist John Benthal (another of Spinozza's subs). As *The Life* was running out of steam, John was hired to play the incoming *Footloose*, and our bond put me near the top of his sub list. When word spread I was subbing Broadway (successfully), my pal Jon Herington asked me to fill in for him on *The Civil War*. But most consequential of all, David Spinozza rewarded my diligence by asking me to sub on his next show, *Fosse*. I was proud to have carved out a spot as a Broadway sub. But, lucky for me, my part-time status was about to change.

During my stint at *Fosse*, I made the acquaintance of pianist John Samorian (who was subbing the Keyboard 1 chair). Guitar and piano sat side by side in the crowded pit, and John and I hit it off immediately. The *Fosse* keyboard book was quite demanding—and the show's high-strung conductor only inflamed the madness. I watched in sympathy as sub after sub melted under the intense pressure and scrutiny. But John Samorian was different. He played the show effortlessly (or at least he made it look that way) with a big smile and a dry brow. *Fosse* was a 3-act dance marathon without any dialog—the music (and choreography) was literally non-stop. The top of the show reminded me of climbing aboard a roller coaster. Once the pulley chain started dragging you up that first hill, there was no turning back. You weren't getting off the ride until it was over.

John Samorian and I bonded in the pit of the Broadhurst Theatre. A few months into the *Fosse* run, John confided he was leaving for a full-time gig with the upcoming film-to-stage adaptation of *Saturday Night Fever*. I was excited for John—and jealous. I'd come of age during the disco era, so the thought of playing those classic Bee Gees songs on a nightly basis sounded like fun. I'd learned to be proactive when it came to potential work, so I seized my opening.

"Hey John, let me know who ends up playing guitar at *Saturday Night Fever*. I'd love to sub on that show."

"Will do," John replied, before adding, "Actually there are two guitar chairs, but I don't think they've filled the second slot yet. I'll check into it for you."

I smelled opportunity. Carpe *disco*.

John followed through on his word, asking *Saturday Night Fever* contractor Bill Meade about the guitar situation. When

Bill confirmed the Guitar 2 designation was still up in the air, John immediately threw my name (and undoubtedly, Sting's) in the hat. Once again, my Sting credit probably helped crack open a door that might have otherwise remained closed. Bill Meade contacted me about the position, and we scheduled a *loose* audition. The musician's union frowns on unpaid auditions, but that didn't stop Bill Meade. He was a bit on the slippery side.

I auditioned for *Saturday Night Fever* at the old Carroll Rehearsal Studios on West 41st Street, right next door to the ultra-sketchy Port Authority Bus Terminal. Bill Meade enlisted pianist John Samorian and drummer Jon Berger to be my backing *band*. Hmmm, acoustic piano and drums...but NO bass. Not exactly the ideal instrumentation for disco music. Bill threw a couple of *Fever* charts on our music stands and counted us off. We hacked our way through "Stayin' Alive" before Bill complained, "Come on guys, you sound like you're sight-reading." (I thought to myself, "Maybe because we are sight-reading?") I figured we should just pick a two-chord tune like "Brick House" and groove, but I knew better than to open my mouth. Next, we tackled one of my Bee Gees faves, "You Should Be Dancing." After we stumbled across the finish line, a deadpan Bill gathered the charts and said he'd heard enough. I had no idea if I'd made a good, bad, or indifferent impression. I thanked Bill for the opportunity as he rushed out the door. He just nodded, and said he'd be in touch.

# Made Man

Bill Meade called a few days later with the verdict: the *Saturday Night Fever* gig was mine. I was ecstatic. Some guys spend years subbing on Broadway without ever being promoted to full-time status. Despite Bill's somewhat questionable reputation, I owe that man BIG time. As they say in the mob, I'd earned my "button."

When I told some of my rocker friends about my new job, they were ambivalent at best. (*Broadway?... Gasp!*) They viewed musical theater with deep skepticism, essentially equating the move with being put out to pasture. One clubdate colleague feared Broadway might "age me." I didn't see it that way at all—if anything, playing four-hour *slugfests* in a tuxedo was aging me. The thought of having a steady job within walking distance of my apartment sounded like the Fountain of Youth (and the Fountain of Dollars). In fact, after spending the last 25 years in various orchestra pits, I'll go as far as to say I probably would've left the music business if I hadn't landed on Broadway. The sporadic and nomadic lifestyle of a freelance musician is too stressful for my constitution; I much prefer the known quantity of Broadway. Plus, thanks to a steady influx of pop music (and electric guitars), musical theater's stodgy stereotype is fading.

Like a farmer, the life of a journeyman musician tends to be seasonal. Let's face it, there are a lot more tours (or weddings) in June than January. Accordingly, I had to pinch myself when my first February on Broadway rolled around and the cash kept right on flowing. My bank account was in a state of shock after being accustomed to hibernating for multiple months of the year.

Not long after starting *Saturday Night Fever*, I bumped into Jim Campagnola, one of my former clubdate leaders. Jim offered a friendly hello and asked how things were going on Broadway. I told him I was quite happy, before cracking a joke about the overlapping repertoire between my show and the typical wedding reception.

"I'm really digging it, but I'm still playing 'Disco Inferno' every night," I laughed.

Jim replied cynically, "Yeah, but you made *more* money playing that song with me."

Technically, Jim was right. A single wedding gig tends to pay a bit more than a single service on Broadway. But there is one BIG difference. I maybe played 50-60 weddings in a *good* year. On the other hand, a steady Broadway chair offers the chance to play over 400 gigs in a year. Eight shows a week, 52 weeks a year—there's nothing more relentless.

However, it's important to note, you don't *have* to play every performance. As per our contract, musicians are only required to maintain 50% attendance. That's a pretty lenient policy, but as the ever-witty David Spinozza observed, "The thing is…if you don't show up, they don't pay you." Sweetening the deal, if a big opportunity comes along, Broadway musicians can apply for a "leave of absence." If Springsteen wants you on his tour, you can take a union-sanctioned hiatus and let one of your subs keep your seat warm until you return. What's not to love?

Additionally, compared to playing in a wedding band, Broadway offered the following perks: no tux, no bow tie (or as drummer Warren Odze calls it, "the collar of obedience"), no schlepping equipment, no long-distance drives all over the Northeast, and no late nights. Ironically, I got a phone call a few years later from the same clubdate boss asking if I could help *him* break onto the Broadway scene. Jim's earlier snark had disappeared. As Mel Brooks warned, "We mock the things we are to be."

The negativity from my peers toward musical theater wasn't all that surprising; hipsters tend to view Broadway as old-fashioned and cheesy (which can be accurate at times). Underscoring this notion, it wasn't uncommon to see steady Broadway players sub out on weekends to accept wedding gigs—with the conventional wisdom being weddings allow musicians to get their ya-ya's out. (Depending upon your specific show, this can be a valid argument. All Broadway productions are not created equal; *Hamilton* bangs a lot harder than *Fiddler on the Roof.*) Although wedding receptions typically start out on the restrained side, they almost invariably devolve into a drunken blowout featuring loud rock n roll. This can be alluring if you've been playing banjo in a Broadway pit all week. As a newbie, I blindly followed suit and continued to play weddings when offered. (It's also not a bad strategy to keep your clubdate position warm in case your show is a flop.)

Then, one tuxedoed night, it hit me: I much preferred playing *Saturday Night Fever* to wedding receptions. Thanks to The Bee Gees, I wasn't playing corny, two-beat show tunes; I was playing killer pop music with a smoking 16-piece band. Not to mention, I could walk to work, I could wear jeans, and I was home by 11pm. I saw the light and broke the cycle of choosing weddings over Broadway.

I bumped into fellow Broadway (and Steely Dan) guitarist Jon Herington one afternoon and lamented musical theater's unjust stigma. He nodded in agreement.

"I don't understand it either," Jon sighed. "The audience purchases printed tickets, they sit in assigned seats, we play well-written orchestrations with great musicians,...and it's a union job with a good salary and healthcare/pension benefits. It's professional showbiz. Wasn't that our goal?"

I couldn't agree with Jon more. Plus, let's be real, if we musicians only accepted gigs involving music we *truly* loved, most of us would literally be starving artists.

The typical evolution of a Broadway show includes years of stripped-down readings, rehearsals, workshops, and untold revisions, before hitting the road for a multi-week tryout in a host city like Chicago, Seattle, or Boston. Mounting an out-of-town production gives the creative team a chance to kick the tires and tweak their handiwork away from the harsh glare of New York. Then — IF the show survives its trial run — it's on to Broadway, where the critics gleefully rip it to shreds. (Just kidding, every once in a blue moon, critics actually like a show.) However, the internet has all but destroyed the theoretical out-of-town grace period. Nowadays, the web is buzzing with gossip about distant, fledgling works by the first intermission.

Meanwhile, the Broadway production of *Saturday Night Fever* was a UK import, so there'd been no need to hit the road;

the Brits had already served as guinea pigs. After three weeks of "previews" (performances in front of a paying audience), *Saturday Night Fever* officially opened on Broadway. As tradition dictates, our show's producer, Robert Stigwood (famed impresario and manager of Cream and The Bee Gees) hosted a big opening night party. I was in heaven, strolling the paparazzi-lined red carpet into The China Club, with the beautiful Patty Murray on my arm.

Patty and I entered the Times Square hotspot and climbed the staircase toward our velvet-roped affair. As we approached the top of the steps, we spied the alpha Bee Gee, Barry Gibb, chatting with an anonymous bigwig. (All three Bee Gees were in attendance for our opening night festivities.) Despite my *lofty* title of Guitar 2, I was completely starstruck at the sight of the hirsute Mr. Gibb. (Remember, The Bee Gees had ruled the earth when I was a college kid in Miami.)

As Patty and I reached the second-floor landing, Mr. Gibb's companion walked away, leaving the Bee Gee in a probably unfamiliar setting: alone. The unaccompanied Barry turned in our direction with a welcoming smile on his face…and time stood still. Was I allowed to speak to my hero? Or should I respect his privacy? Unfortunately, I chose door #2. I panicked and hurried Patty toward the dance floor without acknowledging the King Bee Gee. What a dumbass! I regret *my* choice to this day—and so does Patty. She astutely picked up on Barry's warm vibe, and feared we were borderline rude to our de facto host. Sadly, I have to agree with her. I'd traveled the world with Sting and hung out with the likes of Bruce Springsteen and Eric Clapton, but my swagger was nowhere to be found when I came face-to-face with Barry Gibb. Talk about a missed opportunity.

## *Journey to Whoville*

I was loving my first full-time Broadway gig—then my phone rang. As an official chair holder (no longer just a *lowly* sub), I was a proven commodity and, right on cue, work begat work.

A-list Broadway contractor John Miller was calling to see if I had any interest in joining the upcoming *Seussical*—*The Musical*. According to John, the show was going to be huge, "The next *Lion King;* it will run ten years minimum!" I was flattered by John's overture, but hesitant. I was perfectly happy at *Saturday Night Fever* and wasn't sure I wanted to abandon my wah-wah for a musical based on a series of children's books. (I smell banjo.) Patty and I discussed the pros and cons at length, with Patty leaning toward making the move.

"But The Bee Gees are huge!" I contended.

"Dr. Seuss is *huger,*" Patty countered.

I couldn't disagree with her. Dr. Seuss had been entertaining generations of children since the 1950s. Considering (1) Seuss's global popularity; (2) John Miller's prediction of an extended Broadway run; and (3) the lukewarm reviews for *Saturday Night Fever,* I decided to take the plunge. Goodbye disco, hello Whoville.

Unlike my made-in-the-UK *Fever, Seussical* was a brand-new creation. Accordingly, the producers wanted to float an out-of-town trial balloon before braving NYC. Shows under development typically bring a small core of New York musicians (piano and drums) along for their pre-Broadway beta run—and then flesh out the orchestra with local players. But *Seussical* opened its wallet and added me and fellow guitarist Jack Cavari to the manifest as well. Fortunately, our temporary home was just up the road (relatively speaking) in the city of Boston. The close proximity to NYC allowed me to jump on Amtrak on my day off and come see Patty—or vice versa.

The production offered "company housing" at a corporate hotel 20 miles outside of Boston, but this was a non-starter for me. I wanted the true Boston experience, so I went rogue. I pocketed my housing stipend and rented an apartment near the Berklee School of Music—and maybe more excitingly, Fenway Park. (The Yankees and the Red Sox may be the Hatfields and McCoys of baseball, but Fenway is a treasure.) Bandmates Warren Odze (drums) and Jack Cavari (guitar) followed my lead and rented pads in the same building. Look out Back Bay!

Mid-August, *Seussical* invaded Boston's Colonial Theatre. The venue was only a couple of miles from my *pied-à-terre*, so I was more than happy to walk to work each day. Living in Manhattan had transformed me into a hardcore pedestrian *and* an avid people watcher. Lucky for me, the city of Boston offered plenty to ogle along the way.

Day one, I walked through the doors of the Colonial, guitar case in hand, and saw contractor John Miller sitting behind a long folding table with the creative team (composers, orchestrator, music supervisor, copyist, etc.). In the world of theater, these power players are lovingly referred to as "table cats."

John blurted out (loudly enough for the other "cats" to hear), "Is that the same guitar you played on the road with Sting?"

Once again, my Sting credit was paying dividends—and from that moment forward, my overlords were aware of my flashy resumé. (Actually, I have a feeling they already were. Like it or not, that's how showbiz works.)

Rosy forecasts notwithstanding, *Seussical—The Musical* was

in trouble from the start. The show, an amalgam of Dr. Seuss's greatest hits, struggled to find its focus amid the glut of disparate stories and characters. The creatives searched for solutions, rewriting large chunks of the show while feverishly arranging (and rearranging) the puzzle pieces. Material was cut, material was added, as the overworked cast desperately tried to keep track of the dizzying changes. The actors lived in a constant state of flux—exploring new content during daytime rehearsals, before performing the *original* version of the show at night.

Meanwhile, at the other end of the spectrum, the band was at liberty during the day. One of the unforeseen perks of being out of town was the opportunity to exhale. Since I wasn't in NYC, I was no longer required (or able) to participate in the daily rat race. This may be the best part of being out on the road: you literally have ONE job. Our drummer, Warren, compared the relaxed pace to "being away at summer camp." He was right, it almost felt like a paid vacation. I spent my mornings jogging along the Charles River, and my afternoons practicing the guitar or reading. Adding to the fun, Patty made the trek north a couple of times and we embraced the role of curious tourists. We hiked Boston's historic Freedom Trail (featuring cool spots like Paul Revere's House, The Old North Church, and Bunker Hill), as well as making day trips to Plymouth Rock and bewitching Salem.

As expected, *Seussical* received tepid reviews in Boston. So tepid in fact, the wounded production ended up cancelling the final week of its scheduled six-week run and staggering home to New York. Despite ongoing efforts to right the ship, the show remained a muddle. But retreat was not an option. After four weeks of wobbly previews at the Richard Rodgers Theatre, *Seussical* officially opened on Broadway.

The producers went whole hog for our opening night party and rented out the Central Park landmark, Tavern on the Green. As the company feasted on unlimited food and drink, I huddled in the corner with my fellow guitarist, Jack Cavari, discussing our precarious outlook.

"I pray this thing has a long run," Jack whispered over his cocktail.

"I hear you," I countered. "I figure I've got about 10 years to make a *lifetime* of money."

It was true. I was forty and finally debt-free, but I had zero savings and no retirement strategy. (I'd burned through my leftover Sting money years earlier on the barstools of Manhattan.) I hoped a hit show would at least get me pointing in the right direction financially, but the clock was ticking. Time is an investor's best friend.

Patty and I eventually decided to call it a night and bid our tablemates good evening. As we approached the exit, the Tavern's giant wooden door swung open, and in waltzed TV/Radio icon Larry King, surrounded by his entourage. King was holding court mid-stride and we couldn't help but overhear his newsflash.

"The Times was *not* kind," Larry growled.

I felt my heart sink.

Patty and I stopped off at our corner bodega to buy the early edition newspapers before hitting the hay. Sadly, Larry's reporting was solid; *The New York Times* review was less than glowing. Other critics followed suit, equally unimpressed with the predicted juggernaut. My "can't miss" show was already missing... right out of the gate.

Undaunted by the critics' slings and arrows, our producers

pressed forward with their plans to record a cast album. In a show of muscle, *Seussical* had enlisted heavyweight producer Phil Ramone (Frank Sinatra, Billy Joel, Paul Simon), and über engineer Elliot Scheiner (Steely Dan, Fleetwood Mac, Queen, Sting) to lead the way. The recording session took place at Sony Studios on West 54th Street—which, like most of New York's classic recording studios, is now long gone, replaced by a luxury apartment building.

Typically, non-classical albums are constructed piecemeal over several weeks (or months), but Broadway doesn't tend to roll that way. Accordingly, we put the proverbial pedal to the metal and cranked out the entire *Seussical* cast recording (28 tracks!) in a single day. When I asked our conductor, David Holcenberg, about the kamikaze approach, he smiled and explained the goal was to capture the energy of a live show. This sounded plausible, but I had a sneaking suspicion budget considerations might also be a factor.

The pace of our session was fast and furious, but thankfully the marathon day was punctuated with breathers. Certain breaks were union-mandated, other breaks came courtesy of our producer Phil Ramone. Whenever the energy began to flag, Ramone would burst into the room and attempt to rally the troops. Unfortunately, our producer's pep talks were painfully generic. Fellow guitarist Jack Cavari picked up on the hackneyed rhetoric and started discreetly compiling a list of Ramone's platitudes. With all due respect to the legend, Phil's cheerleading was pretty clichéd. Always the cut-up, Jack nodded at his scribbled sheet of paper and whispered to me, "*This* is all it takes to be a big-time producer? Hell, I could do this."

Ominously, only one month into our Broadway run, the producers resorted to the theatrical equivalent of a "Hail Mary" and tapped TV star Rosie O'Donnell to replace David Shiner as our Cat in the Hat. This celebrity roster maneuver, known as "stunt casting," is typically used to goose ticket sales after a show has exhausted its natural shelf life. But my poor *Seussical* had been in survival mode since opening night, so any and all gimmicks were on the table. In addition to O'Donnell, teen rap sensation Aaron Carter and gymnast Cathy Rigby were run up the flagpole along the way. Rapper Lil' Bow Wow was rumored to be in the mix as well, but he never materialized. As I like to remind people, it's called show BUSINESS.

Although *Seussical*'s future was uncertain, I made a bold decision: I sold my car. Owning a car had been a necessary evil during my clubdate heyday, but those sands had shifted. First, the wedding band industry was shrinking, due in large part to the popularity of DJs (and the glut of shitty bands who'd inadvertently sent potential clients rushing toward said DJs). Second, I was playing more and more Broadway—and fewer and fewer weddings. I crunched the numbers (monthly parking, auto insurance, maintenance, etc.) and realized my car was no longer generating enough of a profit to justify the persistent headache. With much pleasure, I jettisoned my Jetta. Twenty-some years later, I still don't own a car, and I've never been happier. Freedom from the *ball and chain* of automobile ownership is exhilarating.

\* \* \*

*(New York, NY) June 29, 2020—The Broadway League announced today that Broadway performances in New*

*York City will be suspended through the remainder of 2020 due to COVID-19. The League has released updated information regarding performance cancellations and ticketing. Broadway theaters are now offering refunds and exchanges for tickets purchased for all performances through January 3, 2021.*

Jeez—the REMAINDER of 2020! My once-promising year is now officially a bust. Fingers crossed for 2021.

### An Audience with the Queen

As things limped along in *Whoville*, I picked up an ultra-sweet side gig...and crossed a major item off my bucket list.

I was sitting on my couch, waiting for a visit from the cable guy, when my phone rang. I answered. It was *Seussical* bassist, Francisco Centeno.

"What are you doing?" Francisco asked urgently.

"Uh, nothing."

"Good," Francisco barked. "Grab a guitar and come to S.I.R. [rehearsal studios] on 52nd Street."

I was confused. "Why? What's up?"

Francisco spoke quickly. "I'm rehearsing with Aretha Franklin for an upcoming show at Radio City Music Hall and she needs a second guitarist. Get your ass here—NOW!"

Francisco had been Aretha's bassist for years, but I never dreamed his position with the Queen of Soul would benefit me. My heart pounded as I pulled a pair of jeans over my pajama boxers and half-brushed my teeth. Making a split-second (but conscious) choice, I tossed my jazzy Guild hollow-body guitar into a gig bag and sprinted the three blocks to the studio.

Five minutes later, I was at S.I.R. I caught my breath and stated my business to the dude at the front desk. He nodded and directed me to one of the facility's smaller studios. Francisco beamed when I walked through the door and introduced me to his bandmates. Aretha's son, Teddy, was her regular guitarist, but a decision had been made to add a second guitar for the upcoming, *VH-1 Divas Live: The One and Only Aretha Franklin.* The TV show/concert was scheduled to include numerous guest artists, so Aretha needed a guitarist who could read music on the fly. I'm no ace at sight-reading, but apparently Teddy's skills were more limited than mine.

But here's the WILD part: Aretha's musical director, H. B. Barnum, wanted to use legendary guitarist Cornell Dupree for the second slot—and he'd put Francisco in charge of tracking Cornell down. (The soulful Dupree is one of my six-string heroes, with credits including Aretha, Paul Simon, Miles Davis, and Chaka Khan. Remember that buttery opening guitar lick on Brook Benton's "Rainy Night in Georgia"?…that's Cornell.) Francisco ran to the pay phone, but instead of calling Cornell, he dialed MY number. Thank God I was home. When *Frankie* later confided his unilateral, spur-of-the-moment decision, I was incredulous.

"Why would you do such a crazy thing?" I asked.

Francisco shrugged. "Because I like you—plus Cornell can be bit of a pain at times."

I'm still a little freaked out (and impressed) by Francisco's *cojones.*

I was tuning my guitar when the studio door swung open. I looked up to see two beefy bodyguards hurrying a hoodie-shrouded person into the room. Once safely inside, the hood was pulled back to reveal the Queen of Soul, Aretha Franklin. (Twenty years later, I'm getting chills just writing this passage.)

I'd been an Aretha fan for as long as I'd been listening to music, so the term "starstruck" is woefully inadequate. Meanwhile, I'd heard apocryphal stories about the diva's aloofness, so I wasn't sure if I was supposed to acknowledge Aretha—or ignore her. I watched out of the corner of my eye as Aretha and Francisco traded hellos but was caught off-guard when Francisco pivoted and introduced *me* to the Queen. I reflexively extended my hand—and immediately panicked. I feared the gesture might be considered too familiar, so I retracted my paw…just as Aretha moved to reciprocate. (Damn, I'd left the Queen of Soul hanging.) Ms. Franklin awkwardly withdrew her hand, consummating an embarrassing exchange that haunts me to this day. In my defense, I later learned my instincts weren't entirely off-base. Aretha's band members confirmed she was usually pretty cool and detached, but she'd apparently donned a warmer persona to welcome the parade of guests to her VH-1 coronation.

I tried to keep my shit together as Aretha sat down at the grand piano and started noodling. I couldn't believe I was in an intimate rehearsal space with six people—and one of them was Aretha Franklin. Setting the mood, a plate of BBQ chicken wings was perched atop the piano. I knew I was in for a memorable afternoon.

Out of left field, Aretha said she wanted to play "Cherokee"—a dusty jazz standard from the 1930s. I hadn't played this *Real Book* staple since my college days, but a merciful God threw me a bone. Somehow the tune came rushing back to me, magically flowing from my fingers as the band dug in. When we got to the bridge, a scuffling Francisco looked over at me and mouthed, "What's the chords?" I mimed the answers to Frankie as an entranced Aretha tickled the ivories, none the wiser.

Full disclosure: I've been known to ridicule my college education at times, complaining how Miami's jazz-centric curriculum had left me unprepared for the real world. I'm not completely wrong; the academic experience can be somewhat unmoored from practicality. But, after successfully navigating Aretha's obscure request (and putting a smile on her face in the process), my gripes against jazz pedagogy have definitely mellowed.

I'll never know, but I like to think Aretha also appreciated my choice of weapons. Bringing my jazz guitar was a bit of a gamble, but a lot of old-school soul records feature the unmistakable sound of a hollow-body guitar, so my goal was sonic accuracy. Meanwhile, Aretha's son Teddy was wielding a solid-body Les Paul guitar—a hard rockin' axe associated more with Led Zeppelin than 60s R&B. The dread-locked Teddy wore his guitar slung low and seemed to be channeling Lenny Kravitz. Me and my fat-bodied jazzbox served as the perfect foil.

We spent the afternoon unpacking a treasure chest of Aretha's classics. I can't begin to describe my bliss as we jammed on songs including "Chain of Fools," "Daydreaming," and maybe most important of all "Respect" (recently rated #1 in *Rolling Stone*'s "The Greatest Songs of All Time"). There's no telling how many times I'd hacked my way through that well-worn tune at bars and weddings—but performing it with Aretha erased any lingering trauma. Sitting ten feet away from The Queen as she belted out her anthem of empowerment was otherworldly. I thought to myself, "Okay, I can die now. I've finally played 'Respect' the way God intended."

After a few hours of musical ecstasy, we called it day. Aretha seemed happy, but I wasn't sure if my audition had been successful enough to warrant a callback. Regardless, I was determined to stay in the moment. I thanked Francisco (discreetly, but profusely) and floated home.

Nearing my stoop, I bumped into one of my next-door neighbors. He looked at me and tilted his head.

"You okay, Jeff? You seem like you're in a daze."

I smiled, "I just spent the afternoon making music with Aretha Franklin."

"Well, that would explain it," he chuckled.

It was one of the most special days of my life. I felt sanctified—consecrated in the *River Aretha*. Best of all, Francisco called that evening to say the musical director wanted me to come back again tomorrow.

Daily rehearsals progressed. Nobody ever told me I was officially hired, but they kept asking me to return. I've always heard possession is nine-tenths of the law, so I held on tight and continued to show up.

The VH-1 broadcast was conceived as a homage to Aretha, with numerous special guests invited to appear, perform, and kiss the ring. Little by little, other artists started materializing at S.I.R. One day it was Mary J. Blige, another day brought Backstreet Boys and Kid Rock, Philly soulstress Jill Scott made the scene one afternoon; it was a revolving door of heavy hitters. Meanwhile, the band started to expand. Horns, strings, and percussion were gradually added to the mix, ultimately necessitating a move to the big room at S.I.R. for our final days of rehearsal.

The day before the broadcast, kit and caboodle moved to Radio City Music Hall—and believe it or not, I still hadn't officially been hired. Consequently, I felt a sense of trepidation as I approached the security table outside of the venue. I waited my turn as production assistants checked names off their lists and distributed laminates. Reaching the front of the line, I identified myself to a young woman with a clipboard and held my breath. (This might sound ridiculous, but these scenarios are more common than you might think. I have a friend who *used* to work with Aretha. He found out he'd been relieved of his duties when he showed up at the airport to fly to a gig and there wasn't a ticket in his name. Showbiz can be amazingly loose—even at the highest levels.) The assistant eventually located my name, smiled, and handed over my all-access credentials. Whew, I guess I'd passed my two-week audition. I proudly slung that plastic rectangle around my neck and stepped into a dream come true.

I'd visited Radio City Music Hall as an audience member, but this was my first time as a performer. Accordingly, I felt like a conquistador as I glided down the aisle with my guitar on my back. I climbed the short but transcendental stairway to the stage and gazed out into the magnificent auditorium. Playing with Aretha at Radio City? I was psyched.

In addition to the array of pop stars on the bill, the show included an all-star jazz tribute to the Queen of Soul—and I mean "all-star." The sextet featured pianist Herbie Hancock, bassist Ron Carter, drummer Roy Haynes (filling in as a last-minute replacement for Max Roach), trumpeter Clark Terry, saxophonist James Carter, and Russell Malone on guitar. (I knew Russell from his stint alongside my brother in Harry Connick Jr.'s big band.)

The auditorium bustled with activity as the jazzers assembled for their soundcheck. I grabbed a seat amid the fray and watched the scene unfold in awe. Russell Malone saw me in the house and waved me up on stage. I jumped at the invite and hustled to join him.

Russell gave me a hug and smiled, "I see you eyeing my new guitar, Campbell. Check this baby out."

Russell removed his axe and handed it to me. I strapped on the instrument and plucked out a chord or two. The guitar was indeed special, but I was *slightly* distracted. There I stood onstage at Radio City, flanked by my longtime heroes, Herbie Hancock and Ron Carter. This did not compute. Standing between the musical legends made me feel like I'd snuck on to Mount Olympus. (As they say on *Sesame Street*, "One of these things is not like the other.") I quickly came to my senses, returned the guitar to its rightful owner, and scurried back to my seat among the mere mortals. Giddy from my brush with greatness, I sat mesmerized as the jazz titans showcased their effortless mastery.

We did a run-through of the show the next afternoon, sans the stars … except for Kid Rock. The Detroit rapper was the only artist who came to the dress rehearsal and, fan or not, I had to admire his commitment. Meanwhile, NYC vocalist (and fellow Miami alum) Kimberlee Wertz served as a stand-in for ALL of the evening's performers, singing excerpts from every number in the show as the sound crew set levels and cameramen framed their shots. Kimberlee's versatility was quite impressive.

Needless to say, a television broadcast from Radio City with a 40-piece orchestra was a strictly union affair. Accordingly, we took mandated rehearsal breaks whenever the music contractor barked "Take ten!" I've seen it happen repeatedly over the years, yet I'm always amazed by the rigorous enforcement and adherence. When the union says it's break time, it's break time — even if you're knee-deep in creativity. Our conductor H.B. was compliant (he had no choice), but as soon as the *ten* was *taken*, he was ready to resume work. Of course, any large gathering of musicians inevitably includes a few stragglers, but the hardboiled H.B. was having none of it. The minute we were back on the clock, H.B. would frown at the contractor and point to any empty chairs on the bandstand

"I want $50 from here...and from here...and from here," H.B. groused, as he levied his old-school fines for tardiness.

The contractor nodded and took out his note pad. Paychecks were lightened.

Our schedule included a two-hour dinner break before the broadcast, so I strolled home, changed into my tux, and grabbed my lovely date. I was excited Patty would be able to share the special evening with me, but making it happen had required a little legwork. The band wasn't allowed any guests, so Patty had put out feelers for a stray ticket. Unfortunately, the only ticket she could find was of the full-priced $500 variety. We wrestled with pulling the trigger, but ultimately rationalized the extravagance as a combination "once in a lifetime experience" and "good cause." (VH-1 had created the *Divas Live* series to promote their *Save The Music* charitable foundation.) In a case of *imperfect* timing, the day after we purchased the ticket, Patty received a call from one of her earlier queries offering a spare comp. We shrugged—$500 poorer—and stuck with our original altruistic justification. In a win/win, Patty procured the freebie and passed it along to Francisco's wife.

Thirty minutes before showtime, I made my way out onto the massive Radio City stage. Approaching my designated area, I was surprised to see one of Aretha's assistants removing music from our stands and replacing it with a different selection. Alarmed, I asked him what was up. He shrugged and mumbled, "New opener."

Say what? It was only a half-hour before downbeat, and we were getting brand new music? I was stunned. The original plan had been for the band to kick off the festivities (sans Aretha) with an instrumental medley of jazz standards—including The Queen of Soul's latest obsession, "Cherokee." The swinging opener was meant to serve as an *amuse-bouche* for the Radio City crowd before the televised portion of the evening began. But Aretha apparently had a last-minute change of heart—and decided to let her 40-piece orchestra sight-read in front of 6,000 people. Was she screwing with us?

Our jazz mash-up was replaced with another tune from Aretha's trunk, an arrangement of Stevie Wonder's "Uptight (Everything's Alright)." I scanned the multi-page chart and gulped—there was a lot of ink. I was nervous enough; I certainly didn't need the added stress of trying to decipher unfamiliar music in real-time. Complicating the situation further, the song had been arranged with Aretha's voice in mind—but we were going to perform it instrumentally. The logic, if any, escaped me. Meanwhile, our veteran bandleader H.B. didn't seem the least bit flustered. (I'm sure he'd weathered far worse during a colorful career that included Count Basie, Frank Sinatra, and Lou Raw ls.) H.B. pointed to trombonist Fred Wesley—yes, *that* Fred Wesley of James Brown "Hit it, Fred!" fame—and yelled, "Yo Fred, you got the melody?"

"Yeah, I got it!" Fred shouted back casually.

I couldn't believe what was happening. We were going to wing our way through a complex arrangement on one of the world's greatest stages. I suddenly felt like I was in a bar band—a *40-piece* bar band that included four background singers and two dedicated tambourine players.

The house lights went down and away we went. I was struggling to keep up with the fast-moving chart when it hit me, "Hey, wait a minute. I know this song…and it only has TWO chords." I abandoned my efforts to follow the arrangement (which also involved tricky page turns) and decided to rely on my ears. I figured I'd just listen and keep playing until I heard the band stop. I let go of my perfectionist tendencies and channeled my inner slacker; if Aretha didn't care, why should I? I vamped along while watching our conductor like a hawk. Incredibly, my strategy worked. In the end, Stevie's prediction rang true: "everything" was "alright."

After skating through "Uptight," it was officially showtime. Video screens rolled the opening sequence for *VH-1 Divas Live*, then we blasted off for Planet Soul. Aretha, and her army of backup dancers, took the stage to the up-tempo strains of Otis Redding's classic, "I Can't Turn You Loose." The crowd exploded as Ms. Franklin tore the roof off the sucker.

After the opening rave-up, a humongous teleprompter in the back of the auditorium began scrolling Aretha's scripted welcome. She ignored it. Aretha bailed on the carefully crafted introduction and started rambling off the cuff. From last-minute setlist changes to improvised stage patter, Aretha seemed determined to let everybody know who was boss. (Or should I say *Queen*?)

The second song of the night was "Chain of Fools," featuring surprise special guests, Backstreet Boys—or at least it was supposed to be a surprise. The plan was for Aretha to start the number on her own, then, after the first verse, Backstreet Boys would enter from the rear of the auditorium, chiming in on the chorus as they strode down the aisles to join Aretha on stage. But yet again, The Queen went rogue. (Divas gonna diva.)

Aretha crowed, "Put your hands together and welcome the Backstreet Boys!"

Nothing happened as the confused crowd looked around the hall.

Aretha doubled down. "All I need is my Backstreet Boys!"

Crickets.

I glanced over in the wings and saw the stage manager drop his head and shake it back and forth in exasperation.

Aretha's son, Teddy, rode to the rescue and plowed forward with the iconic guitar intro for "Chain of Fools." The band kicked in on cue and Aretha sang the first verse before Backstreet Boys made their grand entrance (as originally planned). The crowd finally figured out what the hell was going on and roared with approval.

Our audience was filled with A-listers, and Aretha made a point to name-check her pals throughout the show—often in the middle of a tune. She'd sing one of her classic lines and then punctuate it with "oh yeah, Billy Dee Williams" or "uh huh, Johnnie Cochran." You had to love Aretha's devil-may-care attitude. She was treating Radio City like it was her living room.

Highlights of the evening included Jill Scott's jazzy "(You Make Me Feel Like) A Natural Woman," Aretha and Kid Rock's duet on "Rock Steady," and Mary J Blige's show-stopping "Day Dreaming." Afterward, Mary J and Aretha teamed up for a powerful take on "Do Right Woman, Do Right Man." Until that evening, I'd been a bit of a Mary J Blige skeptic, but she converted me on the spot. The tattooed songstress prowled the stage in her skintight leather mini dress and knee-high boots, growling and scatting like a boss. I found her incredibly sexy and maybe even a bit scary. (So *that's* her secret!)

Changing gears, Aretha performed the operatic "Nessun dorma," reprising her game-saving moment of glory from the Grammys a few years earlier (also at Radio City). Luciano Pavarotti had been slated to sing the Puccini classic at the awards show but fell ill and called to cancel—30 minutes *after* the broadcast had begun. *"I don't feel well. I can't come. I sing for you next year."* Aretha calmly offered to step into the breach and replace the ailing tenor. Her last-minute rendition stole the show and added another amazing chapter to her legendary career. (For the record, Aretha sang to a prerecorded instrumental track of "Nessun dorma" at the *Divas* concert. Our orchestra was big, but not Metropolitan Opera big.)

Canadian newcomer Nelly Furtado was also on the bill. Her song "I'm Like a Bird" was all over the radio, so she'd been invited to the party. Nelly was a sweetie (and quite lovely), but I'm afraid she was out of her depth among Aretha's all-star lineup. Nelly's performance was spirited but shaky, and the crowd response was polite at best. (I don't blame Nelly. I would've been intimidated too.)

I'd befriended Nelly's bassist/musical director, Dean Jarvis, during the week, and he'd approached me on our final day to see if I had any interest in joining Nelly's touring band. Despite Nelly's rising-star status, the thought of hitting the road had little appeal. (I'd already seen the world a couple of times with Sting, plus I was now the proud owner of a steady job on Broadway.) But I'd learned to never say no right out of the gate, so I played along and gently inquired about the pay rate. I was stunned when Dean replied, "$800 a week...Canadian." That sounded like chicken feed, especially from an artist with a major radio hit. Hell, I was earning *twice* that amount by simply walking three blocks to *Seussical*—and I still got to sleep in my bed every night. My "maybe" quickly morphed into a grateful but firm "No thanks."

Wrapping up the incredible evening, Aretha's guests rejoined her on stage for a group sing-along on "Freeway of Love." I was laying down the groove when I heard the audience erupt. Startled, I looked up and saw none other than Stevie Wonder being escorted in from the wings. *Stevie effin' Wonder!* I'd worked with plenty of big-time celebrities, but I was gobsmacked by the sight of Stevie. I am a HUGE fan. To me, Stevie Wonder is a god. Francisco later joked, "Dude, you should've seen the look on your face when Stevie walked out." I'm sure it was priceless.

"Freeway of Love" spiraled into an extended jam. We vamped on the three-chord hook for what seemed like an eternity, continuing to rock loooong after the TV broadcast had ended. (I guess Aretha wanted to take everybody to *church*.) Hand to God, I eventually grew tired of the bottomless cup of encore. I experienced many emotions that evening, but I did not have "boredom" on my bingo card. Suppressing a yawn onstage with Aretha and Stevie? Embarrassing but true.

When the concert *finally* wrapped, the spent crowd filtered out of the auditorium. I saw Patty standing at her seat, so I waved her up on stage. She gave me a big hug and then we stood with Francisco and stared out into the beautiful venue. I was dazed from my two whirlwind weeks, but I had a clear sense of accomplishment—and gratitude. Francisco had taken an enormous risk when he'd defied his boss and called me (instead of Cornell Dupree) for the gig.

"Frankie, I owe you big time for this" I gushed.

Always the jokester, Francisco replied, "Tell you what Jeff, let me sleep with Patty and we'll call it even."

Before I could craft a sufficiently witty response, Patty interjected, "Hold on there, Francisco…get ME a gig with Aretha, and we'll talk."


I'd set our VCR to record the broadcast, so Patty and I rushed home, kicked off our unsensible shoes, nuked a bag of popcorn, and plopped on the couch. I was eager to relive the magical evening, but my expectations had been tempered hours earlier. Before the first note was ever played, I'd been informed the broadcast truck had run out of audio inputs for the orchestra—and I would be the odd man out. The Radio City audience would hear my musical contributions, but the television audience wouldn't *revel* in a single note of my work. Disappointing.

Nevertheless, I excitedly pressed play on our VCR. The show looked amazing, and the band was smoking. Unlike my non-existent guitar, Francisco's bass was mixed nice and loud. And although I'd been standing right beside him all night, I was (re) impressed by his muscular playing. My VHS recording confirmed Francisco was the driving force behind our 40-piece ensemble. Badass indeed.

Rubbing salt in my ego, my visual presence on the broadcast barely eclipsed my aural presence (which again was zero). I watched the video without blinking, waiting and hoping for a classic money shot of me and Aretha (or anybody else for that matter), but it never happened. Every time a cameraman came close to showing me, the director would cut to another sweeping shot. In the end, I was relegated to anonymous, silhouetted musician for the entire show. *C'est la vie.* I wasn't heard — nor hardly seen — on the telecast, but it was still one of the coolest nights of my life.

## *An Audience with the Dancing Queen*

Meanwhile, back at the *Seussical* ranch, ticket sales were bleak, and rumors swirled of an imminent closing. But as my "can't miss" show circled the drain, our maestro, David Holcenberg, pulled me aside.

"Hey Jeff," David whispered. "I'm involved with an upcoming show featuring the music of ABBA. I was wondering if you might be interested in joining me."

With unemployment breathing down my neck, I responded, "Yeah, sure."

David smiled and said he would pass my name on to the show's contractor.

This was another one of those fleeting interactions that would ultimately redirect and redefine my career. David's new project was none other than *Mamma Mia!*, which would go on to become a global phenomenon and enjoy a glorious 14-year run on Broadway—and alter my life in untold ways. (Money may be the root of all evil, but financial security is a blessing.)

Judgement Day for *Seussical* arrived a week later when the producers officially posted a closing notice. My forecasted "ten-year show" had lasted six pitiful months—and I only had one paycheck left. I held out hope David's job offer might materialize, then the plot thickened.

*Seussical* contractor John Miller approached me in the pit before one of our last performances, looked over his shoulder and leaned in.

"Hey Campbell, I think I have another show for you. Any interest?"

"Uh…maybe," I replied, unsure of my status with *Mamma Mia!*

Miller, a savvy vet of the Broadway scene, picked up on my hesitation. "Have you already been sounded for something else?"

"Kind of," I confessed.

Miller asked, "*Mamma Mia?*"

"Yep, but it's not 100%."

Miller pressed forward. He was assembling the orchestra for *Thou Shalt Not* (a new show featuring heartthrob crooner Harry Connick Jr.) and was prepared to offer me the guitar chair. But the all-powerful John Miller wasn't about to play second fiddle to the whims of *Mamma Mia!* Flashing his hardball, John said he'd need a yes or no "in 48 hours."

I was faced with the proverbial "bird in the hand" quandary. The buzz on *Mamma Mia!* was strong as the show toured America in advance of its Broadway run. Audiences were apparently going crazy over the feel-good musical chock-full of songs from

ABBA's platinum catalog. The *jukebox* musical had "hit" written all over it—but my status with *Mamma Mia!* was ambiguous at best. Conversely, my offer from *Thou Shalt Not* was rock solid. Anybody got a crystal ball?

Patty and I debated the situation *ad nauseam* over our allotted "48 hours." Despite the allure of *Mamma Mia!*, my pragmatic nature kept nudging me toward *Thou Shalt Not*. I've never been much of a gambler, and there were plenty of compelling reasons to play it safe. Topping the list, John Miller was (and is) a Broadway gatekeeper, so staying in his good graces was a no-brainer. Furthermore, I had something of a peripheral relationship with the show's star, Harry Connick Jr. I'd hung out with Harry a few times back when my brother Will was playing sax in his big band. (Matter of fact, Harry graciously sang the first dance at Will and Nora's wedding.) Lastly, Broadway's hottest director, Susan Stroman was helming the production. Stroman was a proven commodity, having directed and choreographed two of the current season's hit shows, *Contact*, and a revival of *The Music Man*. These factors, combined with the guaranteed aspect of the job, made *Thou Shalt Not* seem like the obvious (and rational) choice. But the Broadway rumor mill was teasing ABBA magic. I was torn.

I had a problem, albeit a luxury problem: I had TWO shows to pick from. I desperately needed counsel but didn't feel comfortable discussing my embarrassment of riches with my peers. Hell, most musicians struggle to get a single Broadway offer, let alone two. However, I did know one guy who might be sympathetic to my plight: Charles Descarfino.

Charles was the original percussionist on *Seussical,* but, as the critical floodwaters rose, he'd been offered a life raft from another incoming show, *The Adventures of Tom Sawyer*. Charlie wrestled with his own two-show dilemma before deciding to bail on *Seussical* and cast his lot with Mark Twain. (Sadly, Charlie's move didn't pan out. The upstart *Tom Sawyer* was a total bust and actually closed a week *earlier* than *Seussical*. Double ouch! Showbiz ain't for sissies.)

I called Charlie seeking guidance. To my pleasant surprise, Charlie was already aware of my tentative *Mamma Mia!* offer, and in a position to provide valuable insight. Charlie was good friends with Michael Keller, the musical contractor for *Mamma Mia!*—and confided Keller had reached out to him to inquire about my qualifications. Charlie said he'd sung my praises to Michael before strongly advising him to hire me. I thanked Charlie for the endorsement—and the juicy insider scoop. Knowing I was on Michael Keller's radar was encouraging, but it muddied the issue even further. Was it time for a coin flip?

The clock was ticking down on John Miller's offer, I *had* to make a decision. Choosing head over heart, I went with *Thou Shalt Not*. Patty was on the fence, but supportive, nonetheless. Exhausted from weighing our doubts and fears, we surrendered and went with the "sure thing." (This rationale ultimately couldn't have been more wrong. Stay tuned.)

Swear to God, I was reaching for the phone to call John Miller and accept his offer…when it rang. Instead of dialing, I answered.

"Hi Jeff, this is Michael Keller, musical contractor for *Mamma Mia!* I'm in Chicago with the production right now, but I wanted to go ahead and officially offer you a spot in the band. This is pending final approval from London, but I don't think that's going to be a problem. Welcome aboard."

I hung up in a daze, literally saved by the bell. Armed with this new information, Patty and I called an audible. I phoned John Miller and thanked him but told him I'd decided to go with *Mamma Mia!* John responded with an indifferent, "Okay man, best of luck." This last-minute switcheroo proved to be one of the most pivotal (and prosperous) moments in my life.

After a brutal six months, the much-hyped *Seussical* drew its dying breath. Financial losses were estimated at $11 million, making it one of the biggest flops in Broadway history. But since *Seussical* begat *Mamma Mia!*, I was primed for a soft landing. My new show was slated to start in a mere four months, so I filed an unemployment claim and kicked back to enjoy my summer.

The living was easy with guaranteed work on the horizon. I kept my hustling to a minimum, playing only a handful of gigs. With *Mamma Mia!* rehearsals scheduled to begin late September, Patty and I decided to take a quick vacation before the madness kicked in. Neither of us had ever been to the Grand Canyon, so we made plans to sneak out to Arizona for a few days. We booked our flight for September 12.

## 9/11

We were awakened by our phone on the morning of September 11. One of Patty's high-school friends, Barry Jones, was calling from Kentucky and urged us to turn on the TV. We rubbed the sleep from our eyes and switched on the set to see smoke pouring from a gaping hole in the North Tower of the World Trade

Center. Initial reports were speculating a small plane may have accidentally crashed into the 110-story skyscraper. This theory seemed a little odd; it was a beautiful September morning and there wasn't a cloud in the sky. Patty walked into the kitchen to continue her conversation with Barry as I sat on the edge of the bed, staring at the screen. I was trying to wrap my head around the situation when I saw a second plane plow into the South Tower and explode in a ball of fire. (20 years later, the memory still makes me nauseous.) I no longer wondered if this was an accident.

"We're under attack!" I shouted.

Patty hung up with Barry and hurried back into the room. We stood there stunned. We slowly turned our gaze from the television to our front windows. Living on the 5th floor of a walk-up provided a nice regimen of cardio, and a decent panorama of NYC's skyline. Each morning when we opened our blinds, we were greeted by the nearby Empire State Building, while the Twin Towers stood sentinel in the distance. But that day, our view was one of dread. Black smoke billowed on the horizon.

We hung on every word of the NBC News Special Report. An hour after impact, we gasped as the South Tower collapsed in a mushroom cloud of dust. Thirty minutes later, the North Tower followed suit. A combined 220 stories of office buildings erased. Panic consumed us as we contemplated how many people had been trapped inside. Thousands? In a state of shock, we couldn't comprehend the scope of what we were witnessing. Patty's band had a gig booked that evening at CB's 313 Gallery (CBGB's sister club located just next door), and we actually wondered aloud if our gig *might* be cancelled. But we slowly began to grasp the magnitude of the day's events. No, we would not be playing a gig that night—and there would be no trip to the Grand Canyon in the morning. The world had stopped spinning. September 11, 2001, drew a line through my life. Things either happened before 9/11...or after 9/11.

Broadway went dark for two days. Bridges were closed, tunnels were closed, airports were closed; who the hell was going to come to the theater? In the meantime, the light-hearted *Mamma Mia!* kept chugging toward Broadway. In fact, the cast was in rehearsal on the morning of September 11, and had watched the horror unfurl from their upper floor dance studio in Union Square. But, in the truest sense of "the show must go on," rehearsals resumed the following day.

Nobody knew what came next. Would there be more attacks? The sight of any aircraft overhead sparked fear. Anthrax was mailed to *The New York Times*; rumors of a poisoned water supply circulated. New York City was in a constant state of anxiety as we waited for the other shoe to drop.

Two weeks after 9/11, the *Mamma Mia!* band assembled at S.I.R. studios for our first day of rehearsal. We had no idea what the future held for America—much less our fluffy romantic comedy set to the music of ABBA. But we persisted. One foot in front of the other.

On the final day of band rehearsal, the cast joined us for the traditional *sitzprobe* (German for "seated rehearsal"). This occasion is usually filled with laughter and excitement as the cast and band meet to perform the songs together for the first time. But the mood at our gathering was understandably muted. Underscoring the gravity of the moment, ABBA founders Björn Ulvaeus and Benny Andersson were in attendance to offer moral support. A clearly shaken Björn addressed the entire company, speaking openly about the uncertainty staring us in the face, before expressing his extreme gratitude and pride in the production. Benny nodded along in agreement.

Less than one month after the attacks, *Mamma Mia!* played its first public preview on October 5. The joy from the audience was palpable. Between the much-needed distraction and a damn fun night of theater, the crowd was dancing in the aisles by the end of the show. Despite the positive reaction, I still worried the pall hanging over NYC might have an adverse effect on our long-term prospects. The terror attacks had left people afraid to visit New York (especially by air) — and tourists are the lifeblood of Broadway. An empty city equals empty theaters.

*Mamma Mia!* officially opened at the Winter Garden Theatre on October 18. Typically, a light-hearted, feel-good musical such as ours prompts critics to sharpen their knives. But 9/11 had rejiggered the normally adversarial dynamic between high-minded journalists and fun-loving theatergoers. The last thing Broadway (and NYC) needed was bad press, so one could argue *Mamma Mia!* was graded on a curve. Reviewers seemed to pull their punches, begrudgingly admitting the show was irresistible. *The New York Times* threaded the needle, calling the show "bland, hokey, corny,…square," and comparing the production to a Hostess cupcake — before conceding "when the going gets tough, the tough want cupcakes." I had a feeling we might have a hit on our hands, but I had no idea just how big our *cupcake* would ultimately become.

Our opening night party was held at Bryant Park Grill. I'd been given an extra ticket to the show and after-party, so Patty and I invited our good friend Constance Kazee to join us. (Constance's husband, Jeff, is a great pianist/singer and a dear pal.) Lord knows we all needed a night of diversion, but Constance was carrying the added burden of experiencing 9/11 firsthand. The Kazees are like family, so their pain was our pain. Accordingly, if Constance was interested, Patty and I wanted her by our side for the special night.

Constance managed Morton's steakhouse near the World Trade Center and was on her way to work when the planes went into the buildings. Climbing the subway stairs just after the attacks, Constance came face-to-face with hell on earth. She witnessed a grisly scene normally reserved for combat soldiers or ER doctors. With the city paralyzed, Constance escaped the danger by foot, walking all the way back home to Queens. Con was understandably shaken by the traumatic events, but the woman is a rock. She graciously accepted our *Mamma Mia!* invitation, and the three of us enjoyed a wonderful evening, trying our damnedest to laugh and dance the demons away. I'm normally a wallflower, but my inhibitions were nowhere to be found that night. Dancing took on a much deeper meaning as the *Mamma Mia!* family celebrated a communion of gratitude and life itself. The joyous release was cathartic.

### Somebody Up There

As *Mamma Mia!* gained steamed, the show I almost chose instead, *Thou Shalt Not*, wasn't faring as well. The critics and, more importantly, the ticket-buying public were not impressed. I felt bad for *Thou Shalt Not* but was relieved I'd picked the right horse. One night, Patty was offered a comp to *Thou Shalt Not* and decided to give it a go. I told her to be sure to take a peek in the orchestra pit and find out who'd ended up playing guitar. When I got home from work, Patty was already on the couch.

"So how was the show?" I asked.

"Um, okay," Patty replied. "It had some interesting parts, but they didn't really hang together."

I cut to the chase. "Who was playing guitar?"

Patty exhaled and shook her head, "There was NO guitar."

What? A chill ran down my spine. Turns out, the guitar chair had been completely cut from the production before it reached Broadway. I had to sit down to process my brush with disaster. Damn! I'd come *this* close to accepting a gig that, in the end, wasn't a gig at all. I still shudder to think I almost passed up a multi-year blockbuster for a guitar-less dud. For those of you keeping score, *Thou Shalt Not* closed after only two months; *Mamma Mia!* ran FOURTEEN YEARS! The quick, back-of-the-envelope math is sobering. *Mamma Mia!* resulted in more than 700 paychecks, while *Thou Shalt Not* would've resulted in…ZERO. Whew! The angels were definitely watching over me. My year with Sting may be the crown jewel in my resumé, but financially speaking, *Mamma Mia!* was THE gig of a lifetime.

# Carpenter vs. Architect

As *Mamma Mia!* percolated along (with $27 million in advance ticket sales), I was finally able to put my finger on the unfamiliar sensation I was experiencing: job security. I felt a deep sense of gratitude and vowed to repay the gods by "swinging for the fences" in my free time—which was considerable. Even if I played all eight shows in a given week, my *full-time* job only consumed 24 hours of my life. This sweetheart schedule was largely attributable to my commute...or lack thereof.

Thanks to living in Hell's Kitchen, my walk (yes, walk) to work clocks in at a breezy ten minutes. This substantial perk eliminates all travel hassles—and has been known to generate *loving* ridicule from my suburban/outer-borough co-workers at times. Pre-show conversation among orchestra members frequently includes horror stories of delayed subways, backed-up bridges and tunnels, and the dependable scarcity of parking, so it's not uncommon to be met with sarcastic concern when I saunter in 15 minutes before curtain.

"And how was *your* commute Jeff?"

"Brutal," I fake whine. "The crossing light at Ninth Avenue said, "Don't Walk.""

Cue unison groans.

Living within walking distance of the theater district simplifies my life immensely; I feel like I live in Mayberry. But my convenient midtown address isn't the result of some savvy master plan (or a rich Aunt Mary), it's a happy accident—born of sacrifice and perseverance.

Back in the 1980s, before Mickey Mouse and his Lion King pal chased all the hustlers and porn out of Times Square, our adjacent neighborhood of Hell's Kitchen featured a dicey blend of drug dealers, prostitutes, brazen rodents—and consequently, dirt-cheap rents. This made the area a magnet for starving artists. When Patty first came to town, she moved into a 5th-floor walk-up with a childhood friend from Kentucky, and then held the fort as Hell's Kitchen slowly gentrified.

Meanwhile, after my year of luxury with Sting, I landed in a neighborhood walk-up as well. But unlike Patty, I didn't have to climb any stairs. My cozy studio was located on the ground floor, which afforded me the bonus of a patio—a rarity in vertical NYC. However, despite its pastoral aspirations, my postage stamp-sized garden wasn't immune to the surrounding depravity. My apartment building bordered a seedy playground frequented by junkies and hookers, so it wasn't uncommon to find used hypodermic needles and condoms tossed over the fence into my patch of weeds. But I didn't care—at that early stage, the grittiness was part of the charm. I felt validated by the struggle.

Amid the bustling squalor, Patty and I met and fell in love. After we got married, I gave up my $450 bachelor pad and moved into Patty's larger space. I was plugging along, playing weddings and chasing my rock-n-roll dreams when I stumbled upon musical theater. Broadway turned out to be a good fit for my temperament and, long story *not-so-short*, I'm able to walk to work.

In addition to the easy-to-swallow time commitment, my respectable Broadway salary (and manageable overhead) meant I no longer needed to hustle for extra gigs. Making a living as a musician is tough sledding, so we often become hard-wired to say yes to almost every offer. But with a steady paycheck, I finally learned how to say no. It was liberating. I might not have had "fuck you" money, but I definitely had "no thanks" money.

Presented with large chunks of *me time*, my first order of fence-swinging business was to roll up my sleeves and learn the ins and outs of digital recording. For better *and* worse, the digital genie was out of the bottle, and it was now possible to make professionally competitive recordings on your personal computer. (Cost-prohibitive recording studios were no longer the only option for aspiring artists.) I bought a Mac laptop and a first-generation ProTools MBox, and threw myself at the mercy of Craig Cassidy, soundman for *Mamma Mia!* Craig smiled, patted me on the head, and graciously helped me set up my rig. I was a complete novice, but immediately fell in love with the process. I devoured how-to manuals in the darkened Winter Garden pit, underlining tips and tricks with a yellow highlighter—in between ABBA songs—before rushing home to test-drive my latest discovery.

Back when I was a starry-eyed teenager, I figured performing was the only viable path to becoming a full-time musician, so performing was the path I followed. But after decades of climbing onstage, I found myself craving a new frontier. Like blues legend B.B. King wailed, the thrill was gone. Similar to an actor who decides to move *behind* the camera to direct, music production became my new passion. My life as a sideman had been incredibly fulfilling, but I'd begun to see myself as a mere cog in the machine, more of a skilled laborer than an artist. *Mamma Mia!* was a great gig, but I eventually started to feel like a carpenter hammering ABBA nails night after night. I was restless, I wanted more. I wanted to be a composer, an arranger, a producer...an architect!

Here was the plan: find youthful, talented people who sought the spotlight, help them write and record songs, and ultimately reap the creative and financial rewards. I once heard an industry insider observe, "Behind every young face in pop music is someone with gray whiskers." This truth became my North Star. Staying in the shadows and calling the shots sounded totally appealing. I monitored the comings and goings in the *Mamma Mia!* cast, and if someone's vibe caught my eye, I'd ask if they had any desire to pursue a career as an original artist. If the answer was yes, we'd start working together.

Honing my recording skills and writing/producing music was all-consuming. Meanwhile, my phone kept ringing with sideman work. I much preferred my studio pursuits to performing, so I forced myself to pass on many offers. I burned a few bridges along the way, but I was determined to do what made *me* happy. I didn't want to deprioritize my passion in order to play yet another nondescript, low-paying gig. (I already had decades of those under my belt.) Thanks to Broadway, I didn't need the extra hundred bucks—I needed the *dream*.

That said, accepting certain jobs was a no-brainer. I always made time for nice paydays or resumé builders—and performing with singer Michael Bublé checked both of those boxes. But, as usual, the prestigious credit came from a chance encounter.

### Bublé Wrap

Saxophonist Jerry Vivino (of Conan O'Brien's *Late Night* band) had a weekly gig at Luxia, a cozy Italian restaurant located right across from the Musician's Union building on West 48th Street. Jerry led a killer group featuring bassist Mike Merritt and drummer James Wormworth (both also from Conan's band), plus organist extraordinaire Brian Charette. The scene was loose, the food was great, and Luxia quickly became *the* place for musicians to hang in midtown—many after playing their Broadway shows. Jerry shunned using a PA system, which made the volume ideal for mingling. It felt like you'd wandered into a party at Louis Prima's house in the 1960s. The band played everything from jazz to funk, and with so many musos in the house, Jerry would invite people to sit in from time to time.

Typically, I prefer to hide in the back at open jam sessions. Let's face it, showcasing your wares in NYC can be intimidating. The city's talent pool is incredibly deep, which can make the theoretically relaxed setting seem more like a competition. You can't help but think your skills (or lack thereof) are being judged. I always feel like a magician trying to wow a room of fellow magicians...who already know how to saw a lady in half.

One night at Luxia, Jerry approached and asked if I wanted to sit in. Despite my chronic reticence, I've learned attempting to decline such invitations can often become more of a spectacle than simply agreeing to play a tune or two, so I said yes. A-list vocalist Elaine Caswell (Cyndi Lauper, Bette Midler, Joe Jackson) was also in the house that evening, so she and I joined Jerry's quartet for a sexy, down-tempo version of James Brown's "I Got You (I Feel Good)." Afterward, Jerry segued into Sonny Rollins's up-tempo bop classic, "Pent-up House." I'd played this number back in college but, unlike that day when I'd miraculously divined "Cherokee" for Aretha Franklin, I wasn't feeling lucky. Deciding to quit while I was ahead. I turned down the volume on the guitar, stuck my hands in my pockets, and listened. Faced with the choice of silence or humiliation, I opted for the lesser of two evils. When the tune ended, I told Jerry I appreciated the invite and slipped back into the crowd.

I got a call from Jerry the next day. He thanked me for sitting in, before saying he was putting a band together for a couple of Michael Bublé appearances in New York—NBC's *Today* show and an industry event at The China Club. Jerry wanted to know if I'd be interested in the gig. Like I said, "no-brainer." Bublé was relatively new on the scene, but the hype was huge. After the massive success of Harry Connick Jr., retro-crooners were a hot commodity.

I was doubly excited because Jerry told me multi-platinum producer David Foster was overseeing the project. I salivated at the thought of working with the power-ballad legend—and possibly making a high-value industry connection in the process. *Hustle, hustle, hustle.* Some may think of David Foster as schmaltzy (and they'd have a valid argument), but Foster's mag-

ic touch is behind two of my favorite recordings: Earth, Wind
& Fire's "After the Love Has Gone," and Whitney Houston's "I
Have Nothing." I challenge you to listen to either of those tracks
and not get goose bumps. The man knows how to tug at your
heartstrings.

Bublé was slated to play *Today*'s Valentine's Day broadcast,
so the band assembled a couple of nights beforehand at the default spot for high-level rehearsals: S.I.R. studios. We were told
in advance we'd be playing two cuts from Bublé's new album—
"Come Fly with Me" and "That's All." As a hardcore Frank
Sinatra fan, I was quite familiar with both numbers. Bublé's arrangement of "Come Fly with Me" seemed like a direct *lift* from
the Sinatra recording, but his version of "That's All" had been
contemporized and featured an exposed nylon-string guitar intro. The moment I heard Bublé's take on the classic, I was fanta-
sizing about the TV cameras zooming in on me and my new pal
*Mike* as we duetted our way through the first verse.

Michael was nursing a scratchy throat at rehearsal, so David Foster took charge. After running through "Come Fly with
Me," Bublé, Foster, and I huddled together to review the guitar
intro on "That's All." I'd transcribed (and memorized) the part
from the album and was fully prepared to wow Team Bublé.
Foster nodded in approval as I played and exclaimed "Beautiful!" when I finished. We debated one specific chord voicing, but
after referencing the recording, Foster deferred to my ear. Point
Campbell.

The year was 2003, so digital technology had become an
entrenched aspect of live performance. Consequently, Bublé's
soundman had each individual track from Michael's album at
his fingertips; one click of the mouse...and ANY isolated part

from the studio recording flowed pristinely from the computer. Jerry Vivino had assembled a band of NYC ringers, so we didn't need any artificial enhancement, but budget and space limitations prevented hiring a string section. No problem, Bublé's engineer would simply unmute the string tracks from the album and like magic: orchestral accompaniment. Impressive—and depressive. I know the world only spins forward, but technological advances have cost musicians a LOT of jobs. Much like in the heartland of America, automation has hollowed out our workforce (and pension fund) considerably.

The *Today* show hits the airwaves at 7am (an hour much closer to the average musician's bedtime than the start of their workday) and as a result, the band call was for a brutal 5am. Although the *Today* studio is only a three-block walk from our apartment, I didn't like the thought of schlepping my expensive guitar through Times Square in the middle of the night, so I scheduled a car service.

The groggy band congregated around a coffee urn in the makeshift greenroom as we awaited our marching orders. An excited Michael Bublé, hot tea in hand, stopped by to greet the gang as daylight struggled to its feet. We were eventually corralled into the studio for a soundcheck and—at the ungodly hour of 6:30am—drummer Ray Marchica counted off "Come Fly with Me."

After the run-through, I saw David Foster heading in my direction.

David whispered, "Uh, we have a bit of an issue."

I listened as Foster delivered the bad news. Milking the Valentine's angle, the segment producer had suggested *Today* host Katie Couric sneak into the shot during the instrumental section of "That's All" and dance with Michael. The problem? There wasn't enough room for the pair to canoodle with the guitarist "in the way." (The studio was amazingly cramped. The broadcast doesn't convey the reality of the tight quarters.) Foster shrugged "Sorry," and just like that, Couric was in, Campbell was out. Instead of live guitar on "That's All," the soundman would stream the pre-recorded guitar from his backstabbing hard drive. My big feature...up in *digital* smoke.

In addition to my "That's All" benching, I learned our soundcheck of "Come Fly with Me" had been preserved on video. (Apparently, this is standard operating procedure in case of technical emergencies.) The production crew had huddled and decided our rehearsal recording would be fine for the broadcast, so there'd be no need to re-perform the song during the show. Verdict: I was done before I ever got started. With my services no longer required, I thanked my bosses (the firm of Bublé, Foster, & Vivino) and wandered out in search of a cab. I was back home and in bed with Patty by the time Matt Lauer and my new archenemy Katie Couric welcomed their viewers.

We were also scheduled to play a Warner Brothers showcase with Bublé the following week at The China Club. David Foster told me he was flying to LA after our *Today* taping—and wasn't sure if he'd make it back to NYC for our second gig. Mother Nature made David's decision for him. A giant snowstorm hit the Northeast that weekend, dumping over two feet of snow on New York, paralyzing airports and stranding Foster in sunny California. Lucky bastard.

Despite the massive snow drifts, the presentation went

ahead as planned. The China Club was only two blocks from our apartment, so I put on my duck boots, and slowly navigated the icy sidewalks—shuffling along with extra care due to the hollow-body guitar strapped on my back. I entered the club and climbed the stairs to the second-floor room hosting the event. Bandleader Jerry Vivino met me at the top landing.

"Hey Jeff, great news! David Foster loves you," Jerry beamed. "There's talk of making you Bublé's musical director."

This was indeed an exciting development. I wondered, "Could this be my big break?" Spoiler alert: it wasn't. I never heard another peep about joining Team Bublé. At the risk of sounding cynical, talk is cheap (especially in showbiz), so I've learned to avoid premature celebrations. Rule of thumb: no toasting until the first check clears.

The China Club gig was considerably more relaxed than our fishbowl TV appearance; I felt like I was playing at an office party. I assume there were some bigwigs at the back tables, but the room was mainly filled with rowdy employees from Michael's record label ready to partake in a little "day drinking."

The partisan crowd cheered wildly as we performed a selection of tunes from Michael's new album. Despite comparisons to Frank Sinatra, Bublé's bedside manner reminded me more of Dean Martin. Michael wasn't the brooding type; he was more of an affable master of ceremonies, a "guy's guy" who just wants everybody to have fun.

During one tune, Michael turned to the band and waved us off. The song ground to a halt as Michael sheepishly confessed to the crowd we'd gotten lost in the arrangement. The band wasn't convinced, but Michael assured us we were out-of-sync with the computer-generated playback. (Yes, although we had a full big band, we were still augmenting our sound with the phantom string section from Bublé's album.) We started the song over, but only made it part of the way before Michael stopped us again. He shook his head and insisted the band and the computer still weren't matching up. As Michael apologized to the crowd, band members began yelling, "Turn off the computer! Let's play it live."

Our easy-going frontman bowed to the wishes of his veteran ensemble and agreed to attempt the tune without a digital *net*. The third time was indeed the charm. We nailed the chart and the audience roared as we crossed the finish line. Nevertheless, I was astonished Bublé was willing to absorb TWO false starts in front of a crowd — no matter how biased they were. The move seemed amateurish, which made me wonder about Bublé's long-term chances in the music business. Seven albums, six world tours, and four Grammys later, I guess he showed me.

### Fashion Police Brutality

Large snowstorms tend to wreak havoc on Broadway attendance, and unless shows are cancelled altogether (which is rare), producers have to scramble to put fannies in the seats. To that end, I was offered a couple of last-minute comps to a special President's Day matinee of the Rodgers and Hammerstein revival, *The Flower Drum Song*. The lethal combination of two feet of snow and a Monday afternoon performance had all but wiped out the box office.

Patty and I were enjoying the show's first act when my pager vibrated. Yes, my pager. Today, we laugh at the antiquated technology, but at the time, I felt like George Jetson — or at least a low-level drug dealer. I called the mystery number at intermission and wound up on the phone with pop star Debbie Gibson's manager, Diane — who also happens to be her mother. (I believe they call that a "momager.")

Debbie was doing a show later in the week and she'd decided to add a guitarist. Diane said I was recommended by my pal, bassist Conrad Korsch. (Conrad had worked with Debbie in the past, but by this point, he'd graduated to playing with rock legend Rod Stewart.) Wow, in the span of one week, I'd been called for gigs with Michael Bublé and Debbie Gibson. When it *snows*, it pours.

Gibson was performing at Culture Club, an 80s-themed nightclub in downtown NYC. The gig was essentially a "track date" (where artists use pre-recorded music instead of a band), but Debbie wanted to enhance her sound with live percussion and guitar. I wasn't familiar with Gibson's music, but I certainly knew of her reputation. Debbie always struck me as a fluffy, PG-version of Madonna, but you have to give credit where credit is due. Gibson has the distinction of being the youngest female artist to write, produce, and perform a Billboard Hot 100 number-one single. (Impressively, Gibson was only 17 years old when her "Foolish Beat" topped the charts.) I accepted the terms of the one-off gig and was instructed to learn a handful of Debbie's hits.

The vibe at rehearsal was playful and relaxed. We worked for a couple of hours, honing the abbreviated set until the boss was satisfied. As we dispersed, I asked Debbie about a dress code for the gig. She responded, "Think 80s!"

The afternoon of the gig, I took a cab downtown and climbed

over the trash-covered mountain of blackened snow plowed up in front of Culture Club. (I assume the name of the venue was a nod to 80's icon Boy George.) The interior of the joint was festooned with decade-appropriate memorabilia, including giant cut-outs of PAC-MAN and Rubik's Cubes. We set up on stage and made a little noise for the soundman, before retiring to the glorified broom closet that was masquerading as our dressing room.

I hadn't batted an eye when Debbie specified 80s clothing for our gig. I still had (and could fit into) my threads from Sting's 1987/88 tour, so I was set—or so I thought. A half-hour before showtime, we scattered to change into our stage wear. Debbie eventually exited her dressing area sporting a trendy one-shoulder top and designer jeans. I thought, "Hey wait a minute, that outfit isn't retro." Debbie took one look at my spotted silk jacket (with requisite shoulder pads) and pleated pants and burst out laughing.

"Nice fashion statement, Jeff," she mocked.

I didn't appreciate the ridicule—I was just following orders. I felt like I'd been pranked but held my tongue. Magnifying my frustration, our percussionist had ignored Debbie's 80s decree and was wearing modern attire as well.

We performed to a crowded room of enthusiastic (drunken) nostalgia junkies. Debbie's bubbly music wasn't exactly my cup of tea—and her snarky critique of my wardrobe hadn't helped my disposition. But I'm a pro. I did my job with a smile on my face, packed my gear, collected my check, and thanked Ms. Gibson for the work. Truth be told, I still hold a bit of a grudge. Move over Katie Couric.

\* \* \*

*Mamma Mia!* kept humming along, filling the Winter Garden month after month, year after year. The show was clearly a hit, but I kept my guard up. Musicians are accustomed to living hand to mouth, so our default setting is "worry."

Three years into *Mamma Mia!*, I was chatting with one of our substitute drummers, Ron Tierno, at intermission.

"This is Broadway's next 10-year show," Ron stated matter-of-factly.

"You really think so?" I asked.

"No doubt," Ron said confidently.

Ron knew of what he spoke. He'd played drums for the last resident of the Winter Garden Theatre: Andrew Lloyd Webber's *Cats*. The feline musical enjoyed an amazing 18-year reign—which at the time, made it the longest running show in Broadway history. Today, *The Phantom of the Opera* (Webber's other cash cow) is the current record holder with an unbelievable 34-year tenure. And since the *Opera* is still going strong, nobody has a chance of eclipsing it until the Phantom decides to hang up his mask.

*Mamma Mia!* was an undeniable crowd pleaser, resonating with a large cross section of the public. I'd look out into the house during the show and see mothers, daughters, grandmas—and more importantly, fathers—all enjoying themselves. The "dad" demographic is typically a tough nut to crack in musical theater. (Which brings to mind one of my favorite off-color jokes from back in the day. Q: What's the worst thing about having a mistress? A: You have to sit through *Mamma Mia!* twice. Ba dum tss!)

Our audiences ran the gamut from salt-of-the-earth tourists to the urbane upper crust. Meryl Streep was an early fan of the production—years before she starred in the film. Ms. Streep even sent a gushy note to the cast after attending a performance. The hand-written thank-you card hung on our stage-door bulletin board for months. If it's good enough for Meryl…

Illustrating our impact, I got a phone call from show management inquiring about my availability for a memorial service. A powerful New York real estate developer—and *Mamma Mia!* superfan—had passed away and, among his final requests, he wanted our ingénue "Sophie" (played at the time by Carey Anderson) to sing ABBA's "Thank You for the Music" at his funeral. My bosses asked if I'd be willing to provide musical accompaniment for Carey. I assumed my participation would be *gratis*, so I hesitated momentarily before committing, debating just how bad I'd look if I took a pass.

"By the way, it's a paid appearance," the company manager added.

"Okay, I'll do it."

(I refrained from asking "How much?" I'm not a complete mercenary.)

My mood lifted when I got a follow-up call with the specifics. The gig was in Manhattan, a personal driver would pick me up at my apartment and deliver me directly to the event and, best of all, the pay rate was $500. For one tune? Nice work if you can get it.

I mapped out a tasty acoustic-guitar arrangement of "Thank You for the Music" in advance, and Carey and I ran through the song a couple of times in a secluded office at the synagogue. The service was filled with bigwigs, fat cats, and even a US senator. Carey and I sat among the overflow crowd of mourners, listening to the array of glowing eulogies before heading to the stage to close out the ceremony. Carey's heartfelt rendition served as a perfect postscript to the afternoon — I even got a little choked up myself. As the temple emptied, we were discreetly handed envelopes from a grateful assistant. Carey and I said our goodbyes and started hunting for our drivers.

Once inside my vehicle, I opened my envelope. Instead of the promised $500, I found $1000 — in cash. I assumed I'd accidentally been given Carey's pay as well, so I whipped out my cell phone and called Carey to apologize. She answered, "I was just getting ready to call you. I was afraid I'd gotten *your* money." Yep, Carey had also received an envelope containing $1000. Incredibly, we'd both been tipped an extra $500 on top of our already magnanimous $500 salary. Again, the dearly departed was a successful NYC businessman, so his family could afford the outlay, but wealth doesn't always translate into generosity. (Actually, in my experience, wealth rarely seems to translate into generosity.) I was stunned. I'd made $1,000 for a three-minute performance. It felt great to be appreciated — and, for a change, overpaid. Topping things off, I got a lovely thank-you note from the grieving widow the following week. A total class act.

\* \* \*

*(New York, NY) October 9, 2020 — The Broadway League announces the continued suspension of all ticket sales for Broadway performances in NYC through May 30, 2021.*

*Dates for each returning and new Broadway show will be announced as individual productions determine the performance schedules for their respective shows. The League will provide updates to the public as more information becomes available.*

Damn, now they're saying no reopening until June 2021. FIFTEEN months (and counting) of a darkened Broadway? Unprecedented, scary…and costly! Broadway is the straw that stirs the drink in New York City, with theater patrons filling hotels, restaurants, and tourist attractions. Our industry reportedly generates an annual economic impact of $14.8 BILLION in NYC, with approximately 100,000 workers relying on Broadway for their livelihood. This is devastating.

## Like a Bad Penny

Living in Hell's Kitchen put me only a couple of blocks from S.I.R.'s midtown studios on West 52nd Street—the go-to rehearsal spot for big-time acts back in the day. (A 42-story residential glass tower now stands in its place.) I clocked many an hour in the venerable building, making music with Bob James, Aretha Franklin, Michael Bublé, and *Mamma Mia!*—but oddly enough, not Sting. For some reason, Sting's *Nothing Like the Sun* rehearsals were held at S.I.R.'s Chelsea location on West 25th Street.

S.I.R. was Sting's preferred venue for assembling upcoming tours, so I made a point to stop by whenever I heard the King of Pain was in town. I'd dust off my handy (but true) "just happened to be in the neighborhood" excuse and drop in on my old pals.

I'd first started making my S.I.R. pilgrimages back in 1996 when Sting was preparing for his *Mercury Falling* World Tour. I was struggling professionally at the time, but I still wanted to show my face—and I'm so glad I did. This was the last time I ever saw my dear friend and brilliant pianist Kenny Kirkland. (Kenny passed away two years later from an apparent drug overdose.) I also stopped by the rehearsal facility in 1999 to hang out with the gang before they hit the road on their *Brand New Day* World Tour. Sadly, this turned out to be the last time I saw Sting's manager Kim Turner. (Kim succumbed to cancer a few years later.) Sigh, life is loss.

Fast-forwarding to late 2003, Sting was at S.I.R. rehearsing for his *Sacred Love* World Tour. Unlike my previous visits, I was feeling pretty good about myself. Two years with *Mamma Mia!* had done wonders for my self-esteem (and my wallet). Playing on Broadway might not be as prestigious as touring with Sting, but I was nonetheless proud of my professional resurrection.

I wandered into the studio and saw two of Sting's longtime employees, guitar tech Danny Quatrochi and road manager Billy Francis. I was greeted with open arms.

"What's happening, Jeffrey Lee?" they asked.

I told my pals I was staying busy thanks to ABBA's smash hit just down the street. The two congratulated me, then Billy turned to guitarist Dominic Miller (who was standing nearby tuning up).

"See Dom," Billy cracked. "There is life after Sting."

Dominic smiled and nodded, but it's looking like he may never have to navigate any Sting-free waters. Dominic took over the guitar slot right after me, and he's still on the job some 30 years later. All hail Mr. Miller—the Sting Whisperer!

Sting strolled into the studio and gave me a big hug. We traded updates on our lives, before I eventually got around to mentioning my gig at *Mamma Mia!* Sting hesitated for a moment, but ultimately couldn't help himself.

"I should write a Broadway show," Sting sniffed. "But I'd write a *good* one."

I didn't take the bait. Despite my loyalty to *Mamma Mia!*, I wasn't about to get into a musical theater pissing match with Sting, especially on his turf. I laughed off the harmless (and possibly jealous) dis instead. Ten years later, Sting got his chance to go toe-to-toe on Broadway with ABBA's juggernaut. To be continued.

### *Death By A Thousand Notes*

Although my plate was pleasantly full, I didn't hesitate when *Mamma Mia!* contractor Michael Keller called to inquire about my availability for a side project. My bounty of blessings flowed directly from *Mamma Mia!*, so if Michael wanted me to jump, my response was an enthusiastic, "How high?"

Keller was assembling the orchestra for an all-star, one-night-only concert performance of Stephen Schwartz's *Children of Eden*. (Schwartz is one of Broadway's most successful composers with credits including *Godspell*, *Pippin*, and the massive hit, *Wicked*.) The gala event, organized to raise money for The National AIDS Fund, was scheduled for World AIDS Day (December 1) at Manhattan's historic Riverside Church. I felt honored to be included.

Unfortunately, a one-off charity production usually means a skimpy budget and a severely limited preparation period. True to form, our orchestra was only allotted two partial days (six measly hours total) to assemble Schwartz's complex piece of theater. Keller's orchestra of Broadway ringers (plus me) accepted the challenge and made a valiant effort to ingest the material, but as expected, we ran out of rehearsal rope long before we were anywhere close to being ready. Hell, we didn't even have a chance to play through all the music.

Of course, one of the neglected numbers involved an incredibly difficult guitar part. Complicating matters further, the chart was written for acoustic guitar "with capo." (A capo is a clamping tool used to transpose the key of a guitar. The device allows the guitar to *jangle* in any key signature, but I'm not sure there is a consensus on how to properly write for the capo. Trust me—it's complicated.) The dense guitar chart was far beyond my sight-reading abilities and would've easily taken me a few days to decipher, let alone tame. But I didn't have a few days. Color me cynical, but I've seen this scenario play out so many times I've *affectionately* dubbed it "The New York Trick." Employers call you for a low-paying gig with minimal rehearsal time— knowing full well you will go the extra mile (on your dime) to protect your professional reputation. Flounder at your own risk in this town.

The night before the concert, I spent a few hours (of my free time) attempting to unravel the intricate arrangement. I scribbled out a primitive chord analysis and hoped I could approximate the desired effect. Things didn't pan out that way.

On the day of the show, the orchestra finally had a chance to play through the mystery song at the end of soundcheck. *This* is when I discovered the number was essentially a guitar feature. With nowhere to hide. I felt my face redden as I hacked my way through the exposed part. When the song ended, I exhaled and kept my eyes forward, praying I'd skated well enough to avoid targeted scrutiny. Then I heard a disembodied voice from over my shoulder.

"I really need you on that last number."

I turned and found myself face-to-face with our esteemed composer, Stephen Schwartz. Cue flop sweat. As New York Post gossip columnist Cindy Adams used to say, "Only in New York, kids, only in New York."

I stuttered and stammered, spewing excuses about insufficient rehearsal time and ambiguous notation. The Grammy/Oscar/Tony winning Schwartz listened and nodded—and then let me off the mat when I promised to take a closer look at the piece during my dinner break. I knew I wouldn't be able make any appreciable headway before downbeat, but I was willing to say anything to escape the heat of the moment.

Schwartz wandered away as I made one final attempt to decode the music. But it was a lost cause; there would be no "aha!" breakthrough. After a few minutes of futility, I put down my guitar and surrendered to the inevitable: sucking. Fueled by frustration, I uncharacteristically heeded my inner slacker and pulled the ripcord. *What's for supper?*

I roamed around the Upper West Side in search of sustenance and eventually found a cozy Chinese restaurant. I settled in at a table for one and placed my order. I was skimming my trusty newspaper and slurping wonton soup when I suddenly felt a presence. I looked up to see none other than Stephen Schwartz staring at me icily from across the room. Snagged! *"Of all the gin joints in all the towns in all the world ...*" I averted my eyes and gulped down the rest of my meal before scurrying out the door.

Doomed by our lack of rehearsal, the orchestra (and cast) stumbled through Schwartz's two-act opus based on the Book of Genesis. I knew we were in trouble when "God" had trouble finding his pitch. Lucky for us, the charity-minded audience was in a forgiving mood. I'm my own worst critic, but I felt marginally better about my shaky effort when I overheard Broadway vets in the orchestra complaining about the difficulty of the music. It was nice to know I wasn't the only one flailing.

## To Thine Own Self Be True

I got a call to audition for Peter Cincotti's band. The fresh-faced performer had broken onto the scene a few years earlier by ripping a page from Harry Connick Jr.'s playbook: crooning jazz standards while playing a mean piano. Cincotti's debut album, produced by Phil Ramone, hit the top of the Billboard Jazz chart, making Peter the youngest artist (age 23) to accomplish that feat. But Cincotti was now under the wing of producer David Foster, and his sound was evolving in more of a pop-rock, Billy Joel-ish direction. Accordingly, Peter needed a guitarist.

I was emailed a few tracks from Cincotti's yet-to-be-released album—and explicitly warned that sharing the files with anybody would be punishable by death (joking/not joking). I spent a couple of days acquainting myself with the material in advance of my audition at the newly relocated Carroll Rehearsal Studios on West 55th Street.

I showed up at the designated time, nailed the guitar parts, and had a profound realization: my heart was simply not in it. I mean no disrespect to Peter Cincotti or his music. It wasn't him; it was me...confused, conflicted me. Despite cobbling together a decent career, I still felt like I *had* to pursue all major auditions that came my way. (The cat with the longest list of big-time credits wins, right?) But the thought of going out on the road filled me with dread. I found myself at a critical juncture, torn between the life I was *supposed* to want—and the life I actually wanted. Peter (and his bandmates) seemed impressed with my musicianship, but I was never offered the gig. I'm guessing Peter could sense the lack of fire in my belly. In hindsight, I probably should've politely passed on the audition, but I needed to *go* in order to realize I didn't want to *go*. Lesson learned. As Sinatra said, "You're useless if you're not excited about what you're doing."

\* \* \*

Before I knew it, *Mamma Mia!* had entered its fifth year. (Thank you, Jesus—and Benny and Björn!) I'd never spent more than nine months with a show, so I was in uncharted waters, financially and psychologically. Did I ever get bored? Of course, I did. But name a job that doesn't include a certain amount of repetition. As a seasoned journeyman (and a survivor of the freelance jungle), I knew how fortunate I was to have a steady, secure gig. But I also discovered I was capable of feeling two conflicting emotions at the same time: gratitude and boredom. An astute pal teased, "Jeff, you're wearing golden handcuffs, my friend. You have a stable Broadway income *and* an affordable Manhattan rent? You couldn't walk away even if you wanted to." He had a point. I was happy, but, in a sense, trapped—and a bit guilty of going through the motions. Luckily, I got a wake-up call.

### Carrot on a Schtick

Patty and I met up with Rodney Howard and his lovely wife, Mariana, for a long overdue dinner date. Rodney, a fellow North Carolinian, is a killer drummer with credits including Avril Lavigne, Gavin DeGraw, and Regina Spektor. I've played tons of gigs with Rodney over the years, and he's like a brother to both Patty and me. (Matter of fact, Rodney was the first drummer in Patty's original band.) After settling in at our favorite Thai restaurant, Rodney dropped a bombshell—and relit my pilot light.

"Hey man, did you hear *Saturday Night Live* is looking for a new guitarist?"

I closed my menu and laid it on the table.

"Go on."

"Yep, Dr. Luke is moving to Los Angeles, and the *SNL* guitar slot is open."

A fan since its inception, I held a deep reverence for the *Saturday Night Live* franchise. Hearing the show was in the market for a guitarist gave me a new lease on life. I was strategizing before our dinner plates had been cleared.

I'd done a few gigs with *SNL* drummer Shawn Pelton, so I shot him an email as soon as I got home. He confirmed the rumor, and said I'd need to speak with the show's musical director, saxophonist Lenny Pickett. I contacted Lenny, gave him my spiel, and successfully finagled an audition. We arranged to meet the following week—and my nagging case of apathy was instantly cured.

My *SNL* audition was scheduled for a Wednesday afternoon between matinee and evening performances of *Mamma Mia!* I knew I'd have no trouble making the appointment—you can literally see Rockefeller Center from the Winter Garden stage door. I've always heard "dress for the job you want" so, after the matinee curtain fell, I changed out of my Broadway uniform ("pit blacks") to a hip but understated ensemble (that included a "good luck" leather bracelet Patty gifted me from the MTV Store in Times Square).

I threw my guitar on my back and raced out of the Winter Garden. Being excited and nervous, I'd eagerly accepted Patty's offer to walk over with me; I welcomed her calming influence. As instructed, I met Lenny Pickett at the NBC security desk in the middle of 30 Rock's majestic Art Deco lobby. He greeted me with business-like efficiency and handed over a temporary visitor's pass before leading me to the massive bank of elevators. The *SNL* studio is on the 8th floor, so I was surprised when Lenny pressed 17. Turns out, Lenny's base of operations was in an upstairs corner office overlooking St. Patrick's Cathedral on Fifth Avenue. What a view! I've lived in NYC over 30 years, but the skyline still takes my breath away.

Lenny and I were the only people in the room, so I gleaned my audition would be for "an audience of one." I unpacked my guitar as Lenny rummaged around under his desk for a small practice amp. We had trouble getting the unit to power on (it's always something), but we were eventually able to coax the *beater* into cooperating. Lenny placed a thick folder on the music stand in front of me, picked out a few charts, then turned to his computer and opened his iTunes library. *Aha! Stratocaster karaoke.* Jamming to prerecorded tracks was not how I'd envisioned the afternoon would unfold but rolling with the punches is essential in this biz.

We ran through a few numbers from the *SNL* book, including "If You Don't Know Me by Now" by Harold Melvin and The Blue Notes, and Huey Lewis's "Power of Love." Lenny complimented my reading skills, which are fair-to-middling, but I wasn't going to argue.

After we finished playing, Lenny and I sat and chatted. In addition to my audition adrenaline, I was psyched to be hanging out with *the* Lenny Pickett — of Tower of Power fame. I was a huge fan of the Oakland-based horn band, and Lenny had played tenor sax on many of my favorite "TOP" recordings. (Whenever young players seek my advice about conquering 16th-note syncopations, I point them toward the sophisticated funk of Tower of Power.)

As we traded war stories, I was stunned to hear of Lenny's early, lean years in NYC — *post* Tower of Power. Despite his impressive credentials (and talent), Lenny struggled when he first came to town, playing his share of low-paying gigs like everybody else. Lenny finally caught a break when industry honcho Tommy Mottola asked him to perform (and handle horn arrangements) for the Hall & Oates album *Live at The Apollo with David Ruffin and Eddie Kendricks.* Lenny hit it off with Hall & Oates guitarist G.E. Smith, and when G.E. was named *SNL* musical director, he invited Lenny to join him. Smith ran the band for 10 years before passing the baton to Lenny and, defying the cut-throat nature of showbiz, Pickett is still at the helm

25 years later. Keeping Lorne Michaels happy can't be easy. Hats off to Lenny.

I was surprised by Lenny's willingness to sit and talk…and talk. He didn't seem to have anything pressing on his schedule. Meanwhile I did: an 8pm *Mamma Mia!* My internal clock started tugging at my sleeve, so I snuck a peek at my watch. Damn, it was already after 7pm—my audition had morphed into a two-hour hang. (Assuming my time with Lenny would be brief, Patty had agreed to wait for me downstairs. Oops. She kept to her word but eventually began to wonder if I'd been kidnapped.) I seized the next opening in our conversation and told Lenny I needed to hit the bricks for a bite to eat before heading back to work. He thanked me for coming by, then apologized in advance for an all-but-certain delayed decision on the guitar slot. Lenny said the show didn't need a new guitarist until the fall season, so it would be a while before a final verdict was rendered. I dreaded the thought of twisting in the wind, but the extended limbo wound up being a blessing. The *SNL* "carrot on a stick" kept me motivated and combat ready. The voices inside my head told me to stay in fighting shape—just in case. Lenny called a few months later to tell me he'd hired guitarist Jared Scharff for the gig, saying he felt Jared was the best fit for the band's "gestalt." I hung up, sighed…and Googled gestalt. Of course, I was disappointed, but my summer of focus had been just what the doctor ordered. My mojo was back.

### *I Smell Platinum*

After putting another *Mamma Mia!* to bed, I dashed across the street to Emmett O'Lunneys pub to grab a *near* beer and catch the end of the Yankees game with drummer Ray Marchica and substitute bassist Frank Canino. Between innings, Frank mentioned he was relinquishing his neighborhood rehearsal space. An empty studio? *Boing!* This newsflash started my wheels turning. I was still aggressively pursuing my music production dreams, but I'd grown tired of having clients come to my apartment. Working from home felt unprofessional—plus I hated having strangers around my toothbrush. The thought of a separate workspace made me tingle, but I quickly dismissed the notion as too extravagant. Or at least I tried. By the time I'd walked home, I'd run the numbers in my head and convinced myself I could handle adding a second rent to my monthly nut. I discussed the ambitious yet thrilling idea with Patty, and she was nothing but supportive. (Patty had recently lost *her* rehearsal room, so the timing was perfect.)

The next day, I called Frank's landlord, Joe Baker, to inquire about the opening. (I knew Joe from my time as a sub at Broadway's *Footloose*, where he was the associate conductor.) Joe had converted a three-bedroom apartment on West 52nd Street into a music co-op, and I wanted a piece of the rock. We made plans to meet so I could take a look at the space. Despite the cozy 10' x 10' footprint, it was love at first sight. Joe was amenable to having me as a tenant but said he'd promised "right of first refusal" to a colleague, so he'd need to touch base with her before we could seal the deal. I waited (and dreamed) anxiously until Joe finally called with a green light. I was ecstatic. I had my own recording studio. Look out Quincy Jones!

I loved having a professional workspace. Part business, part treehouse—it was my 100 square-foot kingdom. Best of all, thanks to my Broadway income, my studio didn't *have* to be a money-making proposition. My aspirational goal was to generate enough work where the place would pay for itself, but it wasn't imperative. This relaxed financial dynamic allowed me to be choosy with my clientele. Accordingly, I vowed to only tackle stuff I enjoyed. I didn't want to get bogged down producing uninspiring vanity projects. I already had one job; I didn't need two.

After debating over a name for the place—and floating a few trial balloons, I took the path of least resistance and looked at the corner street sign. Welcome to Studio 52! (Kind of like Studio 54, but two blocks south and much less cocaine. Okay, zero cocaine.)

Studio 52 became an oasis of creativity as I immersed myself in learning all I could about music production. I recruited interesting clients, accommodated friends with recording needs, wrote, practiced, took meetings, and taught the occasional guitar lesson. The joint was jumping.

As an added perk, my studio was only a five-minute walk from the *Mamma Mia!* stage door. I split the bulk of my waking hours between Studio 52 and the Winter Garden Theatre. And if I wasn't at the *office*, Patty usually was. She used the room for practicing guitar, vocalizing, writing, rehearsals, etc. We definitely got our money's worth and eventually came to think of the studio as the north wing of our apartment (albeit three blocks away).

Unlike gigs where the clock seems to be moving in slow motion (or broken altogether), time flew when I was at Studio 52. I'd bury my head in a project and next thing I knew, it was hours later. I was pursuing my passion—and keeping my bills comfortably paid. Life was good.

### Star Pupil

I got a phone call from keyboardist/pal Jeff Kazee. "Hey Campbell, I found a guitar student for you."

I knew Kazee had just returned from doing some dates in London with Jon Bon Jovi, so I assumed one of Jon's kids wanted to take guitar lessons. I played along.

"Oh yeah, who?"

Kazee replied, "Jon."

"As in Bon Jovi?"

"Yup."

I was momentarily stunned. Kazee continued, telling me Jon had an extended break coming up and wanted to use the time to polish his guitar skills. Kazee said he'd told Jon, "I know just the guy!" and gave him my number. I thanked Kazee for the vote of confidence.

The next day my cell phone rang.

"Hi Jeff, this is Jon Bon Jovi. I got your number from Jeff Kazee. I'm looking for a guitar teacher and wanted to see if you're available."

I had to pinch myself. I didn't field calls from rock stars on a regular basis.

"Sure!" I responded. Then I opened my mouth wide and inserted my foot.

"Are you interested in focusing on guitar or composition?"

"Guitar," Jon said firmly. "I already know how to write a hit song."

Oops, talk about getting off to a shaky start. I meant no disrespect; I was just doing my due diligence. I merely wondered if Jon maybe wanted to delve a little deeper into music theory and harmonic analysis. (There's a quantifiable reason why songs like "Wichita Lineman" or "God Only Knows" sound so fresh to our Top 40 attuned ears.) Fortunately, Jon didn't take my question personally. Asked and answered.

Agreeing to meet the next afternoon, Jon said he'd shoot me an email with his info. I know New Yorkers are always supposed to play it cool, but I wasn't *that* jaded. I tingled with anticipation.

I showed up at Jon's SoHo address the following day, identified myself to the doorman, and waited while he called upstairs for clearance. I was granted permission to proceed and pointed toward the elevator. When I reached the top floor, the elevator door opened directly into a stunning two-floor penthouse. Jon welcomed me into his sunken living room and introduced me to his wife Dorothea. I tried not to gawk as I admired Jon's upscale digs featuring wrap-around views of Manhattan. Just by swiveling my head, I could see the Empire State Building to the North, the Brooklyn Bridge to the East, and the replacement World Trade Center sprouting to the South. So, *this* is what 27 million bucks will get you.

I unpacked my guitar and took a seat on the roomy couch. Jon grabbed his axe and we settled in, chatting about his goals before loosely jamming on some stuff. I was impressed by Jon's skills as we noodled around on a 12-bar blues. He was already a damn good guitarist, so I admired his desire to improve. We were scheduled to work for an hour but ended up running a little long. I certainly didn't care; I was in no hurry to exit my luxurious surroundings. Jon eventually looked at his watch and groaned, "Shoot, I need to wrap things up." Jon thanked me, saying he enjoyed our hang and would love to continue meeting. I echoed the sentiment.

"Any chance we could get together more than once a week?" Jon asked.

"Fine by me" I replied. "But people usually like to keep it to one lesson a week due to time or money concerns."

Jon grinned. "Neither of those are a problem for me."

I took the elevator back downstairs and wandered out onto the cobblestone streets of Soho with a few extra bucks in my pocket and a smile on my face. It was a good day.

Jon emailed that evening to arrange our next lesson. He also added he'd dug up a spare guitar so I wouldn't need to bring mine again.

A few days later, I hiked back downtown to reconnect with my star pupil—or as Jeff Kazee joked, "Well, your pupil who's a star." Jon greeted me as I stepped off the elevator and said we'd be working upstairs. I followed Jon up the grand staircase to another beautifully appointed space with a wraparound balcony. (Turns out, this room also doubled as the home theater on family movie night.) Jon handed me one of the two guitars leaning on the couch.

"I found this in the back of the closet," Jon offered matter-of-factly.

The loaner was a gorgeous, vintage Martin acoustic. I grabbed the axe and noticed a Sharpie-scribbled inscription on the front of the guitar.

*To Jon — "Keep Livin' on a Prayer!" Happy Birthday '08*

It was signed: Bob Dylan

Jon played it off. "Richie [Sambora] gave it to me as a gift."

Poker-faced, I mumbled, "Cool."

\* \* \*

Exercise has always helped me maintain at least a semblance of sanity. My first instinct most mornings is to pull the covers over my head and cower, but I've found if I force myself to get up and get moving, life doesn't seem quite so overwhelming. *Mood follows activity.* My favorite form of exercise is jogging; I crave the loneliness of the long-distance runner. (Sorry, but I hate gyms. Wrestling an elliptical machine while a stranger huffs and puffs six inches away from you as club music blares from the ceiling? Hard pass. Like Garbo, I *vant* to be alone.)

One afternoon, I was enjoying a run down the sparsely populated Hudson River promenade when I noticed an *interesting* looking jogger coming in the other direction. The guy had his baseball cap pulled low underneath a hoodie and was sporting mirror shades. The vibe seemed a little janky, so I interrupted my daydreams to pay closer attention. (After surviving a terrifying mugging in the early 90s, my situational awareness stays locked and loaded.) As we approached one another, the dude started veering in my direction. My mind raced, "Shit, what the hell does this creep want? Drugs? A date?" I was preparing to assume a defensive position when the encroaching stranger broke into a big smile. Despite the disguise, I immediately recognized my *assailant*: Jon Bon Jovi.

We exchanged high fives and shot the breeze for a few minutes before agreeing to join forces and add a little more mileage to our workout. I usually like to fly solo, but I was happy to make an exception that day. Rock stars make for fun exercise buddies. For the record, I've also crossed paths with Kanye West and Claire Danes (separately) along the Hudson—but neither of those two offered to keep me company. You win some, you lose some.

Jon and I continued to work together on a regular basis. And although Bon Jovi (the band) was on hiatus, Jon occasionally performed at private events with his five-piece solo project. One afternoon during a lesson, Jon asked if I'd be interested in playing one of his upcoming gigs. (His regular guitarist, Bobby Bandiera, had a scheduling conflict.) I jumped at the offer, but knew I had some big shoes to fill. I wasn't worried about covering Bobby's guitar parts, but I had my work cut out for me in the vocal department. Bobby sings like a bird and has a range that challenges Roy Orbison's. Fortunately, the gig was over a month away, so I had time to hit the proverbial woodshed.

One of the rooms at my studio complex was occupied by a sweet but no-nonsense voice teacher from Russia. After committing to Jon's gig, I cornered the *coach next door* and screamed "HELP!" Giulia smiled her sly Soviet smile, and said she'd be happy to work with me. I spent the next month diligently vocalizing, and—lo and behold—I improved. It's amazing what you can accomplish with a little dedication. Regrettably, my singing is like my golf game: neglected. If I could turn back time, I'd invest much more effort on my voice—and on the driving range.

I ended up doing a couple of gigs with Jon's *unplugged* band, but my skills weren't nearly impressive enough to threaten Bobby's job security. Oh well, it was fun while it lasted—and I was paid quite handsomely for relatively little work. Jon was old school and compensated his musicians accordingly. Along those lines, I shared a story with Jon a year or so later about a friend who'd recently auditioned for a MEGA pop star. I'll be polite and avoid naming names, but this young artist is as big as they get. My pal didn't land the gig, but he wasn't too bummed because the proposed salary was only $1200 a week. (For context, Sting had paid my rookie ass $2500 a week—25 years earlier!) When I related this story to Jon, he was incredulous. Based on the magnitude of the entertainer in question, Jon refused to believe me.

"$1200 a week?" Jon shrieked. "No way Jeff, you mean twelve THOUSAND dollars a week."

I had to chuckle at Jon's rich-guy bubble. I assured Jon I was not mistaken. VERY few gigs pay $12,000 a week. Jon shook his head and kept insisting I was wrong. (I wasn't.)

Being pals with a rock star definitely had its perks. Jon invited Patty and me to attend the premiere of his documentary *When We Were Beautiful* at the Tribeca Film Festival. And when Bon Jovi's new album *The Circle* dropped, I was stunned (and flattered) to see my name mentioned in Jon's "special thanks" section of the liner notes. Patty and I were also given "all access" passes for a concert during one of Bon Jovi's sold-out stands at MetLife Stadium. We hung with Jon in his dressing room before the show, picking at the dinner spread while eyeing the sky as a late spring thunderstorm drenched the steadfast fans. Jon was unfazed. I guess stadium-level performers see precipitation as a bonus special effect, courtesy of Mother Nature. (Remember Prince's dramatic, rain-soaked Super Bowl halftime show in

Miami? Of course you do. I rest my case.) The Jersey downpour eventually subsided, allowing Patty and me to make our way out to our primo on-field seats. Despite my experiences with gigantic crowds on the Sting tour, it was still amazing to stand in the middle of 80,000 people screaming "I'm a cowboy" at the top of their lungs. Jon's seen a million faces...and he's rocked them all.

### Major Minor

I received an interesting email from Jon one day:

> *hello pal, hope you're well*
>
> *I have a strange request. I know and really love a precocious little kid who is having a 10th b-day. She wants to sing a song and accompany herself on a recording and I thought of your demo studio. One little pass with perhaps a drum loop behind it. Her dad is willing to pay but doesn't know anyone. I know it's practically like asking you to do birthday parties, but I'd owe you one... ok I already owe you one. I'll owe you another one...jbj*

I valued my friendship with Jon and was more than happy to oblige. Plus, I was always on the lookout for young talent. (Although working with a 10-year-old did seem to be pushing it.) I told Jon to feel free to pass my contact info along. The following day, I got a text from the father of the "precocious little kid." His daughter Charlotte had written a song—and he and his wife wanted to gift her with a recording session for her upcoming birthday. I told him I was always happy to mentor aspiring musicians, so we made plans to meet.

A few days later, I answered my studio door and came face-to-face with the force of nature known as Charlotte Sabina (accompanied by her dad, Michael). Charlotte was effervescent, cute, and oozed personality. She smiled hello, shook my hand firmly, and looked me directly in the eye as we spoke. (In my experience, adolescents tend to stare at their shoes and grunt monosyllabic responses.) I was taken with Charlotte's passion about music and life; her energy was contagious. We spent a couple of hours recording a quick version of her maiden composition, "Green." I finished the mix the following day and emailed it to Charlotte's family. They were ecstatic with the results and asked if we could continue the collaboration. I was absolutely onboard.

Over the course of the next year, Charlotte and I worked on numerous songs together. She was brimming with ideas, and we became a prolific team (as well as good pals). The situation was mutually beneficial: Charlotte learned the basics of assembling and recording songs — and I learned to let go of entrenched concepts and habits. Charlotte's youthful *new mind* wasn't bogged down with norms or formulas. Her "why not?" approach reminded this old dog that rules were made to be broken. Charlotte helped me get out of my own way and discover new levels of creativity. Jon Bon Jovi had asked me to do him a favor, but, in the end, he'd done *me* the favor. Charlotte Sabina was an inspiration.

As our catalog grew, I'd share mixes with friends to showcase Charlotte's talent and seek feedback. My pal, and hugely talented composer/multi-instrumentalist, Art Hays was especially impressed with the depth of Charlotte's lyrics, chuckling "She's like Springsteen—only better!" (Okay, maybe Art got a bit carried away, but what's a little hyperbole among friends?) Meanwhile, Charlotte's songs had garnered another discriminating fan: Jon Bon Jovi.

I'm not saying Jon was capable of being totally objective, but he knew good music when he heard it. In a show of support, Jon invited Charlotte to serve as his opening act at an upcoming gig. At this point, Charlotte was *almost* 11-years old. Charlotte's dad asked if I'd be willing to play the show. I enthusiastically replied yes before suggesting we add a percussionist to flesh out the sound. I called my friend (and *SNL* drummer) Shawn Pelton to see if he was interested. Shawn was game, so our power trio was set. Jon had asked Charlotte to perform three songs, so she and I picked the repertoire, sent recordings to Shawn, and scheduled a short rehearsal at my studio. All systems go.

The concert took place at Best Buy Theater, a 2,000-seat venue in the heart of Times Square. The show was a benefit for Jon's kids' school, Poly Prep. (Charlotte was also a student at Poly and carpooled with Jon's kids, hence the connection.) On the afternoon of the show, we met at the theater for a quick soundcheck. We set up our gear, ran one of Charlotte's tunes, and then broke for dinner. Since my apartment was only a few blocks away, I headed home, with the plan to meet back at the theater at 7:30pm. Then my phone rang around 6:30pm. It was Charlotte's dad, Michael.

"Hey Jeff, I know we said 7:30, but Charlotte is feeling a little nervous. Any chance you could come back a bit sooner?"

"Absolutely, see you in fifteen."

I threw on my stage clothes, brushed my teeth, and scooted out the door.

I flashed my laminate at the velvet rope and made my way to the dressing rooms. Charlotte seemed pretty relaxed to me, but I wondered if she was just putting on a brave face. We hung out and goofed around, trying to stay distracted until show-time. I had faith in Charlotte but, then again, she was only 11 years old. I kept telling myself she'd be fine (and hoping I was correct).

The crowd cheered as we took the stage, and Charlotte was transformed. She slung her guitar behind her back and yelled to the audience, "Hello New York! Are you ready to rock?" I was no longer worried about Charlotte Sabina. She was a natural; she definitely had *it*. The crowd loved Charlotte's music and her 1,000-watt charm. Record executive Charlie Walk (Beyoncé, John Mayer, John Legend) was in the audience and made a point to track down Charlotte's dad to say, "We need to talk." After our short but sweet set, Jon Bon Jovi took the stage and thanked Charlotte, before cracking to the packed house, "I'll be opening for her one day."

Charlotte continued to write, and I continued to produce, cranking out tune after tune. Charlotte Sabina was definitely Studio 52's top client. As our friendship grew, Charlotte's parents kept urging me to visit their weekend/summer home in the Hamptons—a posh group of villages located on the East End of Long Island. I finally took them up on their offer and purchased a round-trip bus ticket for the hamlet of Wainscott. For urbanites without a car, the Hampton Jitney (a private bus company) is a common mode of travel to and from the popular getaway. A three-hour, no-frills bus ride always seems incongruous with the elegant destination, but the payoff makes the schlep worthwhile.

One visit to the Hamptons and I was hooked. The relaxed vibe provided sweet relief from the city so, with an open invitation to return, I started venturing "out east" whenever possible. We'd hang out at Main Beach in East Hampton, often meeting up with members of the Bon Jovi family for sunning, swimming, football, cookouts, and bonfires with S'mores. On other *less-sandy* nights, we'd drive over to Sag Harbor for top-shelf sushi and after-dinner ice cream cones on the town dock.

But all good things must come to an end. Two years into our collaboration, Charlotte's family decided to relocate to Los Angeles. Between business considerations, the gorgeous weather, and the family's love of surfing, the allure of the West Coast proved irresistible. I hated to see my friends (and favorite client) go. I was convinced Charlotte and I would ultimately conquer the world and fill our shelves with Grammys. Maybe we still will?

### Never a Bride

The paint was barely dry on a new year when I got a phone call from *Saturday Night Live*'s musical director, Lenny Pickett. He was in a jam. Producer Lorne Michaels had decided to add a last-minute show to their post-holiday schedule and Lenny found himself one band member light. The show's guitarist, Jared Scharff, was not only out of town, he was out of the country. Jared had taken advantage of *SNL*'s annual Christmas hiatus and jetted off to South America for a vacation. But thanks to Lorne's impulsiveness, Jared was needed a week sooner than expected — and it was unclear if he'd be able to get back to NYC in time. Lenny was calling to see if I was available to step into the void. Oh hell yeah! Another bucket-list item was in my cross-hairs. Despite being passed over for the gig a few years earlier, I was perfectly happy to play the bridesmaid.

On the Thursday before the broadcast, I met with Lenny in NBC's hallowed Studio 8H. Swoon! It had been almost 25 years since I'd made my debut with Sting on *SNL*, but you never forget your *first kiss*. Lenny greeted me, handed me a folder of music, and outlined my mission. The band had built a large repertoire over the years, and they liked to keep things loose, so I'd need to familiarize myself with ALL the music—and be back at the studio on Saturday *morning*, ready to rock. Lenny told me Jared was trying to find a flight home but until further notice, I was "the man." I accepted the *Live Sea Scrolls* from Lenny and stuck them in my gig bag. Sensing our chit chat had run its course, I thanked Lenny and exited stage left. But after only a few steps, I stopped to unzip my guitar case to double-check I had the music in my possession. Lenny rolled his eyes and sighed, "Jeff, the charts are in your bag. I watched you put them in there." My OCD seemed to trigger Lenny, but I didn't care. I am the poster boy for "better safe than sorry."

I spent my entire Friday combing through the *SNL* music; over-preparation is the closest thing I have to a superpower. And while I knew Jared might make it back to New York before showtime, I couldn't let that notion undermine my focus. Fueling the house-of-cards nature of my deputation, the NFL playoffs were in full swing, and NBC had a do-or-die game on their Saturday primetime schedule. Lenny said if the game ended up going into overtime, Lorne could opt to pull the plug on *SNL* and simply air a rerun. Ah showbiz.

Saturday morning, I walked over to Rockefeller Center with

the Strat of Damocles dangling on my back. Rehearsal was slated for a perky 11am — more than twelve hours before the actual broadcast. (No wonder the cast always seems so elated at the end of each show.) I was in for a marathon day…with any luck. Exiting the elevator, I strode down the oft-televised corridor and entered the studio. Yawning stagehands eyeballed me as I headed for the bandstand, no doubt wondering who the hell I was. I unpacked my guitar, took a deep breath, and plugged into Jared's pedalboard. Complicating my *discomfort* zone, Jared's amp was located in a remote room — so in-ear monitoring was required. A crew member provided me with a pair of guest earbuds, and I began stepping through Jared's various effects pedals. I knew I was nervous but, objectively speaking, something seemed amiss. The guitar tone sounded thin and distant to my ear, but then again, I had no idea what the baseline was.

The scene was hectic, and I didn't want to be high maintenance, but I needed guidance. I asked a guy on the crew if he'd be willing to take a listen and let me know if the rig sounded "normal." He plugged in some headphones as I noodled around on my guitar. After ingesting a few riffs, he looked at me and shrugged, "I think so?" Seeking a second opinion, I turned to Lenny Pickett, but he was multi-tasking and gave the same distracted response. I wasn't convinced things were kosher, but I didn't know what else to do. Meanwhile, groggy musicians were beginning to materialize. I felt a sense of dread (on top of my anxiety), worried I was about to be thrown into the deep end of my dream job with a crippled guitar rig chained around my neck. Fully aware of the power of first impressions, the last thing I wanted was the *SNL* band to remember me as that dude with the lame guitar sound. Then a cheer arose.

I looked up and saw guitarist Jared Scharff strutting across the studio floor. By hook and by crook, Jared had managed to get back from Argentina just in the nick of time. The jet-lagged Jared approached the bandstand and offered a friendly but territorial hello. (We'd never met.) I reciprocated and then mentioned I thought *we* were having some technical problems. Jared plugged in his personal, high-end earbuds, leaned over, and started checking the patch cables between his effects pedals. Within seconds, Jared had identified the issue: a defective wire. He switched out one little plug and voila—full, loud, beautiful sound! (I knew it wasn't my imagination.)

Jared thanked me for being on standby, but since he was back in the homeland, my services were no longer required. I was disappointed *and* relieved. I wouldn't get to add "*SNL* house band" to my resumé, but I was happy to avoid performing with faulty gear. I packed up my guitar, thanked Lenny for the call, and headed home. For the record, the football game indeed ran long, but *SNL* absorbed the delay and hit the air around midnight. Patty and I watched in our pajamas as I drowned my sorrows in a big bowl of Häagen Dazs. So close yet so far.

### *Author, Author*

I was chatting on the phone with my longtime North Carolina pal Bill Baucom when something in our conversation triggered a Sting anecdote. (I've got a million of 'em!) Bill said he'd never heard *that* one before, and offhandedly remarked, "Jeff, you really ought to write this stuff down." Hmmm.

One of my most treasured keepsakes is an embossed, personalized leather binder containing each itinerary from the six legs of Sting's *Nothing Like the Sun* World Tour. I'd long worried about losing the sacred memento to fire or flood, so I finally resolved to make a digital copy of the volume. I bought a new scanner and spent the better part of an afternoon completing the tedious task. Bill's "you really ought to write this stuff down" echoed in my ears as I photocopied my 370 days on the road with Sting. By the time I'd finished the chore, I thought Bill might be on to something. I decided to heed his advice ... and *try* to write a book. (Duck!)

I was a total novice. I'd never studied creative writing or journalism, nor penned anything longer than a four-minute pop tune — and my lifelong exposure to Top 40 lyrics put me squarely behind the grammatical eight ball. (Let's face it, if it were up to red-ink-loving editors, Kris Kristofferson's masterpiece would be titled "Bobby McGee and I.") Nevertheless, I offered up a clumsy prayer to *Saint Memoir* and put pen to paper. (Okay, fingers to laptop.) Oblivious to even the most basic concept of a "word count," I didn't know if I had 50 pages or 500 pages. I wrote daily and completed my first draft in a little over five months. Naively assuming "mission accomplished," I kicked back to read my *work of staggering genius*. Yikes! The manuscript had all the charm of a grocery list. Back to the drawing board.

The best piece of advice I heard during my literary leap-of-faith was the following: "Writing is the act of putting words on paper, editing is the act of making them NOT shitty." Thus began the arduous revision process. Like a musician who plays by ear, I was writing by ear. But I'd read enough books to know what a good book should sound like. (Plus, I had Professor Google at my disposal for grammar and style quandaries.) After suffering through the clunkiest first draft ever written, I set out to make a bad book into a good book.

Patty understood my plight, and lovingly left me alone. She would've sent me to our cabin in the woods — if we'd had one. Instead, I holed up in a metaphorical cabin in our apartment. I'd emerge from my mental bunker from time to time, prompting Patty to gently ask, "How's it going?" Most days I'd sigh and ask for a hug. I felt like I was working on the world's largest Rubik's Cube; every time I'd fix one sentence, I'd break another. I had a recurring image of Humphrey Bogart in *The African Queen*, covered in leeches and sweat as he dragged his boat through the shallow weeds. But like Bogie, I'd traveled too far to quit. I wrote by day and played Broadway by night, while tweaking the manuscript on my iPhone between ABBA tunes. (Thank you, iCloud.)

After my next draft, I decided to let a few close friends take a peek. (Anybody who's ever created ANYTHING knows how scary this is.) My pals were unanimously supportive and provided enough positive feedback to squelch my urge to bail. The gentle but honest input from my beta readers was immensely helpful, as their fresh eyes found flaws and holes (and glaring typos) I'd been unable to see. I welcomed all advice, but, not surprisingly, received conflicting opinions at times. *More detail! Less detail!* I weighed each suggestion but knew attempting to please everyone was the surefire recipe for failure. I ultimately realized *I* was my audience, so I set my sights on writing a book I'd enjoy, and hoped I could somehow craft a page-turner...and not an eye-roller.

## *Location, Location, Relocation*

*Mamma Mia!* was in its twelfth year and I'd successfully walked a groove in the sidewalk between my stoop and the Winter Garden Theatre. But change was in the air. *Mamma Mia!* was beginning to soften at the box office, and with the smell of blood in the water, the showbiz sharks had started circling. The Winter Garden Theatre, owned by the Shubert family, is one of the crown jewels of Broadway and a highly coveted venue, so mercenary producers were itching to measure the drapes.

For the record, theater owners are the true power brokers on Broadway. THEY call the shots ... while almighty producers approach on bended knee. And with the Shubert family owning a total of 17 Broadway houses, they are the undisputed kings of the hill.

Although *Mamma Mia!* was slowing, we were far from dead, so the Shuberts devised a seemingly win/win solution. *Mamma Mia!* would transfer to one of the Shubert's smaller theaters — and free up the Winter Garden for a sexy, new production. I'm not sure if we were asked or told, but the deal got done. It was official: after 12 years at the Winter Garden, *Mamma Mia!* would pack its snorkels and spandex and head six blocks south to the Broadhurst Theatre. Moving a show is an expensive undertaking (it's much cheaper to simply fold the tent), so I viewed our change of address as a vote of confidence.

The Shubert's plan seemed sound, but show business is an inexact science. *Rocky the Musical,* a glitzy, over-the-top production based on the Sylvester Stallone film (complete with levitating boxing ring and slick fight sequence) took over at the Winter Garden and suffered a quick TKO. I felt their pain — but them's the breaks. My humbling experience with *Seussical* had opened my eyes to reality: there are no "sure things" on Broadway; EVERY show is a hit on paper. People don't sink years of hard work and millions of dollars into something they don't believe in. But there is a big, scary gap between theory and execution. Add *Rocky* to the long, bloody list of theatrical good intentions. As Seth Meyers joked on *SNL's* Weekend Update, "*Rocky*...the perfect show for people who love boxing *and* musical theater."

Meanwhile, I figured the *Mamma Mia!* transfer was nothing but good news. The Broadhurst had 400 fewer seats than the Winter Garden, so I assumed a smaller theater would translate into an even longer run for our show. This prediction would ultimately prove wrong.

### Red Sky at Morning

Making good on his threat to write a Broadway musical, Sting piloted his semi-autobiographical *The Last Ship* onto Broadway. My buddy Sonny Paladino was the show's associate conductor, affording me random inside scoops as the production readied for its debut. I wanted (and arguably, needed) to see Sting's *baby*, but I didn't want to appear overeager, so I decided to let the hype dissipate before showing my face. Patty and I eventually scheduled a *Last Ship* date—with plans to meet Sonny afterward for a backstage tour. Sting wasn't a member of the cast (yet), but Sonny had confided the hands-on composer attended every performance. I hadn't seen Sting in a few years, so my stomach was filled with butterflies as Patty and I watched from the half-empty mezzanine. I enjoyed myself, but I'll confess I was a bit distracted by the prospect of a post-curtain *tête-à-tête* with Sting.

When the show ended, Patty and I rushed to meet Sonny at the stage door. Sonny ushered us inside while casually mentioning Sting was *not* in the house that night. (He'd flown down to Ecuador for a stray gig.) Damn, I wish I'd known this piece of information in advance. My desire to support Sting's show was sincere but reconnecting with my former boss had also been one of my goals. If I'd known Sting was going to be *in absentia*, I might've considered rescheduling for another evening—and I certainly wouldn't have spent the entire show nervously anticipating our reunion. I was disappointed.

Sadly, *The Last Ship* struggled at the box office. Critics panned the plot as illogical, and theatergoers steered clear. Sting defended the storyline as "allegory," prompting one snarky pundit to quote playwright George S. Kaufman, "*Allegory* is what closes on Saturday night." In a last-ditch effort to correct course, Sting agreed to join the production. (Uh oh, the dreaded "stunt casting.") I was ambivalent about revisiting the show, fearing I might look like an overzealous groupie, but Patty insisted we return and support Sting. My wife is smarter than I am.

We purchased another pair of *Last Ship* tickets and circled back to the Neil Simon Theatre. After the show, we met Sonny at the stage door again. As we entered, Sonny excitedly whispered, "Paul Simon is here tonight." (Sting and Paul were set to co-headline a world tour starting the following month.) I thought, "Here we go again." I assumed Sting would sequester himself in his dressing room with Rhymin' Simon and I wouldn't get a chance to say hello. Fortunately, I was wrong.

Patty and I were standing onstage with the throng of post-show guests when I saw Sting wander into the dimly lit wings. Reflexively, I marched in Sting's direction. "Hey Sting, it's Jeff Campbell."

Considering the passage of time since our last encounter, I feared Sting might be a bit chilly. I was wrong again. Sting's eyes lit up as he reached to embrace me. "Jeff! I'd have known you right off. Thanks so much for coming."

There were quite a few folks milling about, so I figured my time with Sting would be brief. (After all, I'd spied Paul Simon waiting patiently on the edge of the crowd.) Instead, Sting draped his arm over my shoulder and escorted me around the stage, introducing me to numerous people as "my band mate, Jeff." I was flattered he didn't speak of me in the past tense, I guess my year on the road with Sting had granted me honorary lifetime membership in his band. Patty and Sonny were both witness to Sting's public display of affection and commented on how genuinely happy he looked. I love that guy—still.

I liked *The Last Ship*, but I was obviously in the minority. The beleaguered show only lasted four months.

# Waterloo

Less than two years after moving to our new home, *Mamma Mia!* announced its closing. (So much for my prediction of an extended life at a smaller theater.) The news came as a shock. I'd become so accustomed to playing ABBA songs I'd begun to think we might go on forever. Fortunately, the production gave us a five-month advance notice, so I was able circle the wagons financially and start putting out feelers for other gigs. I'd heard a musicalized version of the Jack Black film *School of Rock* was heading to town, which definitely piqued my interest. I wondered if I could keep my lucky streak alive and possibly finagle a slot in that orchestra. My hopes were quickly dashed when I was told the band for *School of Rock* was already set.

Salting my *Mamma Mia!* wound, I also lost the lease on my beloved recording studio. My landlord, Joe, needed to reclaim the room for himself, so after eight years of creative bliss, I was going to be *studio-less*. (In fairness, Joe did give me four months to vacate the premises.) I looked around for a comparable space but found nothing that fit my budget. One of the most attractive aspects of my studio had been its affordability, so I had no interest in biting off more than I could chew with a new place, and then having to work myself half to death just to keep the lights on. With heavy heart, I removed my shingle. Over the next few months, Patty and I slowly walked our pile of gear back to our apartment—piece by piece. With guitars, keyboards, computers, mic stands, etc. encroaching on our living quarters, Patty and I quickly realized how much we'd depended on the studio simply for storage. The adjustment was tough…and I still miss Studio 52.

That said, as much as I love producing, it is a blood sport. Dealing with artists requires an incredible amount of diplomacy and compromise—and there were plenty of times I didn't see eye to eye with my clients. But since they were the ones signing the check, I'd swallow hard and surrender to their vision (or lack of it). On the upside, I developed a survival skill that serves me well: care…and detach. I'm passionate about my work, otherwise why bother? But the trick is knowing how—and when—to let go. There are a million hills to die on during the creative process, but very few of them (if any) are actually worth it. Like Mick Jagger said, it's only rock n roll.

### Three Heads are Better than Two

I was in the tedious process of dismantling my studio when my cell phone rang. Tangled in cables, I stayed on task and let the call go to voicemail. When I came up for air, I hit playback.

*Hey Jeff*

*This is Michael Aarons.*
*I work with Michael Keller and we're coordinating Andrew Lloyd Webber's new show "School of Rock."*

*They're doing a lab in May and June for about three and a*
*half weeks and then it's eventually going into the Winter*
*Garden Theatre. If you could call me back, I wanted to suss*
*out your availability and your interest.*

*Hope to hear from you soon*

Wow. It felt like Christmas in May. I'd been explicitly told
the *School of Rock* band was already in place, so this was a delicious development. I immediately retuned Aarons's call and told
him I was most definitely interested. His boss, Michael Keller,
had hired me for *Mamma Mia!*, and I'd recently sent him an
email expressing my gratitude for the long-running, prosperous gig. A man of few words, Keller replied, "Hope we can do it
again soon." I'd assumed his response had been a polite formali-
ty. Apparently, I was mistaken.

As it turned out, the *School of Rock* band *had* been set … with
the plan being to use two guitarists. But, thanks to record producer Rob Cavallo, that number needed to be recalibrated. Andrew Lloyd Webber had wisely decided to use a *real* rocker to
help shape the *School of Rock* demos, and he'd tapped Grammy award-winning producer Rob Cavallo for the assignment.
(Cavallo's credits include Green Day, Goo Goo Dolls, and My
Chemical Romance.) Rob did a great job with the demos—but
maybe *too* great for Andrew's wallet. When Andrew's orchestrator started transcribing the recordings, he discovered there were
a LOT of guitars involved. Cavallo had produced his massive
rock texture the old-fashioned way: layering track upon track of
crunchy guitar (courtesy of LA session ace Tim Pierce). Apply-
ing liberal amounts of picking and strumming, Rob had inadver-

tently created a need for a third guitar on *School of Rock*...maybe.

I excitedly called Patty with the breaking news. I still had a few months left at *Mamma Mia!*, but the prospect of sliding seamlessly into another high-profile show seemed too good to be true. Could I actually pull this off? I figured I'd used up a lifetime's worth of luck hitting the *Mamma Mia!* jackpot. But then again, I'd felt the same way after landing the Sting gig twenty years earlier. I've been incredibly blessed but, like they say, "The harder I work, the luckier I get."

Two days later, my elation drifted back to earth when contractor Michael Keller called to "clarify the situation." Keller stressed I was only being hired for the *School of Rock* workshop, explaining Andrew Lloyd Webber had reserved the right to revert to a two-guitar lineup for the Broadway run. I told Michael I understood and was just grateful for the opportunity. My mission was clear: play my ass off and convince Lord Andrew he *needed* three guitars.

The *School of Rock* band assembled for rehearsals at Carroll Studios. I'd been playing *Mamma Mia!* for over 13 years (and focusing on my recording studio for the past eight), so I wasn't exactly in fighting shape. I'd long joked how *Mamma Mia!* had transformed me into a fat, declawed house cat—incapable of foraging for my own *food*. But now my self-deprecating humor had collided with reality. Welcome (back) to the jungle. Meow.

I walked into the rehearsal studio and cased the joint, hoping to score an inconspicuous spot—a nice, safe distance from the harsh glare of the creative team (aka "the table cats"). As I attempted to blend into the scenery, I was greeted by our energetic conductor, Ethan Popp. Sporting lots of tattoos and piercings, Ethan definitely doesn't fit the mold of the traditional Broadway musical director. Ethan grabbed me by the arm and led me to a front and center chair proclaiming, "I want you here." Gulp. My effort to maintain a low profile had failed miserably. Instead, I'd be sitting mere feet from Ethan *and* Andrew Lloyd Webber.

We hadn't received any of the music in advance and, like clockwork, the first chart they put on our stands was a complicated fusion piece written in a 7/8 time signature. I looked at the music and reflexively uttered "shit." I felt somewhat relieved when I heard one of the other guitarists, Tim Quick, softly echo my angst, "Shit is right." After the band stumbled through the odd-metered hazing, we moved on to the tent-pole songs of the show. I could exhale a bit—at least we were back in user-friendly 4/4.

After an hour or so, we took our union-mandated break. I was chatting with my interim bandmates when contractor Michael Keller wandered into the studio. Michael approached and initiated an exchange that confuses me to this day.

"So Jeff, how do you feel about returning to the Winter Garden?"

"That would be awesome…if it ends up happening," I replied cautiously.

"Well, it IS happening!" Michael laughed.

I didn't know how to respond. A week earlier, Michael had expressly conveyed I was being hired for the workshop—ONLY. Any further involvement (specifically Broadway) would be determined at a later date by composer/producer Andrew Lloyd

Webber. But now Michael was acting like the gig was a done deal. I returned to my seat scratching my head.

In addition to electric and acoustic guitar, my duties included recorder. (Yes, the plastic wind instrument we all massacred in fifth grade.) *School of Rock* contained a couple of classroom scenes orchestrated for recorder quartet, and I'd been warned I'd have to *whistle* while I worked. I hadn't given it much thought—until they handed out recorders (with fingering chart and accompanying music) at the end of rehearsal and said, "See you guys tomorrow." I'd survived my pressure-filled day, but quickly realized my evening (and the subsequent month) was going to be spent reacquainting myself with the recorder. Somehow, Patty (and our neighbors) withstood the sonic torture. *Do-re-mi...squeak!*

Luckily, Andrew Lloyd Webber gave us permission to suck—more or less. As the band side-eyed our recorders, Andrew smiled, "Don't worry gentlemen, I want you to sound like children on the instrument." Being professionals, we followed Andrew's instruction to the letter. *School of Rock* ended up running over three years and, even on closing night, our recorder skills still basically sounded like "children."

As a subject of the Crown, Webber usually conceived and unveiled his shows in England before shipping them to America as fleshed-out imports. But Andrew had decided to conjure *School of Rock* in the birthplace of rock n roll: the good ol' U S of A. (Less romantically, I heard speculative whispers of UK child labor laws factoring into Webber's geographic decision.) Interestingly enough, the last time Andrew built a show from scratch in NYC was way back in 1971, when his rock opera, *Jesus Christ*

*Superstar* first hit the boards. Webber was a relative newcomer in those days, so *Superstar* lacked a substantial budget. Consequently, the rehearsal process was a meager affair with minimal props. Wooden boxes and rolling screens were as fancy as it got.

Fast forwarding 45 years later, Webber realized this stripped-down approach had its merits; a limited infrastructure allows more freedom and flexibility to change things on the fly. Accordingly, Andrew decided to shun the traditional protocol of mounting a full-blown out-of-town production before coming to Broadway, and instead chose to keep things simple (and cheap). Opting to "buy local," Webber set up camp at the Gramercy Theatre on East 23rd Street—a funky music venue housed inside a converted 1930s movie theater. Considering my distaste for the road, I felt extremely lucky our "out-of-town" run would take place a mere 25 blocks from my apartment. Amazingly, I was in my fourth Broadway show (maybe), yet I'd still only had to leave town once: *Seussical* in Boston. (*Saturday Night Fever* and *Mamma Mia!* were both hatched in London, so the tweaking process had occurred across the pond.) I took a month-long hiatus from *Mamma Mia!* and settled into my new downtown *office* in the Flatiron District.

Webber stuck to his promise of keeping things loose. Performances were announced online at the last minute, with free tickets doled out on a first-come-first-served basis. Andrew also took advantage of our minimalist staging and, staying true to his word, enacted major structural changes at the drop of a hat. In fact, Andrew cut the show's first song, "The Children of Rock" after only one performance. The tune went from splashy opening number to the trash heap of history in one fell swoop.

*School of Rock* celebrated the end of its workshop with a closing night party at a nearby Gramercy Park bistro. The mood was festive as Team *SOR* toasted its pending move to Broadway in the fall. Just one question: did I make the team? Nobody had confirmed if the production would continue its three-guitar lineup going forward. Off-handed remarks implied I'd be retained, but I didn't want to jump to conclusions. I wanted to hear those three *other* little words: "You are hired."

I returned to *Mamma Mia!* for its final push, unsure if I had a job waiting for me on the other side. I didn't feel comfortable putting the squeeze on my *School of Rock* bosses, so I sat back and anxiously waited for the phone to ring.

### Whirly Bird

Summer was upon us, and my *old* Studio 52 pal Charlotte Sabina was back in town. (She was now the creaky age of 14.) Although her family had relocated to beach-around-the-clock LA, they'd returned to the Hamptons to visit with East Coast friends. My invitation to sneak out and frolic still stood, so I made a point to take advantage of their generosity.

First chance I got, I jumped on the Jitney to East Hampton. Charlotte's dad, Michael, met me at the bus stop and welcomed me to paradise. Michael said we needed to make a couple of stops before we got to their rental house. No problem, I was just happy to be out of the sweaty city. Our first stop: the mansion of Epic Records chairman L.A. Reid. (Charlotte and L.A.'s daughter were schoolmates and good friends.) I was green-eyed whenever Charlotte regaled me with stories of hanging out at *Chez Reid,* rubbing elbows with Jay Z or spending the day on Jennifer Lopez's yacht. After we grabbed Charlotte, we were off to Jon Bon Jovi's Hamptons estate to pick up Charlotte's brother, David (who was best pals with Jon's son, Jake). I'd gone straight from a crowded three-hour bus ride to cruising the homes of the rich and famous before I even had a chance to pee.

I spent a couple of blissful days communing with sand and sea before Broadway beckoned. Despite my fantasies to the contrary, I had to go back to work. The day before I was scheduled to leave, I was sitting on the beach with the usual suspects — which, that afternoon, included Jon Bon Jovi.

"You heading back to the city tomorrow?" Jon asked.

"Unfortunately, yes," I sighed.

"You taking the bus?"

"Unfortunately, yes," I sighed (again).

Jon continued, "I have to go back tomorrow as well. If you want, I can give you lift — I have an extra spot on my helicopter."

My eyes widened. Hitching a ride on a rock star's helicopter sounded exciting … and scary. I'd never flown in a helicopter, and while I was intrigued, I was also wary. I flashed back to my pal, keyboardist Jeff Kazee telling me about his hang with Carlos Santana during Bon Jovi's *Have a Nice Day* World Tour. Jeff said Carlos was warm and charming — and imparted these fatherly words of wisdom: "Stay away from heroin and helicopters." (Santana's fear was well-founded. Two of his close friends, legendary rock promoter Bill Graham and guitarist Stevie Ray Vaughan, had both perished in separate helicopter crashes.)

I'd been toying with the idea of extending my Hamptons visit, but now I was torn. A long, smelly bus ride vs. a luxury helicopter flight with a rock star? I asked Jon if I could let him know. He nodded, "Sure, just shoot me a text. We're leaving tomorrow at 9am from the East Hampton airport."

Driving back to the house, I asked Michael's opinion about Jon's invitation. Should I stay or should I go? Michael didn't hesitate.

"Dude! Grab a bus right back out here the moment you land if you like…but don't pass up this opportunity."

I knew Michael was right. I texted Jon and accepted his generous offer.

I called Patty to share my exciting but somewhat unnerving news. I confessed my apprehension and jokingly rationalized my decision with, "Well, if we crash, at least I'll be in *Rolling Stone* magazine." (*Jon Bon Jovi and an unidentified male died Tuesday when…*)

Michael gave me a ride to the East Hampton airport the next morning. We walked into the pocket-sized facility in search of Jon but came up empty. (We did however glimpse celeb twins Mary-Kate and Ashley Olsen hiding behind large sunglasses, heads buried in their phone screens.) Michael and I walked back outside just as Jon's driver pulled up to the terminal. Jon climbed out of the Escalade with his wife, Dorothea, and daughter, Stephanie, in tow. We exchanged brief hellos and then Jon said, "Let's go!"

We walked through a chain-link gate and straight on to the tarmac as Jon's helicopter was touching down. I thanked Michael for his hospitality as the co-pilot collected our bags and tossed them into the chopper's underbelly. The four of us climbed aboard and buckled into our plush leather seats as the co-pilot closed the passenger cabin door. He jumped back in the cockpit, and in a flash, we were airborne. (I didn't even have time to get nervous.) The blink-of-an-eye experience reminded of the good old days of traveling on Sting's private plane. Get out of the car, get on the aircraft, and hit the skies. Big shots don't waste time in airports like us little people. It is the only way to go.

Over the din of the rotors, Jon gestured toward the complimentary snack basket. I waved him off, mouthing "No thanks." We chatted for a bit, but I didn't want to wear out my welcome by being overly conversational. (The art of *speak when you're spoken to* comes in handy in rock-star circles.) Unlike a jet, the altitude of our trip was low enough to enjoy the scenery, so I gazed out at the lush Long Island landscape as my cabin mates ducked behind their reading material.

Accustomed to a three-hour bus ride, I was thrilled when I spied Manhattan only 30 minutes into our flight. I felt like I was in a dream as we approached the East River Heliport. I looked to my left and saw Manhattan's magnificent skyline, then looked to my right and saw Jon Bon Jovi's chiseled jawline. Damn, I was a long way from Carrboro Elementary School. After touching down, I thanked Jon for the lift and bid him and his family goodbye. I didn't need to hail a cab; I'd simply float home.

But, as they are wont to do, the gods made sure to even the score—quickly. I walked in our apartment and was greeted by a clogged toilet. An out-of-town friend had crashed at our place while I was away, and although she'd probably used a normal amount of toilet paper during her stay, our outdated pipes obviously didn't consider the usage "normal"—and they'd rebelled. (Our building is over 100 years old, so the plumbing can be a little finicky for the uninitiated.) I pushed up my sleeves and grabbed the plunger, while struggling to hold on to a sliver of my glamorous morning. As the saying goes, "It's a short road from the castle to the outhouse."

It was late July and the end of *Mamma Mia!* was coming into view. In a flash of sentimentality, our producers decided to assemble every company member (past and present) for an alumni photograph. I'd planned to participate in the shoot—atop the ruby-red TKTS stairs in the heart of Times Square—but unfortunately the photo session was scheduled for the same morning I was returning from the Hamptons. Despite my allegiance to *Mamma Mia!*, I wasn't going to cancel a long weekend at the beach to be a speck on the back row of a picture featuring hundreds of people. I knew I'd catch some grief over my absence but, thanks to JBJ, my alibi was rock solid.

I strolled into the theater that evening and was making my way to the orchestra pit when I bumped into our conductor, Wendy Cavett. I fought to keep a straight face as I waited for her to lob a fat, juicy *softball* in my direction.

Right on cue, Wendy asked sarcastically, "And where were you today, Mister? The guy who lives closest to the photo shoot…and he still can't manage to show up?"

I reared back and crushed it out of the park.

"Yeah, sorry I couldn't be there Wendy. I was helicoptering in from the Hamptons with Jon Bon Jovi."

My boss dropped her shoulders and rolled her eyes, "Okay…never mind."

## Dovetail

I was about to enter the Broadhurst stage door for a *Mamma*

*Mia!* matinee when my cell phone rang. I looked at the caller ID and saw: Ethan Popp. I was running a little late (by my standards) but stopped dead in my tracks to take the call from the *School of Rock* conductor.

Ethan wanted to know if I was available for a gig on Sunday. He'd been hired to write a musical parody for HBO's *Last Week Tonight with John Oliver* and needed a guitarist. I was torn. Staying in Ethan's good graces was paramount, plus I liked the thought of putting "John Oliver" on my resumé, but it was also my birthday week, and I'd made plans to head back out to the Hamptons with Patty. I explained my dilemma to Ethan and reluctantly told him I better take a pass. He was totally cool and said, "No problem, next time!" Looking to burnish my image with my prospective employer, I shared the story about my previous weekend in the Hamptons — and my glorious flight back to the city on JBJ's helicopter. Ethan responded with his typical wit. "Well, when you see Jon again, remind him he owes me twenty bucks!"

I laughed and seized my opening. I'd been anxiously awaiting word about my fate with *School of Rock* but hadn't wanted to appear pushy. The time had come to push.

"Hey Ethan, while I have you on the phone, what's the latest with *School of Rock?* Did they ever make a decision about adding a third guitarist?"

He responded, "Yeah, dude. You're in. See you in October."

Happy birthday to me! I felt like the luckiest guy in the world. With *Mamma Mia!* closing in mid-September, I'd only have to navigate six weeks of unemployment before jumping right back into the fray with *School of Rock.*

\* \* \*

*Mamma Mia!* took its final bow on September 12, 2015. How the hell did 14 years pass so quickly? With the redundant nature of Broadway, playing a show—especially a long-running show—becomes a blur. (When *Cats* closed after 18 years, guitarist Ethan Fein reportedly summed up the experience with, "It's like it never happened.") Broadway performances are uniform by design; the goal is to build a reliable franchise audiences can depend on—hopefully year after year.

Not surprisingly, this *Groundhog Day* dynamic doesn't appeal to a lot of musicians. One afternoon, I bumped into my pal, keyboardist John Korba—whose credits include Hall & Oates, Todd Rundgren, and Phoebe Snow. In addition to his freelance work, John was associate conductor at the long-running boho smash, *Rent.*

"Hey John, how's tricks over at the Nederlander Theatre?" I asked.

"Like putting caps on bottles," he grimaced.

Sad, but somewhat true. There is an assembly line quality to playing the exact same music in the exact same order every night. But as fellow *Mamma Mia!* guitarist Doug Quinn observed, "Go out on the road with Lady Gaga, and let me know how much her setlist changes from one concert to the next." Doug makes a valid point. Spontaneity is rare in big-time showbiz. Luckily, like my hero Prince, I find "Joy in Repetition." I even have a Museum of Modern Art coffee mug emblazoned with Andy Warhol's ode to uniformity, "I like things to be exactly the same over and over again." Great minds …

The closing night party for *Mamma Mia!* was a blowout.

Our esteemed producer Judy Kraymer even jetted in from London to join the farewell festivities. Kraymer had been the driving force behind the show, persuading Benny and Björn to give Broadway a second chance after their first offering, *Chess*, had fizzled. Kraymer's instincts paid off handsomely—to say the least. *Mamma Mia!* sired 50 productions globally (with the original still running in London), grossed over two billion dollars, and spawned two major motion pictures. The success of *Mamma Mia!* has prompted some to dub Judy Kraymer "the greatest impresario of the 21st century."

Our raucous party fell silent when our beloved producer stepped up to the mic. Kraymer spoke eloquently, expressing sincere gratitude to our hard-working company. But one aspect of Judy's speech confounded me. She opined, "It takes a lot of courage to open a Broadway show—and a lot of courage to *close* a Broadway show." Huh? How does closing a show require courage? I figure you bail when you start losing money. And while nothing's ever as simple as it seems, Kraymer's remark made me wonder if we were shutting down a tad prematurely. I respect and understand artists who want to "go out on top" (as opposed to limping across the finish line), but I felt like *Mamma Mia!* may have had a little gas left in her tank. The "powers that be" clearly thought otherwise. Surprisingly, six years later (and counting), there has yet to be a Broadway revival of *Mamma Mia!* Come on Judy—*Take a Chance, Take a Chance, Take a Chance Chance.*

## Go West, Old Man

After racking up over 5,000 performances of *Mamma Mia!*, I was looking forward to a hard-earned six-week respite between my final lap of "Dancing Queen" and the load-in for *School of Rock*. But Andrew Lloyd Webber split that vacation right down the middle with the recording sessions for our cast album. Despite the *vacatio interruptus*, I was excited about the mission. We were slated to record at historic Avatar Studios (née and now The Power Station), and Andrew had retained multi-platinum producer/Warner Brothers Records honcho Rob Cavallo to helm the project. (Cavallo even went to the trouble of shipping the Marshall amplifiers he'd used on Green Day's wildly successful *Dookie* album from LA to NYC. We never used the amps, but our *Beavis and Butt-Head* band had a lot of fun saying the word "dookie.") Meanwhile, I hoped working with the well-connected Cavallo might open some doors. I still had dreams of breaking through as a record producer, and although my top client, Charlotte Sabina, had moved to LA, she and I were still creating tracks together. (God bless the Internet.)

Charlotte's family had been urging me to come out to California for a visit, and my brief Broadway hiatus provided the perfect window. I debated on whether to travel before or after recording the cast album but decided it would be more strategic to go west *before* I met Rob Cavallo. That way, when we were introduced, I could casually say, "Hey, I was just out in your neck of the woods, working with a young pop singer." A curious Rob would want details…and he'd ultimately make me and Charlotte famous. (Of course, this scenario never occurred, but NYC teaches you to stay ready.)

I snuck out to LA for a few days and had a blast. Charlotte's house was just up the hill from the ocean, so whenever the mood struck, I'd stroll down to the beach for a quick swim without even bothering to bring a towel. Walk a couple of blocks, take a refreshing dip in the Pacific, then head back to the homestead.

During my visit, Charlotte's band had a gig on the books at San Diego's House of Blues. Road trip! The group sounded great, and a couple of record execs were in the crowd. I tried to schmooze the label guys, but I could tell they were glazing over. They didn't care what some graying dude from New York had to say — they were much more interested in conversing with the "talent." One thing is certain in showbiz: the young eat the old.

I hadn't been to LA in quite a while, so I was eager to revisit some of the old haunts from my Sting days. Charlotte's dad, Michael, and I jumped in his car one afternoon, destination: memory lane. The outing was revelatory as my warm fuzzy feelings of yesteryear collided with my older, more mature sensibilities. Sadly, the bloom was off the rose as we trolled Sunset Boulevard. The Strip's magic had vanished — or more likely, my definition of "magic" had evolved considerably. We stopped in the trendy Mondrian hotel for a beverage and found ourselves surrounded by botoxed Barbie dolls in skintight mini dresses and stiletto heels. I felt like we'd stumbled into an episode of *Keeping Up with the Kardashians*. Sigh. Hollywood seemed MUCH cooler when I was in my knucklehead twenties.

Fast forwarding to present day, my talented pal Charlotte Sabina is still in LA. She's in college, she's a competitive surfer, she's an actor (with a lead role in the feature film, *Age of Summer)* and, most importantly, she is still writing and playing music. Keep an eye (and ear) out for Charlotte Sabina. She is a winner.

## *Back to the Garden*

The *School of Rock* band loaded into the Winter Garden Theatre on Halloween. (I should have recognized the spooky omen.) It was wild to be back in the same building where I'd spent a dozen years with *Mamma Mia!* — I was home sweet home. But this time, unlike my previous residency, the band would not be stationed underneath the stage. Instead, we were exiled to a separate room in the basement. (The area had served as the women's quick change room during *Mamma Mia!*)

This was my first experience with a remote pit, and the results were mixed. I was accustomed to being in an open orchestra pit near the audience — a relatively sedate setting that requires musicians to toe the line (more or less). An open pit tends to limit interaction among orchestra members during the show, with players occasionally whispering back and forth. But the default move is to bury your head in a book (or screen) between musical numbers. *School of Rock* changed all that. Sequestered in our isolated rumpus room, there was no need to behave quietly — therefore we were neither quiet nor behaved. I'd compare the raucous vibe to a combination of the *SNL* writer's room and *Animal House.*

We ultimately dubbed our politically incorrect lair, "The Room of Truth" ("The Room of Bullshit" would have been more accurate). We had a lot of laughs — and a few fights — over the course of our three-year reign of terror. I wasn't used to engaging in outlandish horseplay between (and *during*) songs and found the rapid-fire repartee more exhausting than the actual playing of the show. Pit conditions eventually degenerated to the point of sanctioned pre-show *edibles* and "in-flight" cocktails. (Somehow my sobriety weathered the storm.) After 14 years of mature reverence at *Mamma Mia!*, I felt like I was on the road with a debauched rock band. I christened our musical theater/rock-n-roll hybrid, *Annie Get Your Guns N'Roses*.

And while I'm on the subject, I'd like to extend my sincere apologies to ALL the subs who bravely ventured into "The Room of Truth." Subbing is demanding under the best of circumstances, but, more often than not, our scene was the equivalent of a fraternity hazing. To the *School of Rock* subs, please forgive us—or me anyway.

Another downside of being hidden in the basement: out of sight, out of mind. *School of Rock* featured a kickass band of cute and talented kids ON stage, so the hidden *adult* band got zero love. I felt like I was working in the hull of a steam ship, anonymously shoveling coal into the engines of the SS Winter Garden. The job was basically thankless—unless a paycheck counts as thanks. Our private clubhouse may have yielded a relaxed work environment, but, in the end, I missed the interaction and energy that comes from playing in (partial) view of the audience. For me, the remote pit ultimately made the gig less enjoyable.

Nevertheless, I was happy to be employed—and the kids on stage deserved every bit of praise thrown their way. All our young musicians were impressive, and a couple of the players were virtuosic heavyweights. Guitarist Brandon "Taz" Niederauer and drummer Raghav Mehrotra are both *School of Rock* alumni. Remember their names. I guarantee they will have a big impact on the music business. (Google them now if you don't believe me.)

Our opening night audience at *School of Rock* included celebs

Stevie Nicks, Mick Fleetwood, and my old pal Sting. After the show, everybody headed over to the Hard Rock Cafe in Times Square to stroll the red carpet and party hearty. I was thrilled; the Hard Rock is sacred ground in my book. Located in the basement of the historic Paramount Building, the club occupies the same hallowed space where Frank Sinatra drove the bobbysoxers crazy back in the 1940s. (Interacting with NYC's glamorous ghosts is one of my favorite aspects of living in the city.) I combed the club a couple of times looking for Sting, but the humongous venue was packed, and our paths never crossed.

I did see Stevie Nicks from afar, but I wasn't about to bother her. Ignoring celebrities is elevated to an art form by NYC residents. As Rolling Stone Keith Richards once observed, "New Yorkers don't pester famous people, because everyone who lives in New York thinks they're famous too."

Stevie Nicks is name-checked prominently in *School of Rock*, and her song "Edge of Seventeen" is featured in a pivotal scene. Therefore, it wasn't surprising to see Stevie become a repeat customer. She was a big fan of the show, popping in from time to time with groups of friends to cheer us on. One night, our musical director, Darren Ledbetter, had a brainstorm: What if we could get Stevie to play a song with the kids' band? Management loved the idea and urged Darren to approach the rock diva. Darren ain't shy and accepted the challenge. He boldly asked Stevie if she had any interest in making a cameo appearance. She replied, "Sure, let's do it!"

The kids learned Fleetwood Mac's "Rhiannon" and, on an agreed upon night, Stevie snuck in the stage door during the show. The plan was to spring our surprise guest on the audience as a special encore. Company members were told of the event in advance, but we'd been sworn to secrecy. I called a few of my friends and suggested they might want to attend a *certain* Tuesday night show.

In an uncharacteristic gesture of charity, management allowed the band to abandon our subterranean cave at the end of the show and slip into the house to watch Stevie's performance. Broadway orchestras are normally responsible for playing "exit music" as the patrons file out of the theater—but we were off the hook that evening as Stevie Nicks got the final word. After finishing the last song of the bows, I threw my guitar on its stand and raced out into the auditorium. The show's leading man, Alex Brightman, addressed the audience.

"People always ask if the kids are really playing their instruments. The answer is yes." The crowd applauded. Alex took a beat and playfully teased, "In fact, would you like to see us play one more thing?"

The audience cheered loudly.

Alex continued, "Okay, ummm, I think I can do you one better though…ladies and gentlemen, Stevie Nicks!"

The place exploded. The Winter Garden's plaster ceiling seemed at risk.

The prepubescent band kicked into "Rhiannon" as Nicks walked onstage to massive cheers. She took a bow and unleashed her legendary vibrato on the stunned crowd. Chalk up another cool night in NYC.

## *Published*

After five loooong years of mental and emotional elbow grease (and an endless stream of rejections from dismissive agents and skeptical publishers), my memoir, *Do Stand So Close: my improbable adventure as Sting's guitarist* was released by Deeds Publishing. Big thanks to Bob Babcock and the entire Deeds family for believing in me. (Actually, big thanks for believing in me twice! They are my publishers for this book as well.)

Becoming a published author remains one of the proudest moments of my life—and I'm delighted to say I've heard from people all around the globe who love the book. Publishing is very similar to the music business: tough as hell to crack, and even tougher to make a buck. I saw a chilling stat that claimed the average book sells 250 copies. (I'm happy to report I cleared that hurdle early on.) Large advances, best seller lists, Oprah's Book Club, and fat royalty checks are for a select few. Fully realizing this, I regard praise from satisfied readers as my true compensation. Thanks to all for the support.

### Fits Like a Glove

A couple of years into *School of Rock*, I got a call from my good friend (and former *Seussical/Mamma Mia!* conductor) David Holcenberg. David was putting together a workshop for a new show and said he might have room in his budget to add a guitarist. (Typically, shows only hire piano and drums during the early developmental stages.) David wanted to know if I was interested. My 14-year stint with *Mamma Mia!* had altered my life in countless wonderful ways, so my loyalty to David runs deep. Accordingly, I'm predisposed to accommodate his needs whenever possible.

Broadway folk usually jump at workshop offers. The rehearsals are held during the day to avoid nighttime conflicts, creating a gig-friendly schedule that allows top-level (read: employed) talent to sign on. Maybe more importantly, a workshop can be a good investment in your future. Even if you're fortunate enough to have a steady gig, EVERY show eventually closes. (Okay, the verdict is still out on *The Phantom of The Opera*.) Therefore, putting another *potential* show in the pipeline is smart business. But—and it's a big but—not all workshops end up making it to Broadway. And even if the project does make it to the mountaintop, participating in the workshop doesn't automatically guarantee you a slot with the production. Nevertheless, getting in on the ground floor is a solid strategy for cultivating future employment.

That said, I'm somewhat ambivalent about accepting workshops. After years of toiling in Broadway pits, I prefer to spend my free time chasing other muses. I'm not itching to play musical theater night *and* day, but since my patron saint David was asking (and I suspected *School of Rock* had a limited shelf life), I told him I was available if needed. David replied "Great!" and said he'd let me know if the guitar position was approved by the bean counters.

I thanked David for thinking of me and hung up, fingers crossed the mystery workshop would be something fun (or at least painless). My prayers were answered with David's next phone call—in a big way.

"Hey Jeff, I got the go-ahead to add guitar to the workshop, so we're on."

"Thanks!" I replied guardedly.

"Welcome aboard," David chimed. "I'll be in touch about the

schedule. By the way, this is for an upcoming Broadway show about Michael Jackson. Speak soon!"

I hung up with a HUGE smile on my face. I smelled musical bliss...and, with a little luck, another long-running gig.

Talk about your "wheelhouse," Michael Jackson's music is imprinted on my DNA. Neighborhood moms will attest: the backseat of our grade school carpool would explode whenever The Jackson 5's "I Want You Back" or "ABC" came on the radio. I followed the soulful teenyboppers religiously—and stayed onboard as they matured into "The Jacksons" with infectious grooves like "Shake Your Body" and "Can You Feel It." But my dedication grew into obsession when Michael went solo. Michael's groundbreaking *Off the Wall* album (helmed by genius Quincy Jones) rocked my world and inspires me to this day. Then came *Thriller*.

If you weren't in the middle of it, it's difficult to convey the phenomenon of *Thriller*. The album (with cameos by Paul McCartney, Eddie Van Halen, and Vincent Price) was a full-frontal assault on pop culture, devouring everything in its path. "Billie Jean" shot to the top of the charts and stayed there for months. Meanwhile, after some arm twisting (okay, threats) by Michael's record label, MTV finally integrated their playlist and put "Billie Jean" into heavy rotation. The seductive video propelled the song into the stratosphere—and broke down the cable channel's tacit color barrier in the process. A couple of months later, Michael blew everybody's mind when he "moonwalked" across the stage during his performance of "Billie Jean" on the TV special *Motown 25: Yesterday, Today, Forever.* (Michael's dazzling backslide captured the nation's imagination almost as much as Neil Armstrong's actual moonwalk.) For his *coup de grace*, Michael released the "Thriller" video—and the world froze in its tracks. The MTV premiere of the 14-minute opus was one of those seminal events where people remember exactly where they were when it dropped. I was at Chapel Hill's local nightclub, Purdy's (we called them "discos" back then). Purdy's fell silent as the DJ stopped spinning and projection screens unspooled from the ceiling. People stood transfixed as the bashful Michael morphed into a zombie and terrorized his sweet and innocent girlfriend, before leading a crew of funky undead in an unforgettable line dance. It was (and still is) epic.

Our first workshop for the Michael Jackson musical was held in June 2018 at Ripley-Grier Studios on West 38th Street. The producers wanted to keep the fledgling project under the radar, so I'd been instructed to be discreet. In fact, I was asked to sign a non-disclosure agreement. (Am I allowed to disclose that?) The Ripley-Grier lobby featured a large whiteboard listing its current clients along with their respective studios. To ensure secrecy, our project had been codenamed *Westlake* (the name of the Hollywood recording studio where Michael created much of his magic). I understood the stealth strategy in theory—but that cat was going to leap out of the bag the moment Ripley-Grier's other customers heard Michael's platinum catalog echoing through the halls.

Our humble three-piece band consisted of pianist Jason Michael Webb (who was also the musical director), percussionist Everett Bradley, and me. I'd never worked with Jason, but his resumé was impressive and deep. Meanwhile I'd known Everett for years. Everett is an incredibly talented percussionist/vocalist and we'd worked on various theatrical projects together, as well as Jon Bon Jovi's side gig. Everett oozes musicality and his enthusiasm is contagious. (Just ask his star-studded array of employers: Hall & Oates, Carly Simon, The Meredith Vieira Show, Bruce Springsteen, and our mutual pal, JBJ.)

I had an exhilarating week, playing some of my favorite songs in the world. Typically, on the last day of a workshop, a group of industry insiders (producers, theater owners, potential investors) are invited to attend a casual presentation. Days of accumulated clutter is cleared from the room and replaced with rows of folding chairs for the VIP audience. But when I arrived for our *Westlake* finale, the usual sea of seats was nowhere in sight. Instead, two lone chairs sat ringside. I felt a twinge of panic and asked David Holcenberg about the lack of turnout. He smiled and explained it wasn't necessary to woo supporters…we didn't need any. The Michael Jackson Estate was overseeing the production. Wow, no groveling. What a luxury!

Just before showtime, a fashionable couple entered the room and took their seats. I immediately pegged the tanned duo as powerful, wealthy, and Californian. Bullseye! I later learned the identity of our guests: über Hollywood lawyer/manager John Branca (chairman of The Michael Jackson Company and co-executor of the Michael Jackson Estate) and his lovely fiancée.

At that early juncture, there was no choreography, no blocking, and no costumes. Street-clothed actors stood in front of music stands, reading from their scripts — and *sanging* their asses off. Despite the skeletal staging, there wasn't a dry eye in the house by the time we closed with "Man in the Mirror." Our esteemed playwright Lynn Nottage (the only woman to have twice won the Pulitzer Prize for Drama) approached the band afterward with tears streaming down her face. Lynn whispered, "I had no idea I would be *this* moved." Trying to be as objective as possible, I thought we had the makings of an incredible piece of theater.

David Holcenberg called the next day and said Mr. Branca was very pleased with our efforts and the project would be moving forward. I couldn't wait to do it again.

\* \* \*

Late summer, *School of Rock* announced it would be closing in January. (Considering our union contract only requires one-weeks' notice, a five-month warning is quite humane. On the cynical side, it also gives producers a chance to goose ticket sales with unending ads blaring "FINAL MONTHS!") Once again, it was time to put my head down and squirrel away some rainy-day funds. Bidding adieu to any frivolous nights off, I vowed to grind out as many performances as possible until closing. This was bad news for my subs (and their wallets), but desperate times call for desperate measures.

Juggling my dual loyalties, the Michael Jackson team re-assembled for its next workshop—but this time we went bigger. Instead of one week, we did six. Management also added a drummer to the lineup and dumped our cryptic moniker *West-lake,* officially rechristening the budding venture: *Don't Stop 'til You Get Enough.* Six weeks gave us time to put more meat on the bone, and the show slowly started coming into focus. (We also eventually added bass and a second guitar to the mix.) Going forward, the plan was another round of NYC rehearsals in the winter, an out-of-town residency at Chicago's Nederlander Theatre in the fall, and a Broadway opening in March 2020.

As advertised, *School of Rock* wrapped in January. We enjoyed a respectable three-year run, but after my 14-year marathon with *Mamma Mia!*, *School of Rock* felt like a sprint. Lacking an ounce of sentimentality, I skipped our perfunctory closing night party, mothballed my recorder, and set my sights on *Don't Stop 'til You Get Enough.* Unfortunately, two events were conspiring to throw a monkey wrench into my best-laid plans.

First, Actor's Equity (the actors union) called a strike prohibiting members from participating in developmental workshops until the issue of profit sharing was addressed. I was sympathetic to the cause, but the work stoppage put our *Don't Stop* rehearsals on ice while labor negotiations unfolded. Then, as we hung in limbo, HBO released *Leaving Neverland*, a documentary alleging sexual abuse by Michael Jackson.

The Equity dispute was eventually settled, but the shutdown gobbled up ten precious days of rehearsal. Switching into salvage mode, we pressed forward with an abridged workshop and, maybe more ominously, a dark HBO cloud hanging over our heads. The brutal combination of lost rehearsal time and negative publicity ultimately took its toll. When the smoke cleared, our Chicago run had been cancelled altogether and our Broadway opening was pushed to the summer of 2020. The production also dumped its potentially suggestive title, *Don't Stop 'til You Get Enough*, and renamed the show: *MJ.* The safer, more innocuous branding was probably the right move. Attempting to choose another song title would've been an exercise in futility — *every* pop song contains sexual innuendo. (It's not a bug, it's a feature!)

Doing the painful math, instead of a manageable six-month gap between my final *School of Rock* paycheck and my first *MJ* paycheck, I was now staring at more than a year of unemployment. (And keep in mind, this was long before anybody had ever heard the word COVID.) Oh well, when the going gets tough, the tough get subbing. I knew returning to the thankless world of a Broadway sub (after almost 20 years) would be difficult, but I underestimated the looming shock to my system.

# At This Performance, The Role Of...

I reached out to my employed peers, hoping to find a few stray crumbs of work on the sub market. The scene is highly competitive but, in addition to my Broadway credentials, I have a secret weapon: my home address. Our apartment is a ten-minute walk (or a five-minute run) from EVERY theater. When Broadway chair holders assemble their sub lists, adding a Manhattan-based player to the roster (if possible) is always a smart move. In last-minute emergencies, it never hurts to have someone who can show up at the drop of a hat. *That me!*

First in line: *King Kong*. Guitarist Sean Driscoll tossed me a bone and slotted me into the ambitious but struggling production. Critics loathed *King Kong*, but I dug it. (Sorry not sorry, the 20-foot-tall animatronic puppet was amazing.) Thanks to comps through *School of Rock*, Patty and I saw the show during previews, and were thoroughly entertained. Isn't that the goal? Snobs be damned, *King Kong* is the ONLY show I've ever attended where I wasn't sneaking peeks at my Playbill, wondering how many songs were left until intermission. I didn't look at my watch a single time during the show. In fact, I was surprised when the curtain fell. I thought, "Already?"

Watching *King Kong* was pure fun; playing *King Kong* was

brutal. The cinematic score presented some of the most challenging music I'd ever tackled. One chart in particular ("The Cobra Fight") was a mixed-meter nightmare, with random bars of 3/4, 4/4, 5/4, and 6/4 scattered across a single page. *Count or die!* In addition to the difficult music, my job description included electric guitar, acoustic guitar, classical guitar, baritone guitar, and banjo. (My rotator cuff is still barking from all the quick changes. Pro tip: bend your elbow when lifting.) Adding to the madness, the guitar chair involved an elaborate effects pedalboard that required lightning-fast stomp box moves. Little did I know, this tricky *tap dance* was a preview of coming attractions.

Despite a month of meticulous preparation, my first crack at *King Kong* was terrifying. Nausea washed over me as the show started—and the queasiness never subsided. If such a thing were allowed, I would've raised my hand after one or two songs and asked to be excused. I struggled throughout the show; even the easiest of passages become difficult when your hands are shaking. I thought, "What the hell is going on?" Then I remembered…oh yeah, it's called adrenaline. Welcome back, Jeff!

Fortunately, technology had improved exponentially since my last round of subbing…in the previous century. (Holy shit, make that the previous millennium!) As a result, getting my hands on the necessary prep material was much less of a chore. Instead of borrowing the music folder and running to a nearby copy shop, you're emailed a PDF. Instead of bringing a cassette player to the pit to record the performance, mp3s are readily available for download. Best of all, conductor videos are now the norm. Thanks to the digital age, subs can sit in front of their lap-

tops and basically recreate the pit experience at home (sans anxiety). This is a huge advantage, "cockpit simulation" is essential
to subbing success. It's a given you'll be nervous come showtime,
so the fewer surprises the better. Twenty years after my first subbing experience, the sage advice still rang true, "When you think
you're ready, practice two more weeks."

After ingesting *King Kong*, I waded into *Ain't Too Proud — The
Life and Times of The Temptations*. The Motown tuner was right
up my alley, so I was confident I'd be a good fit. For me, the key
to conquering a Broadway book is internalizing the music to an
extreme. I want to be able to *look* at any of the charts and instantly hear the music in my head. This was a piece of cake with
*Ain't Too Proud*. I never turned the page and thought, "Gee, how
does 'My Girl' go again?" But there is a double-edged aspect to
performing such a familiar catalog: everybody in the audience
knows how "My Girl" goes as well. Mistakes will be noticed.
*Ain't Too Proud* was a walk in the park compared to *King Kong*,
but as guitarist extraordinaire Jon Herington notes, "There are
no easy Broadway shows. They're ALL hard."

Despite being in my comfort zone musically, the Temptations show did have one tricky wrinkle: band choreography.
Gulp! Class was in session as 50 or so aspiring *Ain't Too Proud*
orchestra subs assembled at New 42 Studios in Times Square to
learn the show's remedial dance routine. "5, 6, 7, 8!" The moves
were simple enough — but the thought of shaking my booty on
a Broadway stage was nevertheless intimidating. (For what it's
worth, thanks to the mirrored walls in the studio, I can safely say
I was far from the worst dancer in the room. But trust me, the
bar was quite low.)

Toward the end of *Ain't Too Proud*, a pre-recorded underscore takes over as the musicians exit the orchestra pit *en masse* and creep up to the stage. The band stands hidden behind a giant screen while the actors take their final bows. Then, halfway through the encore of "I Can't Get Next to You," the partition rises to unveil the 16-piece *ATP* orchestra (dressed in matching white suits) moving and grooving in *approximate* unison. The crowd explodes when the band appears. One cast member told me the "band reveal" was his favorite part of the show.

My debut ON the Broadway stage was a blur; I felt like the proverbial deer in the headlights. But after a few repetitions, I actually started looking forward to my moment in the sun. Seeing a theater filled with happy people—all on their feet, clapping and singing along at the top of their lungs never gets old. And as a bonus, it was nice to occasionally be recognized by fans as I exited the stage door.

That said, over the years I've learned working *under* the stage is much less stressful than working *on* the stage. Pit musicians typically receive minimal love from the audience, but on the upside, we aren't required to put on a happy face night after night. (I've been there with Sting; feigning enthusiasm when your tank is on empty exacts a toll.) Sheltered from the glare of the spotlight, I can wear jeans and a t-shirt to work, and if I don't feel like shaving (or smiling), I don't. One evening at *Mamma Mia!*, an elderly lady leaned into the orchestra pit after the show to praise the band. I thanked her and was gushing about how much I loved my job when she interjected derisively, "You'd think you'd dress nicer!"

I kept my nose to the sub grindstone and dug into *Beetlejuice* next. Learning a show requires a ton of study, so I was beginning to feel a little loopy by my third mission in less than three months. But I had to keep the train rolling. Subbing is usually more famine than feast; accordingly, you need multiple shows in your quiver to have any chance at earning a meaningful income. My head seems to hold four or five shows max, but I've encountered fearless warriors who were juggling eight or nine different books. I bow to these high-IQ masochists.

*Beetlejuice* haunted the Winter Garden Theatre, so I was back "home" yet again. Between *Mamma Mia!*, *School of Rock*, and *Beetlejuice*, I spent over 16 years walking through the Winter Garden stage door. But this time, things were different. I wasn't family, I was a guest. It was a strange sensation.

After holding a steady Broadway chair for almost two decades, reacclimating to the sub dynamic was challenging. In addition to combating performance anxiety, I detected a subtle vibe from certain orchestra members who seemed to resent subs who acted too comfortable or familiar. I eventually learned to read the room and dial back my conviviality when necessary. There is a fine line between confidence and hubris—and subs need to know how to find the sweet spot. You're expected to be self-assured yet deferential. Music schools should require a minor in psychology.

At my final performance of *King Kong*, I was making water-cooler conversation with one of the assistant conductors, Chris Haberl.

"Sorry to hear you guys are closing," I offered sympathetically. "You got anything else cooking?"

"Thanks, I'll be okay," Chris replied. "I'm also the associate conductor over at *Jersey Boys*."

I nodded—and pounced.

"Cool! If your guitar player ever needs a sub, please give him my number."

"Will do," Chris smiled.

The original production of *Jersey Boys* enjoyed a highly successful 12-year run on Broadway before closing, downsizing, and reopening at a smaller off-Broadway theater only a few months later. Despite off-Broadway's lower pay scale, I found *Jersey Boys* 2.0 appealing. First, it was the story of Frankie Valli and the Four Seasons, which meant the show featured 60s and 70s pop music (my strong suit). Second, the revamped *Jersey Boys* had dropped anchor at New World Stages, which is on the same street as our apartment. The walk from our stoop to the stage door takes five minutes — tops. It doesn't get much cushier than that.

I figured my off-the-cuff *Jersey Boys* pitch probably fell on deaf ears — until I got an email from the show's guitarist, Joe Payne. Joe said my timing was perfect, he just happened to be in the market for a new sub. Jackpot! Time to initiate another launch sequence: new songs, new instruments, new pedalboard…and MORE dance steps! But now that I was an experienced hoofer, I wasn't worried.

I should've been.

*Jersey Boys* and *Ain't Too Proud* were both choreographed by Broadway veteran Sergio Trujillo, so I assumed the demands would basically be the same. Think again Fred Astaire. The *Jersey Boys* dance steps — created a dozen years BEFORE *Ain't Too Proud* — were considerably more complicated and required a lot of homework on my part. (I'm sure our downstairs neighbor heard the floorboards creaking throughout the day and wondered, "What the hell is going on up there?") You'd think Trujillo's choreography would've become *more* ambitious over the years, but it was just the opposite. Surprisingly, the older routine was the harder routine. I'm guessing Sergio eventually tired of watching *Jersey Boys* subs butcher his fancy footwork and vowed to keep future band choreo as simple as possible. Smart plan. It may seem counterintuitive, but many musicians are horrible dancers.

Like *Ain't Too Proud*, my first pass at the *Jersey Boys* choreography was a trip (in more ways than one). I remember looking down at my feet during the encore and noticing one of my shoes was untied. In spite of being extra careful, I ended up stepping on the wayward shoestring and came very close to falling flat on my face. *Down goes Frazier!* The crowd—and band—would've loved that. Going forward, I made damn sure my laces were securely double knotted.

Playing *Jersey Boys* was a revelation. Up until then, I was a casual Frankie Valli fan at best. I liked his 70s era stuff like "Who Loves You" and "December 1963 (Oh What a Night)"—but I'd dismissed Valli's falsetto-laden 60s work as gimmicky. However, after immersing myself in the *Jersey Boys* score, I saw the light. "Sherry," "Big Girls Don't Cry," and "Walk Like a Man" are irresistible ear worms. Then there's Frankie's masterpiece, "Can't Take My Eyes Off You." In my opinion, this is one of the greatest pop tunes ever written. Music aficionados may scoff, but I rank the sweeping composition right up there with Springsteen's "Born to Run."

With *King Kong* closed, I was down to three shows in my rotation. *MJ* was still nine months away, so I wondered if I should try to add a couple more books to the equation. Zach Dietz to the rescue!

### When in Doubt(fire)

Keyboardist Zach Dietz and I worked together at *School of Rock*, so our friendship had been forged by fire—blistering "Room of Truth" fire. Like me, Zach had jumped back into the part-timer pool, and we both found ourselves subbing at *Beetlejuice*. One night during intermission, Zach and I were hanging out, chatting about our futures. I told him I was treading water, waiting around for *MJ* to crank up in the summer. Zach countered, telling me he was going to be conducting *Mrs. Doubtfire*, which was coming to Broadway in the spring. I congratulated him— and was stunned by his response.

"What's your availability look like, Jeff?"

Confused, I reiterated I was starting *MJ* in July.

Zach came back with, "Well, what about before July?"

Wow. Was Zach hinting he'd be willing to hire me for *Mrs. Doubtfire* on a temporary basis? Broadway chairs are highly coveted and aren't usually doled out to people who are just passing through. Could I be so lucky?

Zach elaborated, saying he'd love to have me onboard, even if for only four months. I was flabbergasted. Zach said he'd check with *Doubtfire*'s music supervisor Ethan Popp and keep me posted. I'd worked under Ethan at *School of Rock*, so he knew what I could bring to the table. Nevertheless, I assumed landing the interim position was a long shot at best.

For the record, hiring a Broadway musician on a temporary basis isn't unprecedented—but it is somewhat rare. That said, an argument can be made for the seemingly unorthodox move. Assembling the right combination of musicians for a show's crucial incubation period makes total sense, as early input from the band helps shape the show's musical character. (The printed page is simply a jumping-off point. Composers and orchestrators expect musicians to "romance the ink" and turn those little black dots into listening pleasure.) After a show officially opens, subs are quickly added to the mix and, believe it or not, the original lineup is rarely together again. With so many moving parts, it's important to establish a solid template from the get-go. The solution? Hire a killer band to get the "party" started.

I was psyched to learn music supervisor Ethan Popp was in my corner, but he still needed to run my name—and the delicate issue of my limited participation—by *Doubtfire* composers, Wayne and Karey Kirkpatrick. Deferring to Ethan and Zach, the Brothers Kirkpatrick gave their blessings, and I was granted a dispensation. I alerted my bosses at *MJ* of the offer, and they said, "Go for it…but see you in July!" I was over the moon. The light at the end of my subbing tunnel had just gotten four months brighter.

*Mrs. Doubtfire* was slated to hit Seattle's 5th Avenue Theatre for a six-week tryout before arriving on Broadway in March. There was talk of shipping the entire *Doubtfire* band out west, but, in the end, only the basic rhythm section (keyboards, bass, and drums) made the cross-country trek. I was disappointed…and relieved. I could've used the steady paycheck, but the Seattle run stretched across Thanksgiving and Christmas, and I was more than happy to be home for the holidays. Once again, I'd somehow avoided going out of town with an incoming show. *Mrs. Doubtfire* would be my fifth Broadway chair—and *Seussical* was still the only show that had required me to pack my bags.

I continued to keep my sub plates spinning…while also digging into the fourth *MJ* workshop. In a delicious twist, *MJ* and

*Mrs. Doubtfire* were rehearsing at New 42 Studios at the same time, so I felt like King of the World as I rode the elevator between the 4th and 6th floor on my breaks, hanging out with BOTH of my shows. *MJ* was shaping up nicely and the Broadway buzz was building. At the end of our latest three-week lab, the producers invited a few industry movers and shakers to attend a presentation. VIPs, theater owners, fellow producers, and select celebrities packed into New 42 Studios to take a peek at our emerging piece of theater. By the encore, the entire audience was on their feet cheering—with smiles on their faces and/or tears in their eyes. A veteran theater producer leaned over to me and beamed, "Broadway's never seen anything like this." July here we come (or so I thought).

\* \* \*

I rang in the New Year with great anticipation; 2020 was looking like a real winner. I played my final shows as a sub during January and February (adios choreography!) and readied for *Mrs. Doubtfire.* The show's contractor, John Miller, had been intimating my chair would include multiple "doubles." (A double is any *additional* instrument written into your part.) The good news? You are compensated for each instrument you are required to play. (For you math nerds out there, your first double pays 12.5% on top of your base salary, with each additional double adding 6.25% more.) I was intrigued by the rumored fat payday, but also worried about which foreign objects I'd be expected to fake my way around—mandolin? banjo? zither? I bargained with God, "Just no wind instruments please." I hoped my recorder days were behind me.

I was thrilled when I learned my *Mrs. Doubtfire* book included FIVE doubles. Ka-ching! (Pop quiz: Five doubles? a 37.5% bump in pay.) But my excitement grew exponentially when I got the specific breakdown. In addition to guitar, I'd be playing (wait for it)...guitar. Huh? Yep. My *Doubtfire* duties would entail: Fender Stratocaster, Fender Telecaster, Gibson Les Paul, Gibson 335, acoustic guitar, and nylon-string guitar. Holy cow! I was going to be paid to play six *different* instruments — and they were ALL guitars. (Adding to my elation, I already owned each of these axes, which meant no out-of-pocket expenditures.)

Typically, a Broadway guitar part generically stipulates "electric guitar," and the player is responsible for choosing his weapon. But the *Doubtfire* music team (orchestrator Ethan Popp, along with composers Wayne and Karey Kirkpatrick) spoke fluent guitar. They were sonic sticklers and knew exactly what they wanted. This may sound like overkill to the layperson, but I assure you it isn't. Different musical styles call for different guitars. (Any craftsman worth their salt knows to use the right tool for the job.) If you want a clean, funky sound, use a Strat; if you want country twang, use a Tele; if you want heavy rock, use a Les Paul, and so on. I couldn't believe my good fortune. I remarked to our contractor, John Miller, "Wow, I've *never* seen this before!" Miller replied dryly, "You know who else has never seen this before? The producers!"

*Mrs. Doubtfire* band rehearsals were scheduled to start in late February at Carroll Studios. I'd never attempted to transport six guitars at one time, so I was perplexed. I looked into hiring a cartage company but ended up taking the cheap way out: I enlisted Patty to be my assistant beast of burden. I figured I'd order a car service and we could wrangle three guitars each.

I'd done numerous rehearsals at Carroll and was painfully aware of their cramped elevator, so I called the front desk in advance to inquire about using the freight elevator for my arsenal of axes. A staff member commended my foresight and told me the service elevator was located in the loading dock next to the building entrance. "Just give us a call when you get here."

On the night before our first rehearsal, Patty and I grabbed my guitars and Ubered over to Carroll Studios for load-in. When we arrived, I phoned the front desk to request the freight elevator. The guy said, "No problem, I'll send someone right down." Patty and I waited (and waited) in the cold night air — sidestepping the large rat scurrying around the loading dock — but the elevator never came to life.

We finally surrendered after 20 minutes or so and headed back out onto the sidewalk toward the building's lobby — resigned to cramming ourselves (and my six guitars) into the tiny passenger elevator. As we reached the entrance with our bulky payload, the glass doors swung open. Perfect timing! We looked up to see a good Samaritan patiently holding the door for us. Patty and I did a double take when we realized our doorman was none other than Broadway wunderkind Lin-Manuel Miranda (creator of *Hamilton* and *In the Heights*). Lin smiled and nodded as Patty and I squeezed into the building. I love New York.

The *Doubtfire* band spent a couple days at Carroll, familiarizing ourselves with the music before moving into our new home, the Stephen Sondheim Theatre. Most Broadway houses are creaky, operational antiques, but the Sondheim, constructed in 2004, is a sparkly, modern facility. I was looking forward to spending the next four months in 21st century comfort — then COVID came knocking. Life, as we knew it, stopped.

*NYC "rush hour" 2020*
*Eighth Avenue and West 50th Street*
*(Wednesday, April 1 @ 5pm)*

# Flying Blind

It's important for ME to remember just how scary things were when the pandemic first hit NYC. COVID-19 wasn't a slow-rising flood here, it was a tsunami. Our daily existence changed overnight—and the unknown was overwhelming. Would food supplies be disrupted? (We still have a tower of canned goods stacked in the corner of our kitchen. I dubbed it "The Shrine of Fear.") Would police and firemen fall ill and be unable to do their jobs? Would the fabric of society tear apart? What did "shelter in place" actually mean? Would New York City become a *Mad Max* hellscape of marauding gangs? These anxieties may seem overblown now, but at the time, they were very real.

My college pal Doug Travis lives a couple of hours north of the city. Doug is as even-tempered as they come, incapable of hyperbole. Nevertheless, he called to express his concern over our safety, offering to drive down and "rescue" Patty and me if things got dicey. I told him, without a hint of sarcasm, "If we reach that point Doug, the National Guard probably won't let you past the city limits." We simply didn't know what to expect.

Fortunately, the worst-case scenario didn't come to pass, but life was VERY different. Manhattan emptied out. I've never seen anything like it in my 35 years as a New Yorker. The city that never sleeps slept. (Patty compared the eerie quiet to a Sunday morning meets New Year's Day.) Our Hell's Kitchen apartment building has 10 units, but for a stretch, only two of them were occupied. The vacant hallways made us feel like squatters. Streets were practically traffic-free, jaywalking was *de rigueur*—there was certainly no need to wait for the "Walk" light. The only thing missing was tumbleweeds.

Masks weren't available for months, so I wandered around the city wearing a DIY, origami-esque contraption consisting of a folded handkerchief and two rubber bands. Adding to the *fun*, my strict mask compliance resulted in an ongoing battle with fogged-up glasses. (I eventually learned to rub dishwashing liquid on the lenses before leaving home.)

Shopping became an adventure. Without a car and a spacious pantry to stockpile food, we had to make trips to the market on a near-daily basis. (Ever try carrying a week's worth of groceries for five blocks and up five flights of stairs?) Arriving at the store—IF it was open—you had to wait in line to enter. Social distancing ran this town. Once you finally got inside, the formerly mundane task of grocery shopping suddenly felt like a nail-biting scene from *Mission Impossible*. My internal clock would tick down as I frantically tried to gather the items on our list at record speed. (For whatever deep-seated psychological reasons, toilet paper shelves were picked clean.) More often than not, I'd hit the panic button and bail before my task was complete. My desire for fresh air outweighed my desire for tortillas bent on playing hide-and-seek.

But even after escaping outdoors, the sidewalks felt scary too. Did that sneezing passerby just hand me a death sentence? Looking for any silver lining, at least the city's notorious *aromas* came in handy. "Loss of smell" was a common COVID symptom, so I could count on the streets to provide free self-checkups. *Sniff... ewww... I mean, yay!* Returning from the shopping safaris, we'd wipe down our groceries (and mail), wash our hands vigorously, and then head back to the couch to continue bingeing Netflix. We were fully on guard—and fully unemployed. Like I said, scary.

Dinner also became an adventure. For over two decades, my Broadway schedule had dictated an early bird supper. (I felt like a retiree at *Del Boca Vista*, but I'd quickly learned midnight dinners wreak havoc with your digestive system and waistline.) Consequently, Patty and I rarely dined together pre-COVID. Our urban, on-the-go lifestyles typically involved spontaneous, *separate* meal choices—so the art of making a grocery list and planning dinners was a foreign concept. But with no gigs to disrupt our days, husband and wife started breaking bread as one. Like many, we spent the first few months consuming way too much comfort food, basically self-medicating with carbs, before eventually realizing we weren't on holiday—and our bathroom scales didn't give a whit about some stinkin' pandemic. We didn't go hardcore, but we did resume our exercise routines and made a conscious effort to eat more responsibly.

The shutdown closed all non-essential businesses, forcing us to deal with the respective monkeys on our backs. Patty's drug of choice is Starbucks iced tea, but the ubiquitous chain shuttered when the *latte* hit the fan. Fortunately, a sympathetic insider slipped Patty an industrial-sized Starbucks tea bag to help her navigate detox. Each morning, Patty would carefully ration a few leaves from her junkie stash into a tea ball and brew her fix. Meanwhile, I had to grapple with my New York Yankees addiction. Major League Baseball cancelled the first four months of its season, so I was forced to watch "Yankees Classics" reruns. On the bright side, my Yankees always won, but the "encore presentations" quickly proved unfulfilling. Sports is built on suspense and drama; there was none.

Exacerbating the COVID clusterfuck, Patty had to make an emergency trip home to Kentucky during the height of the pandemic. Patty's older sister sustained a traumatic brain injury in a car accident decades ago and, due to a lack of better options, now resides in a long-term care facility. When COVID hit, the building was placed on complete lockdown and Patty's sister was sequestered in her room. She'd had NO visitors in over six months, and the isolation was making an already tough situation even tougher. So, despite the risk, we agreed Patty *needed* to go on a mission of mercy. Donning a mask, a face shield, and gloves, Patty boarded a flight to Louisville.

Patty wasn't allowed inside the facility, but she showed up each day with a folding stool to sit outside her sister's window. The two visited through the glass for hours on end, attempting to diffuse the loneliness in some small way. No miracles (or physical contact) occurred, but Patty's presence proved therapeutic. After 10 days of separated togetherness, Patty climbed back on United Airlines (in full protective gear) and flew home. Mission accomplished—but only in a Sisyphean sense. Her sister's lockdown continued with no end in sight. For Patty's troubles, as per New York State protocols, she was required to quarantine in our cozy apartment for 14 days upon her return. *Nothing* was easy with COVID.

We went through the motions of day-to-day life, trying to pretend things were normal. But they weren't. Reality would slap me in the face each morning when I opened the blinds to see a deserted sidewalk dotted with blue-masked warriors. (God bless the brave minimum-wage employees who kept our city functioning on a skeletal level.) Reality would also slap me in the face each evening—at 7pm specifically—when New Yorkers raised their windows and voices in unison to honor our tireless health care workers. Intentions were pure, but I think the daily scream therapy (coupled with banging on pots and pans) helped the pent-up masses cope with the ongoing insanity. Emotionally and psychologically, I compared the situation to being trapped in a mine or lost at sea. I knew panicking would only make matters worse, so I strived to ignore my omnipresent anxiety. But I kept telling Patty, only half-jokingly, "This shit needs to end so I can get started on my *post*-traumatic stress."

### Thanksgiving Tears

Eight months into the pandemic, a dark year became darker when my father died unexpectedly on Thanksgiving morning. Less than a week earlier, Dad experienced shortness of breath and, fearing COVID, dialed 911. The EMTs examined my father and suspected his problems were heart—not COVID—related. Dad was admitted to the hospital and tests revealed serious heart blockage. My father's cardiologist laid out the stark options: undergo "risky" open-heart surgery or *try* to manage the issue with medications. At age 84, Dad was wary of major surgery, so our family made a group decision to pursue the meds route. After a few days of treatment, my father was released from the hospital on the Wednesday before Thanksgiving. I called to check on him that afternoon and he greeted me with his signature upbeat, "Hey buddy," before expressing his extreme happiness to be home. He asked if I wanted to FaceTime, but I replied, "You rest, we'll do it tomorrow for Thanksgiving."

The following morning, Dad collapsed at the breakfast table with my mother at his side. (They were married 64 years.) EMTs were called, but they were unable to revive my father. Patty and I were still tucked in, watching the end of the Macy's parade when my older brother, Mike, called with the heartbreaking news, "He's gone."

There's a hole in my life—but thankfully, no loose ends or regrets (except for that tabled FaceTime). Dad and I had candidly discussed our mortality for years, and we closed each conversation with "I love you." As we grew older, we openly acknowledged one of life's sad realities: if things go according to "plan," children bury their parents. It sucks, but it's part of the gig. I sure didn't want my parents to endure burying me.

I would not be the man—or the musician—I am without my father's loving guidance and unconditional support. Dad was a great role model, teaching me to lead with honesty, respect, and all-out effort. His death was a huge loss, but I try to focus on gratitude. My dad lived until he died, and he didn't suffer. I was lucky to have him as long as I did.

Alas, with the pandemic raging, our family made the painful but prudent decision to postpone having a memorial service for my father. Nobody wanted to risk compounding our grief with a serious illness (or another death). I'm certain Dad would've agreed wholeheartedly. He was as selfless as they come.

\* \* \*

*COVID UPDATE: On December 11, 2020, the U.S. Food and Drug Administration issued the first emergency use authorization (EUA) for a vaccine for the prevention of coronavirus disease 2019 (COVID-19)*

A vaccine!—and only ten months into the pandemic. (I'd feared it might take years.) Things are finally moving in the right direction. Fingers crossed for humanity.

## Jabbed

According to the calendar, it's March once again. (In a sense, it feels like last March never ended.) Unbelievably, the lights of Broadway have been dark for an entire year. These have been tough times indeed, but Patty and I have managed to remain healthy. Enhancing our gratitude, on the anniversary of the Broadway shutdown, we became eligible for the vaccine. As soon as we rolled out of bed, we jumped on our laptops and steeled ourselves for a marathon day of *fishing*. (We'd heard tales of people spending hour after frustrating hour refreshing their browsers in search of an appointment.) Luckily, our fears were unfounded. We were able to schedule vaccinations through New York State's website in a matter of minutes—but unfortunately the earliest appointment was six long weeks away. Looking for a backup plan, we logged onto our corner pharmacy's website to check their availability. Miraculously, we were able to snag shots for the very next day. Topping things off, I got a call from

Walgreens late in the afternoon asking if I could "Go ahead and come in now." I threw on some shoes and was there in a flash. Urban living involves many sacrifices— but convenience isn't one of 'em. Bottom line: on my FIRST day of eligibility, I had a Pfizer vaccine in my arm by 6pm. It was an emotional moment. (Patty got her first shot the following morning.) Four weeks later, we both received our second dose. Thank you modern medicine.

\* \* \*

Six months after my father's death, with our family fully vaxxed and the COVID risk at a manageable level, we held an overdue, and deeply cathartic, memorial *picnic.* An overflow group of loved ones gathered outdoors on a picture-perfect spring day to celebrate the life of Jim Campbell. There were no tears or somber speeches—just hugs, laughter, snacks, and plenty of ice-cold beer. Dad would've loved it.

\* \* \*

*(New York, NY) May 5, 2021 – With guidance from Governor Andrew Cuomo, based on current health trends and subject to continuing improvement of public health and vaccination rates, as well as the state's final approval of each theater operator's health and safety protocols, the Broadway League announces that Broadway shows in New York City will resume ticket sales this month for Fall 2021 performances.*

Hallelujah!!! Broadway is reopening in the fall; I'll finally be going back to work. On the downside, *Mrs. Doubtfire* and *MJ* are no longer separated by a four-month cushion. Instead, they are on a collision course. And since I still haven't figured out how to be in two places at the same time, I've regrettably played my last note at *Mrs. Doubtfire*. My scheduled four months of fun and profit with the *Doubtfire* gang turned into two measly weeks. I knew this could happen, but I'm bummed nevertheless.

Before COVID-19 flipped the world on its ear, friends kept asking "What if *Mrs. Doubtfire* is a hit?" Inquiring minds wanted to know if I'd forsake *MJ* and stand pat. That was a good question but, in a word, nope. Objectively speaking—at least from a financial standpoint—the *best* Broadway gig is the one that runs the longest. But at this point of my career, I can afford to be choosy. If *Mrs. Doubtfire* outlives *MJ*, I'll have no regrets. My life-long love of Michael Jackson's music runs deep, so I can't imagine a better fit for my skill (and mind) set. If *MJ* winds up being a box-office bust, hopefully my pals at *Mrs. Doubtfire* will let me come back and sub.

I'm reminded of a passage in my book, *Do Stand So Close: my improbable adventure as Sting's guitarist.* During the European leg of Sting's *Nothing Like the Sun* tour, we crossed paths with Michael Jackson's *Bad* tour in Paris. Michael's keyboard-ist/musical director, Greg Phillinganes, had invited Sting's sax-ophonist, Branford Marsalis, to hang out one afternoon—and Branford asked if I wanted to tag along. Being a big fan of Phillinganes's body of work (Stevie Wonder, Eric Clapton, Anita Baker, etc.), I eagerly accepted. The three of us sat around Greg's hotel room, comparing notes and trading tales from the road. To my surprise, Greg seemed somewhat blasé about his high-profile gig with the King of Pop. When pressed, Greg confided he was frustrated his commitment with Michael's tour had prohibited him from signing on with Eric Clapton's upcoming tour. I sympathized with Greg's luxury problem but didn't share his sentiment. Even with further reflection, I stand by my previously published comment in *Do Stand So Close*:

> *I'll burn in Guitar Hell for saying this, but if I had to play a song night after night, I'd choose "Billie Jean" over "Layla."*

God must have been listening—or I'm clairvoyant. Either way, I'm now positioned to play "Billie Jean" (as prophesied) "night after night"…and hopefully for many years to come. I couldn't be happier.

> *(New York, NY) May 11, 2021—MJ, the new Broadway musical inspired by the life of singer Michael Jackson, has announced a February 1, 2022, opening at the Neil Simon Theatre. Previews will begin December 6, 2021. Tickets will go on sale to the general public on Tuesday, May 18 at 10am ET.*

*MJ* to the Neil Simon Theatre? Talk about coming full circle. I worked at the Neil Simon when I first moved to New York—as a candy salesman. A mere 35 years later, I'm heading back to a building where my NYC dreams set sail. But this time, instead of being stationed in the lobby with a soda gun and a tip jar, I'll be underneath the stage rocking out. Hollywood studios would probably dismiss my fairytale ending as too syrupy, but the poetic plot twist is not lost on me.

# Startin' Something

After being adrift for almost two years, I'm finally back to work. We held our first band rehearsal this morning at Carroll Studios—and I couldn't stop smiling. It felt great to *have* to be somewhere…hell, anywhere. It made me realize how much I'd missed having structure and purpose in my life. (On the other hand, I'd never lost sight of how much I missed having an income. My weekly bills made sure of that.) The *MJ* cast has been hard at work for the last couple of months, methodically assembling the show with the help of a skeletal band (piano, drums, and percussion). I would've loved to have been involved, but the creative process can be brutally slow; it wouldn't make sense for producers to pay a roomful of musicians to sit around and twiddle their thumbs while the theatrical caterpillar struggles to escape its cocoon. Accordingly, the full orchestra isn't added to the equation until a week or so before the first public performance. This condensed time frame guarantees a pressure-cooker environment, but that's why we're called "professionals."

* * *

Ahhh—breathe deep. The day that seemed like it would never arrive has arrived. *MJ* debuts tonight at the Neil Simon Theatre. As a recovering perfectionist, I'd prefer a longer preparation period, but that's not how showbiz works. *Saturday Night Live* producer Lorne Michaels summed it up best. "We don't go on because it's ready, we go on because it's 11:30."

I'm proud to say I've been onboard with *Westlake/Don't Stop 'til You Get Enough/MJ* since the first note was played. But with repeated delays and setbacks, the project began to feel like a tantalizing mirage floating just beyond my grasp. Magnifying my angst, the Neil Simon Theatre unveiled their huge, eye-catching *MJ* marquee right *before* the COVID shutdown. Consequently, a 12-foot-tall *en pointe* Michael Jackson—complete with fedora, sequined glove, and sparkly socks—has been staring down on me for two long years. Each time I passed the neon-orange billboard, I'd look up and sigh, "One of these days…"

Well, today is that day.


The streets of New York are bustling with holiday tourists. The slow-moving hordes can be frustrating for us on-the-go locals, but after enduring last year's deserted, joyless sidewalks, I've promised God I'll never complain about crowds again. Come one, come all!

Unfortunately, the specter of COVID-19 still looms large. We're heading into year THREE of the pandemic—and we ain't out of the woods yet. There was a brief moment back in the summer when I thought we'd rounded the corner, then mutations of the virus started popping up. The "Delta" variant continues to burn through the land, and now we're dealing with a new, highly transmissible iteration called "Omicron." (I'm beginning to hate the Greek alphabet. I pray Broadway can weather the latest *letter*.)

Out of an abundance of caution—and an existential desire to keep the lights on—all Broadway employees are required to be fully vaccinated. We are also tested three time a week, and mask use is compulsory. And, at least for the time being, audience members must show proof of vaccination and wear masks throughout the performance. I look forward to the day where these protocols are a distant memory, but "distant" might be a stretch for me. The COVID scars run deep.

I know life is filled with crazy twists and turns, but I NEVER expected to go 650 days between gigs. Tonight is both a finish line and a starting gate. My emotions are complex to say the least. I'm psyched, anxious, relieved, stressed…and melancholy. This is the first professional triumph I haven't been able to share with my father. Dad was always so excited, proud—and curious. (Whenever my parents visited NYC to see one of my Broadway shows, Dad preferred sitting in the orchestra pit with me rather than in the audience.)

I want to bask in the glory of the moment, but I'm wary of dropping my guard. My last Broadway outing (*Mrs. Doubtfire*) only made it through three performances before the sky caved in. But I have to put my fear on the shelf. It's time to tune out the distractions—and inherent artistic doubt—and focus on the mission at hand. As The Isley Brothers sang, "I got work to do."


I slung my *MJ* laminate around my neck, grabbed my jacket, kissed Patty goodbye, and set out on my *grueling* ten-minute trek to the Neil Simon. Nearing the theater, the sidewalks started getting congested. I thought, "It's Monday night, who are all these people?" Then it dawned on me: this pulsing mob was flocking to *MJ*. I was stunned (and thrilled) when I noticed the line was wrapped around the block. The impressive turnout couldn't be the result of positive word-of-mouth from satisfied customers—we hadn't had any customers yet. The mass of humanity was based solely on the Michael Jackson brand. Wow!

Squeezing through the energized crowd, I slipped in the stage door and made my way downstairs toward the orchestra pit, nodding to the flurry of still unfamiliar faces on our crew. (Unfortunately, polite nods have temporarily replaced smiles in our masked society.) I pulled my guitars from my locker and strutted to my designated spot in the dugout. I plugged in my trusty axes, threw a sincere and grateful glance skyward...and began noodling on some mindless picking exercises as *MJ* readied for take-off. Then, a disembodied voice started booming through the house PA system—saying the sweet words I'd been longing to hear:

*"Welcome to the Neil Simon Theatre and MJ the Musical. Out of courtesy to the company, please take this time to silence all mobile phones and electronic devices. The taking of photographs or the use of any recording devices is strictly prohibited. We ask that you show your love for Broadway by keeping your mask over your mouth and nose while you are inside the theater—unless you are actively drinking something. The MJ band is being conducted by Jason Michael Webb."*

Hell yeah...let's do this!

## *<record scratch>*
# We Interrupt This Program 2.0

Well, *MJ* made it through all of SIX (!) performances before COVID swamped our company and forced a shutdown. Much like athletics, if you don't have enough healthy players to field a team, you have no choice but to forfeit. And since *MJ* is a brand-new show, our bench isn't deep enough (yet) to cover mass absences. This is beginning to feel like a slasher film. Just when you think it might be safe ...

Management scheduled a ZOOM call to discuss the situation. I logged on warily, fully expecting to hear "See you guys in March"—so I was relieved when our producer announced a *mere* two-week hiatus. (To underscore how dire the circumstances were, *MJ* preemptively cancelled 15 shows during the lucrative, tourist-rich Christmas season.) Other Broadway productions encountered similar staffing problems due to COVID, triggering last-minute postponements as well. (*Moulin Rouge!* actually pulled the plug on a performance after patrons were already in their seats.) Not surprisingly, ticket holders were furious over having their holiday festivities yanked out from underneath them. Sure, their money was refunded, but high-and-dry theatergoers were left on the hook for other ancillary expenses, ranging from the relatively small (parking garages) to the large (hotel rooms and airline tickets). It was a PR nightmare. Meanwhile, some shows (including *Jagged Little Pill, Ain't Too Proud*, and even the monolithic Radio City Music Hall *Christmas Spectacular*) threw in the towel and closed their doors permanently.

After returning from our unplanned *holiday*, the *MJ* company switched to DAILY testing. Fortunately, unlike regular civilians, I didn't have to stand in long lines at Urgent Care or City MD—or one of the ubiquitous mobile testing vans or tents canvassing Manhattan. The Broadway League wisely developed a private testing infrastructure for all theater employees—featuring multiple sites scattered around Times Square. As a resident of Hell's Kitchen, it couldn't be any easier for me. Each morning, I receive a text from Mobile Health containing a registration link. One click and a personal QR code is generated on my iPhone. I wander over to a testing facility of my choice, flash my info-laden barcode for scanning, have my nostrils swabbed, and move on with my day. I'm in and out—two minutes tops, with the results emailed to me within the hour. I quickly reached the point where I'd open my communiqué without a second thought. Like clockwork, each message read "Your COVID result is: NOT DETECTED."

This wasn't surprising. I have no social life; I live like a monk. No restaurants, no bars. I'm either at work, the grocery store, or on my couch—and I always wear a *MJ*-issue KF94 mask in public (even outdoors if I'm in a crowd). Consequently, when my throat started tingling, I dismissed it as a run-of-the-mill January cold. *I got 99 neuroses but hypochondria ain't one. Hit me!*

I rolled out of bed on Saturday morning and walked over to get my daily checkup. Twenty minutes later, I was back home enjoying a second cup of coffee when my email dinged. I casually opened it and froze: "Your COVID result is: DETECTED."

It was a gut punch. I immediately texted *MJ*'s COVID safety officer, Kim. "Could this be a false positive?" She replied, "Unlikely" and suggested I get retested with the more-sensitive Rapid PCR version. I asked her if I should reveal my status to the workers when I returned to the testing center. Kim said, "Absolutely."

I put my shoes back on and hustled over to Times Square again. Feeling like I'd somehow been a bad boy, I sheepishly told the receptionist of my diagnosis. She shrugged and directed me to a PPE-swathed staffer. I informed my "swabber" I'd tested positive 30 minutes earlier and was back for confirmation. She shrugged too. Just another day at the office.

After receiving my positive result, my first order of business was launching Operation Substitute…stat! Normally, orchestra subs aren't brought into the mix until a Broadway show has been up and running for a month or so—and subs NEVER play the show without riding shotgun in the pit a few times beforehand. But in light of the pervasive COVID threat, the *MJ* band had been urged (read: commanded) to assemble an emergency back-up roster…if only on paper. I'm a world-class worrier, so I didn't need prodding. Although I was still trying to learn how to play my parts properly, I set my pride aside and made a warts-and-all recording during our first week of performances. My execution was uneven, but I plowed forward, distributing mp3s and charts to my deputies—along with a heaping helping of caveats. New productions are constantly evolving as the preview process unfolds, so *MJ* was a moving target, but at least my squad would have a fundamental grasp of the show if pressed into service. My Boy Scout tendencies paid off when the doomsday scenario became a reality. (Pardon me while I take a moment to pat myself on the back.)

I always made a point to get swabbed relatively early in the day (10am-ish)—in case disaster struck and I had to wrangle an eleventh-hour sub. (For the record, my second test indeed confirmed my infection.) Complicating matters, I'd managed to test positive on a matinee day, so I needed an intrepid strummer in my chair by 2pm...instead of a slightly less desperate 8pm.

I alerted Jonno Linden, one of my presumptive subs, to my Code Red. Thank God, Jonno was available—and equally vital, COVID negative. Lucky for us both, Jonno had taken the initiative to familiarize himself with the music...on the outside chance he'd be summoned from the bullpen. Bless him. Jonno's diligence made our incredibly difficult situation surmountable. We talked through the trickier passages by phone before Jonno rushed uptown to the theater. He took another COVID test on site—and then buckled into the hot seat.

Early in our run, I'd fretted continuously about getting COVID and being branded as the guy who "broke" the show. Ah, I miss those days of innocence. I am currently the sixth person in our 12-piece band to contract COVID since we started a little over a month ago, so this frantic drill is nothing new. Chaos has become the norm.

Thanks to Jonno, *MJ* went on as scheduled. But I'm flattering myself; *MJ* would have gone on even if my chair had sat empty. Guitar 2 is important, but not "full refund" important. Fact is, I've never seen a show cancel a performance due to a missing musician—which, to be fair, is a rare occurrence. (Broadway weeds out undependable types real fast.) If necessary, orchestras can crawl across the finish line with the most skeletal of crews. Hell, piano and drums could get it done in a pinch.

OK, so I'm out; Jonno is in. Next on deck: test Patty. We broke the seal on a home test (supplied by *MJ*) and followed the directions. Ten minutes later, we had our verdict: Patty was "clean." New problem. Isolation is recommended when one household member tests positive, with CDC guidelines suggesting separate bedrooms and bathrooms. Ha! In NYC? Who do they think I am? Jon Bon Jovi? Our "floor-through" apartment is bigger than a lot of the glorified closets that pass for living quarters in NYC, but true isolation would be impossible for us. (We'd kill for separate bathrooms.) So, it's come to this: we're wearing masks inside our own home, using FaceTime to say "goodnight" from opposite ends of the hallway...with our windows open (in January). Fortunately, the radiators in our 120-year-old building are up to the task. Matter of fact, muscular steam heat systems were developed in response to the Spanish Flu epidemic of 1918. The goal was to make apartments unbearably hot, thereby forcing tenants to open their windows even in the dead of winter. True story. (Viruses hate fresh air!)

My second question to *MJ*'s COVID safety officer was an obvious one: When can I come back? There was a flicker of good news. For better *and* worse—unlike our actors, and horn section—I'm able to perform my duties while masked. And although this means I *get* to wear a mask for three straight hours every night in our cramped orchestra pit, it also means I'm eligible to return to work sooner than most. With the ever-evolving protocols, I only have to sit out five days...provided my symptoms disappear, and I can produce two negative test results 24 hours apart. Kim counted Friday (onset of symptoms) as Day Zero, therefore Saturday was considered Day 1. Come on Wednesday!

I felt a little sick for the first two days; low fever, light cough, runny nose, and I slept a lot, but I've definitely punched the muso clock feeling exponentially crappier. Unfortunately, in this *golden* age of COVID, that's not how Broadway rolls anymore. "The Show Must Go On!" is no longer our *cri de guerre*—and I'm a musical theater leper until further notice. Meanwhile, I'm thrilled to report my Pfizer vaccines (and booster) did their job as advertised. I felt fine by Day 3. Now the waiting.

## TEST RESULTS COUNTDOWN:

**Day 5**: Positive. Damn, no early parole.

**Day 6**: Positive. (Patty is sniffly and scratchy but amazingly still negative.)

**Day 7**: Positive. Frustration building.

(Patty now tests POSITIVE. On the bright side, husband and wife are no longer required to isolate. We clearly weren't doing a very good job anyway.)

**Day 8**: Positive. Sigh. I should've never gotten my hopes up—you'd think I would've figured this one out over the years. Plus, I've now used up all my paid sick days. The meter is running. (Thankfully, Patty's symptoms are resolving. Go Pfizer!)

**Day 9**: Positive (still). Compounding my anxiety, we're scheduled to record the *MJ* cast album at The Power Station this coming weekend (which would be Day 16 & 17 in COVID speak). I'm officially in the bargaining phase with God.

**Day 10**: Are my eyes playing tricks on me? Is there a pink line or not? I send a photo to our COVID safety officer Kim for a ruling. The call on the field stands.

NEGATIVE! (Like JBJ crooned, "I'm halfway there.")
Another negative tomorrow and Exile on 49th Street is over.

**Day 11**: Negative again!!! No doubt about it. Sweet relief. Damn, that was the longest 10 days of my life. I am back in the game!

Tonight, come 8pm, I will be in my chair playing "Beat It" with a HUGE smile on my (masked) face.

First things first: gratitude. When COVID exploded two years ago, NYC became scary as hell. Patty and I personally know a handful of people who died from the virus, and peripherally, many more. Therefore, it is vitally important to acknowledge this fact: I did not spend ONE minute of the last 10 days fearing for my life. I never woke up gasping for air in the middle of the night wondering if this was "it." Kicking the bucket never crossed my mind—and my symptoms never progressed past "mild cold." My deepest thanks to the scientific and medical community. Vaccines work!

Now where were we? Oh yeah . . .

\* \* \*

*"Welcome to the Neil Simon Theatre and MJ the Musical. Out of courtesy to the company, please take this time to silence all mobile phones and electronic devices. The taking of photographs or the use of any recording devices is strictly prohibited . . .*

Hell yeah . . . let's do this! (again)
Dear Lord, PLEASE let it stick this time.

# Epilogue

An old adage claims, "Do what you love, and you'll never work a day in your life." Well…yes and no. I wouldn't change a thing (okay, maybe a few), but turning your passion into your vocation is a double-edged sword. Human nature dictates *any* pursuit that generates your paycheck will become tedious, if not exasperating, at times. (I wonder if Tiger Woods still thinks golf is fun?) Nevertheless, I achieved my childhood dream: I spent my life as a professional musician. There were good times, there were bad times, and of course my amazing meteor ride with Sting.

For years I grappled with the timing of my Sting success, fearing my crowning achievement had come too early in the grand scheme of things. I felt like an athlete who'd won the Super Bowl or the World Series in their rookie season, and then—despite respectable longevity—never made it back to the big game. It was bittersweet. But blessed with perspective, I no longer sweat the front-loaded arc of my career. Who cares *when* I played with Sting? Opportunity knocks when it damn well pleases—IF it knocks at all. And with that being the case, I'd always choose "too soon" over "never."

Was I supposed to have my most prestigious gig so early

in my career? I guess the answer is yes. Did I peak at the ripe old age of 28? I guess the answer is maybe. But resting on my Sting laurels was not an option. I *had* to keep going, so I did. And that's when the real struggle began. Relocating from North Carolina to NYC in my mid 20s took a lot of guts—but in hindsight, *staying* in NYC was the true test of courage. Faced with essentially starting over—sans the rock-star glamour I'd become accustomed to—I swallowed (or channeled) my pride and renewed my vows with New York City. I humbly ground out a hit-and-miss living for ten bumpy years—plus got sober to boot—before ultimately finding redemption and, more importantly, contentment on Broadway.

Trying to excel at anything comes at a steep price. Many sacrifices are required. But after five decades of chasing the dream, I've finally conquered my need to conquer the world. I'm ready to recalibrate my priorities and *attempt* to introduce some balance into my life. (Balance? What a concept!) Next on the agenda? Playing Frisbee in the backyard with my dog. All I need is a Frisbee, a backyard, and a dog!

*To Patty — thanks for 30 years of love. 159 more please!*

As this book was going to press, my dear mother, Nancy, passed away. Two days gone and I already miss her terribly.

One of the few (or possibly only) upsides of the Broadway shutdown was a chance to spend meaningful time with my mom. After my father died, my two brothers and I took turns caring for Mom, and thanks to my COVID hiatus, I was able to make multiple trips down south to visit her. Mom and I spent our days tag-teaming the morning crossword puzzle, working in the yard, watching classic film noirs, and—her favorite—making leisurely trips to the grocery store for bargain hunting and socializing.

As noted, my parents were married for an impressive 64 years. Sadly, the blessing of a long marriage often means one spouse will eventually have to brave their day-to-day existence without their lifelong partner at their side. This lonely, unbalanced challenge proves difficult at best, and sometimes insurmountable. At 84, my mother dealt with numerous health issues, but her biggest underlying condition may have been a broken heart. Rest high, sweet Nancy. I love you.

# Acknowledgments

Special thanks to my generous and whip-smart beta readers: Mark Sloan, Jonno Linden, Vince Fay, Art Hays, and Patty Murray. Your input was invaluable. Your eyes, ears, brains, and hearts helped make my book better.

Thanks to:

Patty, Will and Nora, Mike and Cindy, Brian Dennis, Tony and Ronda Bowman, Tom and Sue Merkel, Jeff and Constance Kazee, Rodney and Mariana Howard, Paul and Deb Adamy, Sharon and Jule Rousseau, Mark Sloan and Michelle Van Parys, The Bugs Gang, Steven Robinson, Shirleene Robinson, Bill Baucom, Jim Henderson, Bob Christian, Greg Darden, Carter Minor, Morgan Davis, Doug and Kim Travis, Karen Henry and Jack Fowle, Keith and Elaine Crittenton, Tim Hildebrandt and Joanne Martin, Andy Church, Barbara Thornton, David Holcenberg, Ethan Popp, John Miller, Michael Keller, Michael Aarons, Warren Odze, Ivan Bodley, Sting, Tom Herrmann, Sandy Aquila, Dolette McDonald, Jack Morer, Mike Olsen, David Bulitt, Vic Garbarini, Jon Bon Jovi, Bob Lefsetz, and Branford Marsalis.

Thanks to a lifetime of dear friends and bandmates:

David Tyson, Floyd Knight, Curtis "Brother" Wilson, Stephen Hartsell, Robin Wilson, Bill Bolen, Larry Duckworth, Tim Smith, Scott Sawyer, Luther Rix, Bob Quaranta, Paul Rich, Tommy G, Steve Gelfand, John McNally, Jon Albrink, Amanda Homi, Jim Campagnola, Peter Valentine, Jon Herington, David Longworth, Art Labriola, Mike Mancini, John Benthal, John Samorian, Martyn Axe, Phil Edwards, Ian Breck Stewart, Johan Nilson, Chris Parker, Jack Cavari, Steve Marzullo, David Nyberg, Myles Chase, Rob Preuss, Doug Quinn, Ray Marchica, Wendy Cavett, Darren Ledbetter, Zach Dietz, Brandon Ethridge, Brian Koonin, Tim Quick, Micah Burgess, Pete Donovan, Gary Seligson, Cameron Rasmussen, Sean Driscoll, Mike Bono, John Putnam, Hiddy Honari, Larry Saltzman, Conrad Korsch, Tony Tino, Art Hays, Kenny Soule, Steve Count, Paul Ossola, Yves Gerard, Dean Moody, Lane Sparber, and Evan Gluck.

To Bob, Jan, Mark, Matt, and the entire team at Deeds Publishing.

Thanks for your continued faith in my work. (Extra thanks for the nudge, Bob!)

*In memory of Jim Campbell, Nancy Campbell,
Larry Riggsbee, Anita Adsit, and Billy Francis*

*I miss these incredible people.*

# About the Author

Jeffrey Lee Campbell, originally from North Carolina, is a guitarist, composer, producer, and author. Jeffrey has been a professional musician for 50 years — 35 and counting in New York City. In addition to touring the world with Sting, Jeffrey has performed with artists including Sammy Davis Jr., Aretha Franklin, Michael Bublé, and Jon Bon Jovi. A grateful journeyman, Jeffrey has played guitar on countless recordings, jingles, and Broadway shows. His globetrotting memoir, *Do Stand So Close: my improbable adventure as Sting's guitarist* received praise from critics and readers around the world.

contact: jeffreyleecampbell.com

*Also by Jeffrey Lee Campbell*

CPSIA information can be obtained
at www.ICGtesting.com
Printed in the USA
BVHW031643060422
633551BV00008B/451

9 781950 794737